*To my husband,
companion afield and in time*

# The only
# GOOD BEAR
## is a
# DEAD BEAR

## A COLLECTION OF THE WEST'S
## BEST BEAR STORIES

Jeanette Prodgers

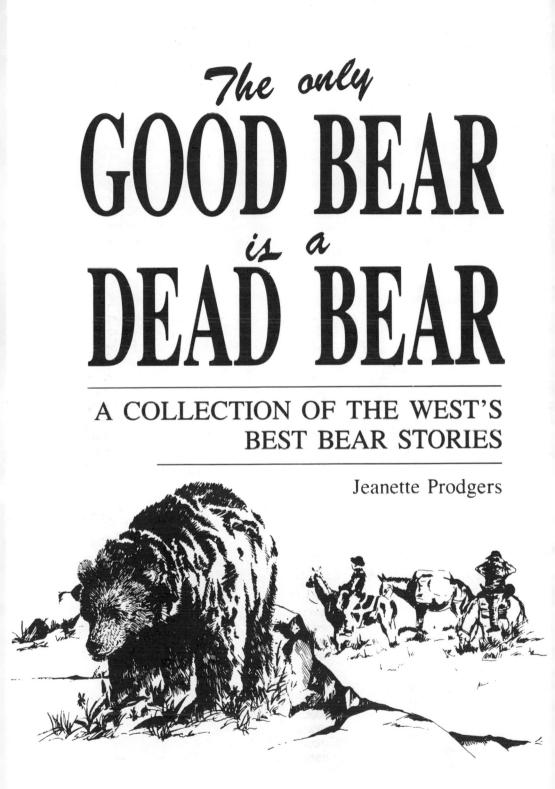

The passage on page 72 from *Tough Trip Through Paradise*
(by Andrew Garcia, ed. by Bennett H. Stein,
The Rock Foundation, 1967) is reprinted with
permission of Houghton Mifflin.

Library of Congress Catalog Card Number 86-90513
ISBN: 0-934318-96-4

Published by Jeanette Prodgers,
2715 Ottawa, Butte, Montana 59701

Publishing consultant:
Falcon Press Publishing Co., Inc.
Helena and Billings, Montana

First printing 1986
Second printing 1992
Third printing 1993

# Table of Contents

# Preface

In a thoughtful essay about wilderness written more than 40 years ago, the late great naturalist/philosopher Aldo Leopold noted the fact that the outstanding achievement of wilderness, the grizzly, was "retreating steadily toward the Canadian border." In 1909 when Leopold first saw the West," there were grizzlies in every mountain mass." By the early 1940s, an estimated 6,000 grizzlies survived in the U.S. with 5,000 of those in Alaska. Only five states had any at all. "There seems to be a tacit assumption," Leopold wrote, "that if grizzlies survive in Canada and Alaska, that is good enough. That is not good enough for me."

"Relegating grizzlies to Alaska is about like relegating happiness to heaven; one may never get there." He added that, "if education really educates, there will in time, be more and more citizens who understand that relics of the old West add meaning and value to the new."

The first evidence of grizzlies in what is now the Continental United States was recorded by Spanish explorers on the coast of California in 1602. They saw and described grizzlies feeding on whale carcasses near present-day Monterey. Later (1690), Henry Kelsey, an explorer in the employ of the Hudson's Bay Company, wrote in his journal that he had observed "a great sort of bear which is bigger than any white bear and is neither white nor black, but silver haired like our English rabbit." The first sighting of the plains grizzly took place in the prairie west of Winnipeg, Manitoba, and was concluded by the killing of two bears for their meat, which Kelsey pronounced good.

The first recorded sighting of grizzlies in Montana was made by members of the Lewis and Clark Expedition (1804-06). They observed plains grizzlies, killed them for scientific evidence and in self-defense, and were much impressed with their size and ferocity.

In recent years there has been a resurgence of interest in "the great bear" perhaps as a corollary to the rebirth of interest in conservation which culminated in 1970 with Earth Day activities. The new environmentalism spawned many specific pieces of legislation reflecting public concern, among which was the Endangered Species Act of 1973 and subsequent amendments. The grizzly bear now had the protection of federal law, or so it appeared to its supporters. Every state had to react to a federal listing which nominated species as threatened or endangered. Each state was now called upon to provide data defending its choice of designation.

Montana for many years sold a bear license entitling a sportsman to take one bear of either species, black or grizzly, either sex, and offered spring and fall hunts. By 1967 the grizzly was listed separately and sportsmen were required to purchase a trophy license and to report their success or lack of it to the Department of Fish and Game. Thus Montana had ten years of experience with legal grizzly hunting seasons to back up its claim that the grizzly was threatened, but not endangered.

Since then, Montana has set quotas and limited hunting areas in an attempt to fine tune this controversial management proposal. Animals as potentially dangerous to life and property as grizzlies must be treated differently than a rare frog or endangered butterfly species. The grizzly requires special consideration.

Montana has had a long acquaintance with the "great white bear." Though they are no longer common on the plains, occasional stragglers wandering eastward out of the front range of the Rockies in recent years invade isolated ranches and small towns along the foothills to the dismay of residents and Fish and Game officials. Incidents such as these remind us of the differences between Montana and Kansas. Apparently grizzlies are far more adaptable to living in close proximity with man than man is to cohabiting with them.

Descendants of the early pioneers who waged war on all predators to protect their livestock and their lives may be inclined to agree with the anti-bear philosophy that still exists. "Shoot, shovel, shutup." That is the slogan of many rural folks and rural sympathizers who live in the nearby towns and cities and express their hatred for the bears in violent fashion. It is expressed several ways. Bears may be perceived as anti-business because there is opposition in some areas to logging, road-building, and subdividing in prime grizzly habitat. Or bears may be hated because they are feared—recent human deaths and maulings by grizzlies in Glacier and Yellowstone national parks have rekindled earlier fears of possible attacks on innocent citizens. As more and more people invade the backcountry, it is expected that more "bear incidents" will occur. This all makes for gory headlines and sensational accounts in outdoor magazines.

As an old Ozark hillbilly once observed, "Down here in the hills, we'uns is generally down on what we ain't up on." Research on grizzly biology, habitat requirements, and behavior is fairly recent, probably beginning with the pioneer studies by the Craighead brothers in Yellowstone National

Park between 1959-1971. Controversies spawned by the abandonment of artifical feeding policies of the Park Service and subsequent declines in bear numbers have dominated the discussions of professional biologists, agency administrators, ranchers, hikers, bear lovers and bear haters for the past 25 years and show no signs of abating.

Where once we had almost no good information and very few people concerned about the plight of the grizzly, now we can number bear researchers by the score and wads of information are being produced, not all of it mutually acceptable to the folks charged with responsibility or those just plain interested. Grizzlies make good copy, as the journalists have noted, so we can expect to see excessive coverage of all human encounters, fatal or not, with grizzlies.

This collection of stories should help us understand our long-standing fascination with these magnificent creatures (or vicious brutes). It also gives us insight into our preoccupation with our continual attempts at their destruction, exposes the exaggerations and excesses, and casts doubt on the sportsmanship involved. In the latter case we may be annoyed by the accounts of wanton slaughter, set guns, traps, poisons, and the use of dogs. We may wonder at use of bear meat for human food, and the sale of hides, until we reflect that bears are currently being poached for sale of gall bladders, claws and teeth as well as hides. Things haven't changed all that much you may conclude, but at least the early settlers had more reason to try to recoup their losses than we do.

If we learn from these fascinating and little-read accounts some lesson in tolerance, humility, and perhaps a sense of responsibility for this unique creature, the author will have been justified in her long, arduous task. Similar contributions need to be made for Canadian and Alaskan grizzlies. As we settle the foothills and valley floors and invade the backcountry with bulldozers and backpacks, the remnant populations of grizzlies will be further reduced. How we resolve this dilemma may well tell us what kind of people we really are!

Dr. W. Leslie Pengelly, Missoula, Montana

# Introduction

$B$ecause the fate of bears, especially grizzlies, living in the remaining western wilderness, is uncertain, this book was compiled to recount the West's long-going war against bruin. *The Only Good Bear Is A Dead Bear* features western frontier bear stories which, for the most part, have not appeared in any other major bear story collection. Many accounts were taken from old newspapers because frontier editors often considered bear stories quite newsworthy. Even obvious bare-faced lies made good news copy before the days of radio and television. Other accounts were excerpted from books or magazines.

When selecting stories for this book, I generally used unfamiliar accounts rather than those often-told tales of Lewis and Clark and Hugh Glass. Although there are a few stories told by noted men such as Theodore Roosevelt, most of the tales were related by average western pioneers, including trappers, hunters, businessmen, women, children and politicians.

During the frontier days, the philosophy that "the only good bear is a dead bear" was the prevalent attitude among pioneers. Bears were considered pernicious predators to be shot on sight. They served no useful purpose other than offering exciting adventure to thrill-seekers who needed to boast of their bravery. Few pioneers ever defended the bears' right to exist. Furthermore, pressure from the frontier livestock industry often forced state governments to post bounties for predators, of which bears were included. Therefore, not only did a frontier bear slayer become a hero, he also became a few dollars richer.

Bears received respect only in print. That is, they were sometimes called Mr. Bear or Mr. Grizzly or Bruin with a capital B; but most often they were referred to as brutes, beasts or monsters. In practice, they were killed or harassed at every opportunity. Due to braggadicio, rarely was a "small" bear ever killed—even if it was a cub—it was usually a "big" cub. Most of the mature bears encountered or killed were either "huge" or the "largest of their kind". Actually, size of the bear didn't really matter that much as long as bruin was dead and the bear slayer had its pelt as proof. Female bears with cubs or cubs themselves were considered worthwhile trophies. Even members of the early-day Boone and Crocket Club, the prestigious conservation organization, regarded any and all bears as fair game.

To western pioneers the bear personified wilderness, and wilderness was something man had to conquer with his technology to make a safe and habitable home for more humans. After the pioneers "civilized" the wilderness, their great-grandchildren began to value the remaining untouched land for its own beauty; and the bear became a symbol of wilderness to them too. However, this symbol held different meaning for some descendants than it did for their forefathers. Wilderness no longer seemed such an adversary now that people had the comforts of the city to protect them against the harshness of nature. To some, wilderness became a wondrous world, and the bear represented all that was mystical there.

Antipathy toward bears persisted well into the 1940s, when grizzlies were already extinct in many western states and dwindling in Montana, Wyoming and Idaho. The remaining grizzlies in the Rocky Mountains hid in the deepest wilderness and generally evaded man. Since bears were scarce they posed little threat to humans. In conjunction with their scarcity, sportsmen and others began to value bears as important elements of the natural environment, and laws were enacted to protect bruin from total extinction in the West.

Slowly, negative attitudes toward both bears and wilderness shifted and eventually evolved to the philosophy of today's wilderness supporters. However, tradition dies hard, and there are still people who carry that deep-seated fear and hatred of bears with them that they inherited from their ancestors or invented for themselves. Although the average citizen is unlikely to encounter black bears in the wild, and even fewer will see grizzlies, many will fight to save what they cannot see, and others will fight to eradicate that which they do not know. Both sides fight for a symbol. Those who seek to protect bears envision them as the wildest part of wilderness. Those who seek to destroy bears perceive them as threatening forces of untamed nature.

*The Only Good Bear Is A Dead Bear* simply presents an historical documentation, in the form of stories, some true and others contrived, of the West's previous prejudice against both black and grizzly bears. Some of the stories are funny; some are frightening; some are sad; and some are downright shameful, but they all speak of a past when bears were plentiful.

As a final note to the reader, these stories have been reprinted in their original form, with minimal editing in cases when clarification was necessary. Hence, purists will have to pardon the incorrect grammar, out-dated spelling, and improper syntax in some of these tales. Instead, enjoy them for their content and flavor.

# Close Encounters of the Worst Kind

$S$ome of the West's most exciting frontier bear/human encounters that were ever recorded are included in this chapter, with the notable exceptions of Lewis and Clark, Hugh Glass and other well-publicized adventures. Although there were some terrible maulings, a few of which resulted in human death, most encounters ended with bruin's death. The number of hair-breadth escapes is all out of proportion to actual maulings— the result of an exaggerated perception of danger. Almost every horrible confrontation in this chapter involved a grizzly. Most often, the bear was a mother protecting her young or a startled or wounded bear.

While it is true there were more bears for humans to encounter in the frontier days, it was the pioneers' attitude toward bears that caused much of the trouble. Bears were considered adversaries to be killed outright. An attitude of shoot first/think later caused many men to take careless shots at bears, endangering their own lives. Misdirected shots, often wounding bruin, only served to enrage the animal and force it to defend itself against a human assailant.

As it can be seen by reading the following bear stories, men were so anxious to prove their prowess by securing a bearskin that they often abandoned common sense in the excitement of the encounter. While it is understandable how a man could easily get excited when he realizes he has accidently roused a bear, it is a different matter when a bear hunter who is purposely pursuing bruin loses reason as was often the case.

Pioneers often created their own problems by shooting simply because they saw a bear. It didn't matter whether the bear was as big as a horse and their weapon inadequate, or their marksmanship poor; man felt compelled to shoot despite the odds against a clean kill. Shots were fired at cubs without considering the mother's possible and most likely nearby presence; and there were those would-be bear hunters who, with reckless abandon, pursued a wounded bear into the brush.

Many men were mauled due to their own folly; whereas the bears usually attacked men out of self-defense or because they perceived a threat in man's presence. In many cases, if the bears had been left alone, tragedy probably would not have happened as often as it did.

# A High Price To Pay

*In 1881, a hopeful young Swedish immigrant trying to earn enough bounty money to acquire a ranch determined to kill a livestock-killing bear. Accompanied by two friends, Peter Haelstrom found and shot the bear. However, the young Swede did not escape unscathed. His hair-raising story written by William Flynn appeared in the May 31, 1934 **Rocky Mountain Husbandman**.*

During the autumn of 1881, herds of farmers and stock raisers in the vicinity of Warm Springs [Montana] were harassed by a giant cinnamon bear which wrought havoc among their cattle and sheep. Almost weekly the great creature executed night raids and with cunning bordering on the diabolic, eluded all hunting parties which endeavored to end his costly forages.

At last, becoming desperate at their lack of success and the mounting toll the bear took from their possessions, ranchers offered a $100 reward to the person or persons who would kill the animal. Even this added incentive, which caused more and more hunters to shoulder their guns and take the trail of the bear which was marked by fallen, torn, and bloody carcasses of partially eaten stock, did not end his activities.

Among those who were attracted by the reward was one Peter Haelstrom, only two months from his native Sweden, who was making his home on a ranch not far from the Warm Springs mound. Guest and dependent of his brother, Haelstrom believed the reward, should be [sic] kill the bear, would enable him to make at least a start in acquiring a ranch of his own.

His thoughts were fired by memories of a flaxen-haired girl-wife he had left in Sweden.

If he should successfully hunt the bear, he reasoned, and win the reward, he could more quickly send her word that he had found a haven of security and a place of happiness and peace in the land to which he had journeyed.

By dint of much persuasion, Christian Jorgenson and Andrew Peterson, countrymen of the ambitious young Swede, agreed to join him in the hunt. Haelstrom offered a share of the reward, should their undertaking be successful, but once having given their word, they generously refused to accept any part of the money. The sport and adventure of the hunt would be sufficient compensation for their trouble, they explained.

Early on the morning of September 15, the three hunters left Warm Springs and worked north from the mound. In a large pasture known as Peterson's field, they found the trail of their quar[r]y. Huge paws had left impressions in the soft ground and the crushed grasses of the meadow showed a plain trail leadnig [sic] toward the Mount Powell foothills.

Proceeding with all possible haste, the hunters followed the tracks. The bear was traveling slowly, loggy and overburdened from a night's feasting on several kills. When the hunters followed the animal's tracks into the brush-covered foothills below Mount Powell, the fresh condition of the trail showed their quar[r]y to be not far off.

Haelstrom was in the lead. He held his rifle ready in his hands as he cautiously proceeded through the tangle of underbrush and willows. He was forced to move slowly, following the trail and at the same time attempting to search the terrain ahead for the first sight of the bear. Jorgenson and Peterson followed not far behind.

Suddenly Haelstrom saw the bear. The animal, crouched on its haunches, front paws swinging in short, jerky circles, glared at him from a tangle of brush not 10 feet away.

The leader raised his rifle and fired. A plunk of lead striking flesh gave proof the ball had not missed.

Motionless for a moment, the bear remained poised. Then with a growl of rage and pain, he turned and plunged into the brush.

Haelstrom's two companions rushed to his side. "I shot him," he cried excitedly. "Follow the blood. We will finish him yet."

Throwing caution to the winds, the three men crashed into the underbrush. This time Peterson took the lead. Haelstrom followed several paces behind as Jorgenson, almost stumbling over his heels, brought up the rear.

Making no attempt to conceal their movements, the three hurried on. Blood showed plainly on the leaf and wood matted ground. The trail grew more distinct as the wounded animal moved more slowly, weakened from loss of blood.

Crimson spots led the men around a dense clump of willows. Slipping and stumbling on insecure footing, Peterson hurried around the turn in the trail and paused, searching for further signs.

A shuffling sound, a short, choked-off moan caused him to retrace his steps and look back. The sight that met his eyes froze him with terror and horror.

The bear had leapt from the shadow of the tangled willows. He had launched himself in a furious attack upon Haelstrom. With all the agile swiftness of his breed he had been upon the man before he was aware of his danger.

The force of the bear's attack had knocked Haelstrom down, as he lay, half stunned, a wide swinging paw armed with long pointed claws raked across his face and left behind a welter of blood and torn flesh.

Dangling by a thread of skin, the man's upper lip hung away from his face. His nose was torn and a great gash on the right side of his face extended from ear to breast.

Haelstrom attempted to bring his gun to bear on the enraged animal. But he could not turn quickly enough.

Once more the creature was upon him, his ferocity increased by the smell of flowing blood. With a deep-throated growl he again pounced on the helpless man.

His great jaws opened and exposed shining, blood-flecked teeth. With a crunch of breaking bone they closed upon the man's head.

Jorgenson and Peterson raised their guns to fire, but they feared to miss their aim and wound the man. Helpless, they watched the bear's jaws, their strength increased by insane rage, close over the face of their companion.

Twice the bear shook the man as a terrier would shake a rat. Then he dropped the body and stood for a moment over his kill.

Peterson raised his rifle. He fired. Once more the smack of lead ball striking flesh gave proof the bullet had gone home.

A stiffening flood of strength seemed to flow through the animal's body. He rose still higher and seemed to poise majestically. Then his indomitable wild will released its hold and the creature slumped upon the body of his last victim—dead.

With frantic haste the two young men attempted to move the carcass off their fallen comrade. Their very haste defeated their efforts and it was some moments before they were able to drag Haelstrom from beneath the great weight of the bear's body.

When they did so, all hope that the man might be alive turned to dismay. The scalp was raked back from the bone. The splintered skullcap showed above a welter of blood. In the midst of a gorry [sic] mass of blood and flesh and hair they saw jelly-like particles of tissue.

Hastily improvising a stretcher by slipping broken branches through the sleeves of their coats, the two men carried their wounded companion to Warm Springs. A superficial examination disclosed faint heart beats.

Stumbling and reeling from exhaustion and shock, they brought Haelstrom to the Warm Springs hospital and sought the medical aid of Dr. Mussigbrod. But the surgeon was absent from the institution.

Although believing their mission hopeless, but spurred by the indication that Haelstrom still lived, they commandeered a wagon and team and took him to the Sister's hospital at Deer Lodge. Dr. [A.H.] Mitchell was called.

But there was little he could do other than ease the suffering of the wounded man. He bathed his cuts and placed a dressing over the gaping wound.

As Dr. Mitchell finished his work, Haelstrom opened his eyes.

"Am I going to die, doctor?" he asked. The words fell haltingly and indistinctly from his torn lips.

Dr. Mitchell bent lower to catch the faintly spoken words.

"Yes," he said, "rest, my boy."

Haelstrom's eyelids slowly dropped. Those near his bedside believed him dead. But a faint, hesitant rising and falling of his chest showed he still lived.

As the doctor and attendant watched his breathing grew more faint. At last he again opened his eyes. The watchers bent nearer.

"Well, I killed the bear, anyhow," they heard him mutter. Then his eyes closed and he had gone once more and still alone to seek a haven of peace and happiness.

# A Bird In The Bush Is Better Left There

*M. D. Hatheway, an early-day western printer and prospector, was ferociously attacked by a bear while bird hunting one afternoon in the early 1860s. When retrieving a grouse he shot, Hatheway was fiercely charged by an angry bear that followed the "finder's keeper" law of life. The old prospector, however, had a strong will to live and put up quite a fight. He even survived to read his own obituary. His story was printed nearly forty years later in the May 13, 1906* Anaconda Standard.

It is seldom recorded that a man has an opportunity of reading his own obituary or has the ability to whip a bear in a hand-to-hand encounter. M.D. Hatheway, an old-time printer of Montana and a man whom every early-day resident of the territory knew and respected, was one of these, and he has often told the story to his friends. Mr. Hatheway was a printer of the good old school of hand composition. He had the virtues of the old-time print and he had his faults. He was capable of filling an editorial chair and had been known to do the mental work of the devil, all in the same office. He was one of the founders of the Helena *Independent,* when that paper was published at Deer Lodge [Montana] in the early '60s, and he had worked on nearly every pioneer paper in Montana. Where he is at the present time I do not know, but I was told recently that several years ago he made a comfortable stake out of a mine in the Tobacco Root range, and had gone back East to spend the remainder of his years in peace and plenty with the folks he knew when he was a bare-headed, freckled-faced boy in knee breeches made of homespun cloth.

The last time I remember seeing him was nearly 15 years ago, when he sat in front of a store in Twin Bridges [Montana] and showed to a crowd of curious people specimens of tellurium ore which was valued at thousands of dollars to the ton. " And I have a place where it can be taken out by the hundreds of tons, and it is all as good as this," he asserted, proudly. "When I make my fortune I am going to buy a carload of the best bourbon whiskey that the state of Kentucky can produce. Then I am going to set it up right here at the crossroads at Twin Bridges, where the roads from many sections meet. I am going to knock the head out of each barrel, hang a tin cup on its staves, and sit right down here in comfort and watch the fellows that come along and drink all that is good for them. It will be good whiskey, and it will not contain two headaches to every swallow, either, as does the greater part of the stuff which is sold to prospectors."

But Mr. Hatheway's pay shoot of ore all went out with another shot, and, although he spent many months in Bear gulch trying to find it again, his efforts were futile, and finally he abandoned the claim, hopeless and broken-hearted for a spell, only to have his spirits rise in hope a few days later when he again stumbled upon some rich float which once more set him to gophering like a badger. Finally he did strike something rich which enabled him to ship a few carloads before the shoot pinched out and he is said to have gone back to his old home with a bank roll aggregating nearly $20,000, all of which was taken from the earth in a few months and contained in a few carloads of ore.

But I am telling another story. The one promised was how he mastered a bear single-handed, and how he came to read his own obituary notices. It was just 30 years ago this summer when the northern end of Madison county enjoyed a boom in its quartz ledges and prospectors from all parts of the state were attracted there by the phenomenal showings which were made on the surface. It was in that summer that the town of Pony [Montana] had its first boom and people gathered there by the hundreds. Houses were built rapidly and it might be said that Pony grew faster than any mushroom, for it was created, named and was doing business during a single afternoon. The mines first discovered were rich in gold, on the surface, and it was not long until every square foot of ground within a dozen miles of the town was located. Mr. Hatheway was one of the early prospectors to reach the camp, but he was not lucky enough to find anything to suit him, so he and a considerable number of friends drifted over to the South Boulder, where another district, Mammoth, was being developed. There the prospects looked good to the party, and the boys went into camp, intending to do a considerable amount of work on the claims they had located. Provisions were scarce, and it became the duty of one of the members each day to go hunting in order to keep the camp supplied with meat. Some of the younger men in the party would go deer hunting occasionally and generally bring in meat after being gone for a few hours. Even then Mr. Hatheway was an old man, so when his day to hunt would come he would content himself with taking his shotgun and prowl around in the brush along the creek, shooting prairie chickens, pheasants and grouse. One day he shot a grouse from a clump of brush and walked into the thicket fearlessly after the bird. Before he had taken a dozen steps where the brush was the thickest he heard a savage growl, and, looking up, startled, he saw a cinnamon bear heading for the dead grouse, growling fiercely, with every hair in its body raised in anger.

Mr. Hatheway was perfectly willing that the bear should have the grouse; he was not particularly fond of the birds, especially when they had to be secured at the risk of life, so he retreated precipitately. The bear pounced upon the bird, tore at it savagely for an instant and then, tossing it aside as worthless, the ferocious animal made for Mr. Hatheway, who was vainly trying to hurry through the entangling brush to the comparative safety of the sidehill above the creek. But the brush was so thick that progress was slow, almost impossible when one was excited, and presently Mr. Hatheway slipped and fell backwards. The bear was less than a dozen feet away, coming on mercilessly with jaws wide distended and growling in anger. Taking the only chance left, the helpless prospector threw his gun to his shoulder—it was long before the day of breech-loading shotguns— and fired his last charge of shot full into the eyes and mouth of the approaching brute.

It might be said that it was a foolhardy trick, for the shot was No.6 and intended for no other use than to kill birds. Its only immediate effect was to make the bear more angry, and when the smoke cleared from Hatheway's vision he saw the bear in a perfect tantrum of rage, slapping his face to get rid of the stinging pellets and burying his nose in the earth to ease the pain.

"Had I kept still for a minute," said Mr. Hatheway, in telling the story, "it is possible that he would have turned around in his pain and misery and moved off in a different direction, concerning himself most with his hurts, for a bear, like all other animals and some men, can only think of one thing at a time. But I did not do so. I tried to hurry from the brush, and the first move I made attracted the bear toward me. He let a growl out of him which fairly made by [sic] blood curdle in horror and came after me with a greater determination than ever. I realized I was powerless against him, and the thought came to my mind that my last day had come. However, I was determined to sell my life as dearly as possible, and when I felt the hot breath of the bear in my face I made a jab with my shotgun and succeeded by a scratch in putting out one of his eyes. This made him hesitate for a moment again and I got still farther out of the thicket before he was on me once more. This time he was mad clear through, and the first swipe he made he sent the gun spinning out of my hand and so high in the air that it landed outside the thicket and was found days afterward more than 100 feet away. When I lost my gun I realized that I had a hopeless fight on my hands, but I was still undaunted. The bear rushed over me, knocking me down and walking the full length of my body, digging in his paws and scratching with his sharp claws at every step. The pain was excruciating and I think I fainted for a few minutes, but I was soon brought back to consciousness by an acute pain in my wrist and when I opened my eyes the bear had my left wrist in his mouth and was gnawing it savagely. Then I took a desperate brace on myself and began fighting for my life, for I knew if I could not find some method of fighting off the cruel beast my fate would be to be eaten alive.

"How I lived through the horror of the next few minutes I can never tell. I could distinctly hear the crunching of the bones as the bear tore at my arm despite the faintness which the pain brought over me. I could feel his hot breath blowing in my face, and it seemed as if it would burn me, so intense was it with hate. Then, for a wonder, some passing noise attracted the maddened brute's attention for a moment and he dropped my arm, now broken and crippled beyond mending, and gazed in the direction from which the sound came. This gave me another opportunity for my life, and I was prompt to take it. Like all other miners of those days, I wore shoes, the soles of which were thickly studded with hob nails. My shoes were especially heavy and the nail heads were exceedingly long and sharp. Like a flash the thought came over me, 'Kick his head off!' and I can tell you that I tried to do so. Before the bear could look around from an impatient survey of the matter which had disturbed him, I had planted both of my hob-nailed boots square on the wound made by the charge of bird shot early in the fight and made the bear whimper in pain. I quickly followed up my advantage and landed with both feet again, with a desperateness that sent the bear bowling over on his back. I remember seeing a dun-colored ball of fur vanish in the darkness which came swimming before my brain and then I knew no more for a century it seemed.

"When the boys returned to the shack that night they did not find supper ready, for it was one of the duties of the hunter to prepare the evening meal, and they wondered greatly thereat, for generally I was punctual in the observance of my duties. Some one else got supper, and, as I was still absent at nearly bed time, one or two of the boys started out to find me. They knew the general course I usually took in my bird hunts, and they followed it. Just at dusk they came to the thicket where the bear and I had mixed it up so fiercely, and the bent-down appearance of the bushes showed them that something had been doing. They crawled on their hands and knees through the thicket and were soon at my side. The bear had decamped. One of the boys staid [sic] and watched me while the other brought a hatful of water from the near-by stream. This was poured on my face and it revived me, but I was very near the spirit land from pain and the rough treatment of the bear. Evidently the old cinnamon had returned to the fight after I had kicked him over on his back for the last time, for there were several bites on me which must have been inflicted after I had become unconscious, for I do not remember having them when I fainted.

"While the boys rigged up a crude litter to bear me to camp I took stock of my injuries, which consisted of an arm crushed from the wrist to the elbow, three broken ribs, a dislocated shoulder and nearly a dozen savage bites, and I verily believe that if I had not fainted the bear would have killed me when he came to the attack for the last time. I have always thanked Providence for losing my consciousness at that time, for I think the bear believed he had killed me and went away satisfied that he had wrecked dire vengeance on at least one of his natural enemies—man. But he paid the penalty of his attack upon me the next day, for one of the boys took his trail at daylight, and two hours later his hide was stretched on the side of our shack.

"As soon as a wagon could be secured from the valley I was loaded into it and taken to the ranch of Dr. I.S. Stafford, on Willow creek, 14 miles away, and there my injuries were dressed.

"About four months later I came to Butte [Montana], and the first man I met I used to know started back in horror as if he had seen a ghost. 'Great Scott, Hatheway!' he exclaimed, 'I thought you were dead. Come and take something and convince me you are alive.' I did so and the bartender nearly had a fit and swore he had 'em. Then I investigated matters and found the report had been generally circulated throughout the territory that I had been killed by a big bear on South Boulder. I was pretty well liked in those days, and the papers all gave me a good sendoff, and I have the pleasure, which few men ever have, of reading the good things the press had to say of me after I was reported [to] be dead. I have them all in a scrapbook and am preserving them for future reference."

# "Murder, Save Me"

*One old-timer's close encounter with a bear scared him so much that he never fully recovered. That man was Hiram Steward, hunting companion of prominent frontier dentist Dr. William Allen. The two men were hunting near the Big Horn Mountains when they saw some bear tracks. Following the trail, they located the bear's den and tried to entice the bear out by bombarding it with rocks. Disregarding common sense, dauntless Steward entered the thicket and the maddened animal charged him. Dr. Allen wrote about this thrilling experience in his book* **Adventures With Indians and Game—Twenty Years in the Rockies,** *but the following account was taken from pp.14-17 of George Shields' book* **Hunting in the Great West,** *published by Belford, Clarke and Company in Chicago and New York; copyright 1884.*

On another occasion Allen told us he was out hunting with old Hiram Stewart [Steward], a noted hunter and trapper, who had spent more than half his life in the mountains, and had killed more bears and other large animals probably than he had hairs on his head. It was in May. As they were crossing a coulee one day, in which the brush grew thick, and in which there remained some patches of old snow, they saw where the ground had been disturbed. Passing along, they saw a hole in one of the snowdrifts, which looked as if some one had set down a coffee sack full of rocks. But there was a row of such holes, and on further examination they were forced to conclude that they had discovered a bear track, and the largest one, they both agreed, that they had ever seen. They followed the trail to where it led into a dense jungle of box elder, water beech, rose bushes, etc., at the head of the coulee.

They walked around this, and seeing no trail leading out of it, concluded the bear must be in there. They threw rocks and clubs into the t[h]icket to start him out, but he would not start. Then Allen got down on his hands and knees, and pushing his gun ahead of him, crawled in. He could not see any bear, but after he got in about twenty feet he heard such an unearthly growl as convinced him at once that the outside air would be healthier for him, and slid out backward, much faster than he went in. Then old Hi. said he would go in. Allen told him he had better not, but he would not listen to caution and crawled in. He had not gone far when he met the old leviathan coming out, and raising his rifle, took a hasty aim and fired. This ball entered the bear's breast and knocked him down, but Hi. saw at once that he was not dead, and attempted to throw the shell out of his rifle. But an accident to a gun almost invariably happens just at the most critical moment. Or, if a fellow ever pulls the wrong trigger, it is sure to be when the fine shot are in that barrel, and the buckshot in the other, and the deer gets away again. Joe's [Hiram's] shell stuck in the chamber of his rifle, and refused to budge. He knew he had no time to fool away in swearing at his bad luck, so he slid out just as fast as the nature of the ground would permit, but before he got out the bear had recovered from the effects of the shot sufficiently to get up and start after him. Hi. wore an old buckskin suit that had been in the service for years, and that was so stiff from having been daubed with blood, grease, molasses and other animal and vegetable matter that he could take it off and lean it up against a tree, and it would stand there until he wanted it again, just the same as if he were in it. He was sadly handicapped in this race by a game leg that was about two inches shorter than the other, and when he got out of the thicket there was not a tree in reach large enough to climb, so he started up the hill side with the bear at his heels, growling and roaring at every jump, and Hi. yelling "Murder, save me, shoot him, kill him quick."

Allen said the spectacle was so ridiculous that had it been his own funeral instead of Hi's, that was coming off so soon, he must have laughed all the same. Notwithstanding Hi's old coat was stiff as a shingle, it stood out behind until you could have played bill[i]ards on it, if the bear hadn't been in your way. At every jump Hi. made he would career over toward the side his game leg was on, just as a chair goes over when one leg falls out of it. Finally Allen braced up so that he could shoot, and turned his Winchester loose on the grizzly. The first shot caught him behind the shoulder, and the second in the neck, but he paid no attention to them more than to stop and scratch the spot with his paw, and then go on after Hiram. But the third shot, fortunately, caught him at the butt of the ear, and dropped him in his tracks.

By this time Hi. had reached the ledge of rocks that he had started for at first, and which he thought would save him. He had just grasped a thin shelf that stuck out, to pull himself up by, but it broke off, and let him fall to the ground just as the bear dropped, and in his death struggle he caught Joe [Hi.] with one of his hind feet and threw him more than twenty [f]eet down the hill. Joe [Hiram] gathered himself up, rubbed the mud off his face and hands, felt of arms and legs to see that they were all whole, looked at the great monster, which now lay dead, and as soon as he could recover his breath enough to speak, said, as he shook with terror from head to foot: "Great God, twenty-five years in the mountains, and I never cum [sic] as near gettin' killed as that."

He laid down on the ground, and it was more than an hour before he was able to walk. Allen said his face was as white as the snow in the coulee, excepting the space around his eyes, and that was yellow. Poor old Hiram never recovered from this terrible shock, and died a year afterward. Several who knew him claim that the scare was the direct cause of the sickness that ended his life. He was a mental and physical wreck from that time to the day of his death. Allen took from the bear one hundred and eighty-seven pounds of oil, and his skin when stretched and staked out on the ground measured over nine feet wide by ten and a half in length.

# "Heavy Eyes"
# Ignores His Vision

*In his book* Friends Of My Life As An Indian, *James Willard Schultz told of an encounter his friend Frank Monroe had with some grizzlies near Two Medicine Lake in 1889. Frank Monroe, alias Heavy Eyes, was son of Hugh Monroe, Rising Wolf, the first white man to traverse the eastern slope of the Rockies between the Saskatchewan and Missouri rivers.*

*Schultz and William Jackson, half-breed scout, were on a hunting trip with Heavy Eyes when the latter was attacked by a grizzly which crippled him. This account was excerpted from pp. 15-23 of that book, published by The Riverside Press—Houghton Mifflin Company in Cambridge; copyright 1923.[1]*

. . . In this first autumn month of 1889, Heavy Eyes, his nephew, Blackfeet Man (whose white name was William Jackson), and I, after long and strenuous work in our hayfields, decided that we must have a good hunt, and, leaving our women to look after our ranches, we struck out for the mountains with team and wagon, camp equipment and saddle horses, and at noon of a warm still day arrived here at the foot of this lake [Two Medicine Lake].

"You two are enough to set up the lodge and get things in shape, and, while you are doing it, I will go up on the ridge and kill a deer," Heavy Eyes said to us.

"Yes. Go, and hurry back with meat: we need it," I replied.

Away he went upon his pinto hunting pony, across the outlet of the lake, and up the steep quaking-aspen ridge.

We had finished putting up our lodge when we heard a shot, and then three more in quick succession, and later, several more. "That means meat; good, fat deer or elk meat," Siksikaiquan [Jackson] exclaimed.

"Yes, and he will soon be in with it. Let's start a fire and have a good bed of coals ready for broiling some ribs," I replied.

We gathered a lot of dry cottonwood branches, made a good fire of them, and watched for our hunter to return, and after a long time saw him riding down through the scattering quaking aspens to the river. He was swaying in the saddle, hanging on to the saddle horn with both hands, his hat was gone, and of his clothing but a few shreds of his shirt remained. We ran to meet him, and, just as he came to the near shore of the river, he fell from his horse in a dead faint, the bloodiest, worst-torn man that we had ever seen, his face, right hand, right shoulder, and right leg terribly mangled. We brought water in our hats, bathed him, and he came to, murmured, "Nitsi kim' atsistutoki, nitap'okaiyo" (Did me wrong, real-bear[2]), and fainted again.

We saw that his injuries were far too serious for us to attempt to heal, so Siksikaiquan ran to throw bedding into the wagon, and hitch up and take him to the agency [Blackfeet Reservation], away down on Badger Creek, while I again bathed and then dressed his torn flesh and broken bones as best I could. He came out of his faint as we laid him on the bed in the wagon, and then away they went; and, loading my heavy Winchester, I crossed the river, climbed the ridge, and without trouble found the place of the bear fight. Below a wide, thick growth of service-berry brush the ground was trampled, torn, and splotched with black dried blood, and from there two bloody trails went west along the ridge. Following these, I came to a damp ravine, thickly grown with broad-leaved, brittle-stemmed bear weeds, and there found four distinct bear trails. I followed them on, soon losing the two that were not bloody, and later losing these last when I passed out of the quaking aspens and into heavy pine and fir forest. And though I hunted three days for the wounded bears, I never found them. On the fourth day Siksikaiquan returned and told me that the wounded man had nearly died from loss of blood, but the Government physician reported him now in a fair way to recover, though he would be crippled for life.

It came to me now, as I sat there thinking of the old times, that I never had heard the victim tell of his encounter with the bears; so I went to camp to ask him to relate it. I found the old men sitting all in a row on the river-bank, passing the pipe, and Curly Bear called out to me: "Come. You are just in time to hear Heavy Eyes tell us about his fight here with the real-bears."

"For that very thing was I coming," I replied, and sat down with them and took a turn with the big pipe.

"Well, as I was saying," Heavy Eyes began, "we decided, we three, to come up here and have a good hunt. The night before we started, I had a powerful vision: I saw myself standing upon a big log in a heavy forest, standing there looking for game. Away to my right, some thick brush shook and swayed, and, watching, I saw two big real-bears come out of it and straight toward me. As I was about to raise my rifle to aim at one of them, he called out to me: 'Stand as you are, for we have come to talk to you.' I was very much surprised to be so addressed, by a real-bear, in perfect Pikuni language.

"They came on and on toward me, and, when quite close, sat up on their haunches, and the one said to me: 'We heard you talking about going to Two Medicine Lake to hunt, you and two others. Well, go, kill all the grass-eaters that you want, but don't shoot at any of our relatives. I warn you now that you must not attempt to harm them. If you do, you will be sorry for it so long as you live!'

"Now, my friends, only that evening, just before going to bed, we had been talking about real-bears, saying that we hoped to find and make a big killing of them during our hunt. And these two had heard our talk; there could be no doubt of it! More surprised than ever, I tried to think quickly what I should say to them, and, before I could make up my mind, they suddenly disappeared, my shadow came back into my body. I awoke with a loud cry, and found myself sitting up in bed, my body wet with perspiration.

"Said my woman: 'Why that terrible yell? Are you sick?'

"'Not sick, I am all right,' I replied, and she at once slept again. But I didn't. I lay awake the rest of the night, thinking constantly of my vision, and, when morning came, decided that I would heed that real-bear's warning. I told none, not even my woman, about my vision.

"We made so late a start that day that we were obliged to camp for the night on Willow Creek, and so did not arrive here until noon of the following day; and, as soon as we unhitched the team, I left Apikuni [Schultz], here, and Siksikaiquan, to set up the lodge and make a good camp, and rode up on to the ridge, across there, to try to kill a deer.

"When I came to the game trails up there and found no fresh deer tracks in them, I was surprised. Then, following one of the old beaten paths, I saw that it was being used by bears, real-bears, and that accounted for the absence of the deer: they don't like, as you know, to rest and feed about where sticky-mouths are plentiful.[3]

"I rode higher up on the ridge, and came to a steep rise on it where the service-berry brush was actually black with its heavy load of ripe fruit. I was very hungry, and got down off my horse to eat some of it, and, to prevent the animal leaving me, I made four or five turns of his bridle rope around my left arm. I moved from bush to bush, picking and eating the largest, blackest berries, and thought that I had never had any so sweet and juicy as they were. Suddenly, my horse snorted. I looked back at him, saw that he was staring at something on the ridge above me, and, looking that way, I saw a big real-bear standing up on his hind feet, clawing together top branches of the brush and stripping them of their fruit, leaves and all, with his big, sticky-lipped mouth. I thought at once about my vision, the warning that I had been given, but that bear was so fat that I wanted him; there was enough fat on his body to furnish cooking grease for my woman all winter. Within me there seemed to be two voices, one saying repeatedly, 'Don't shoot at him! Don't shoot at him!' And the other saying, 'Shoot! Kill him! You want all of that fat for your woman and children!'

"I surely felt that I should not shoot, but something stronger than my will made me raise my rifle and fire at the bear. I heard the bullet spat into him. He gave a terrible roar of pain, and at that three more bears rose up close by him, and stared about, trying to learn what had hurt him. He had gone down out of my sight in the brush, and, thinking that I had killed him, I fired at one of the others, and he roared like a mad bull and came for me. I fired at him again and again, knew that my bullets struck him, but he kept coming. He sprang upon me, bit me, and we fought one another down the steep ridge, my horse following, for his bridle rope was still wrapped around my left arm. I was hurt very badly, bleeding plenty, and so was the bear. I knew that I had only two more cartridges in the magazine of my rifle, but I fired them as I got the chance, which only made the bear roar with pain and come at me again. He sprang upon me and began mauling me, and I saw my horse fighting him, kicking him fiercely, and became unconscious. When I came to life, I saw that I was under my horse, who was still kicking the bear, and I knew that I was again going to faint. I wanted to cry out for help; my voice was going: 'Pinto horse,' I whispered, 'fight hard for me,' and I knew no more.

"Again I came to life, to life and terrible pain. Blood was running from my face, from my torn and mangled shoulder and breast, from my crushed hand. My horse was standing close by me, his haunches torn and bleeding. I called upon him again for help, and he stood quietly while I crawled to him, and after many failures at last I got up into the saddle with my rifle. Why I hung on to it, useless as it now was, I don't know. I was too weak to guide the horse, so I told him to take me to camp, and he did his best to take me straight there. Just as we crossed the river, I fainted again, but then Apikuni and my nephew were running to help me. They brought me to life, washed and dressed my wounds, my nephew hurried me down to the agency, and that white doctor set my broken bones.

"There, my friends! That is what I got—crippled for life for not obeying the warning of my vision!"

# Chewed By A Grizzly

*A surprised mother grizzly savagely attacked an equally surprised Colorado man in 1890, leaving him critically wounded. In an attempt to save himself, the man wrestled the bruin until he was overcome with pain. Then he played possum. His unusual story was reported November 6, 1890, in the* **Livingston Post.**

Mr. Best, of Durango [Colorado], came very near losing his life recently by being devoured by a ferocious bear, and his escape is probably the most miraculous that ever occurred in the history of the state, says the *Denver Republican*.

Mr. Best was up Lightner creek looking for horses and was coming down the side of a steep canyon about 10 miles from town, and as he drew near a portion of the trail where the brush and undergrowth was very thick he heard a crackling and smashing of the scrub oak on one side.

Suddenly a low growl met his ear, and without further warning the brush parted and Mr. Best was confronted by a large, ugly-looking silvertip or range bear, that stood hardly two feet away. For a moment bruin stood as if considering what tactics to pursue. Then raising herself upon her hind feet and waving her paw in the air, she rushed for Mr. Best, who totally unarmed, knew not how to escape the infuriated animal.

As she approached closer and closer until he could feel her hot breath in his face, he managed to catch her by the feet and being possessed on ordinary occasions of enormous strength, which now in this exciting moment became superhuman, he held her feet in such a manner that she was unable, although trying her best, to strike or tear him with her claws.

For a moment both paused for wind and Mr. Best was looking for some way to let go, but no way was found. The bear, finding herself powerless to crush her victim, as he had held her feet so widely apart that she could do nothing with them, saw her way clear to end Mr. Best's career by eating his head and face, which, as both his hands were employed in holding her feet, she could do and he could not prevent it unless he should turn her feet loose, and then she would have more advantage than before.

Slowly she leaned her ugly face toward him and then opened her enormous mouth and took Best's head inside and leisur[e]ly began to crush in his head and his face with her teeth. Mr. Best was, of course, unable to stop her, and was compelled to let her pursue her man-eating course.

Finally, overcome with pain and loss of blood, Mr. Best fell backward, the bear falling on top, and being now so weak that he could offer no further resistance, bruin, ffnding [sic] herself free, proceeded to tear and lacerate Mr. Best's face and scalp.

While she was inflicting her punishment upon him she heard, as well as did her victim, who had not yet lost consciousness, a lot of noise from the brush, accompanied by a few sharp growls, which evidently came from her cubs. Leaving Mr. Best, she started to investigate the trouble there and disappeared.

Mr. Best, half unconscious and blinded by the blood that was flowing from the many wounds that had been inflicted on his face and head, was unable to rise, but turned over on his face and tried to think what to do.

Just as he had determined to try and find his way to some ranch or camp he heard the bushes crash and knew that the bear was returning.

Having heard that they will not bite or touch anything they think dead, he resolved to find out, and as the bear approached again he kept perfectly still. Bruin came up and waited for him to jump or move, and seeing that he did not she bit him on the arm, and then finding he did not move she nosed him a little, and after a few farewell bit[e]s grunted to her cubs and plunged into the brush.

Mr. Best succeeded in dragging himself to a tie ranch five miles distant and medical assistance was summoned. The physician found the man in critical condition, and his recovery is still uncertain.

# At Close
# Quarters With Mama

*When A.E. McCartie and several friends returned to retrieve two bears they had killed the day before in the Crazy Mountains, McCartie came within 100 yards of a very protective mother grizzly and cubs. As she started after him, McCartie shot her in the neck with his muzzle-loader; but the shot failed to stop her charge. This gory story, written as a dispatch from Livingston, Montana, appeared in the June 20, 1892* **Anaconda Standard**

A.E. McCartie, who has been in the employ of George Coe at his ranch on Shields river, was brought down to Livingston [Montana] Thursday evening and placed under the care of the county physician for treatment. McCartie's injuries are the result of an encounter with a huge grizzly and are sufficiently thrilling for him, in case he recovers, to raise the hair on the head of young America in years to come as he relates the tale of how he was almost killed by a female grizzly on Monday last. For several weeks past bear have been prowling around the ranch of Mr. Coe and only a few days ago a band of five came down near his house where they finished the remains of a dead calf and then returned to the hills.

On Sunday James Killorn, James Murphy and McCartie decided that, as there was about two feet of snow in the hills, it would be a good day for bear, and shouldering their guns they started for Crazy mountains. After traveling a few hours, Killhorn [sic], who was a few feet in advance of his companions, came within 20 feet of five grizzlies stretched out on a ledge of rock. Sneaking back to where his companions were, he informed them of his discovery and the three advanced cautiously for several yards, when the bear scented them and started. The party succeeded in killing a yearling and an old one, and leaving the carcasses, returned home. The following morning Coe, Murphy and McCartie hitched up a team and started up to bring the meat down. Leaving their teams at the foot of the mountains they separated and started up on foot to where the dead bear had been left. McCartie was meandering along slowly and had just emerged into the edge of a small clearing, when on the opposite side and about 100 yards from him he saw a female grizzly and three cubs. The only weapon he had with him was a muzzle-loading rifle, and, not feeling prepared to tackle such big game with this, he was thinking of retreating and finding his companions when the bear sighted him and made for him. McCartie waited until she was within good firing distance and then took good aim and fired. The bullet lodged in her neck with sufficient force to knock her down, and as soon as she fell McCartie turned and started to run. But in jumping from the log on which he was standing his foot caught on a smaller log, throwing him head first into the snow. Before he could regain his feet the bear was upon him, clawing and biting, and, had it not been for the opportune arrival of Coe, would soon have killed him. Coe had been attracted to the spot by the firing and emerged into the clearing just in time to see the bear land upon McCartie. Raising his rifle he fired three shots into her body in rapid succession, at which the animal gave a howl of pain and releasing her hold upon her victim, fled into the timber. Just at this moment Murphy came over to learn the cause of the firing, and as he stepped into the clearing the three cubs returned in search of their mother and were shot in one, two, three order by Murphy. McCartie was found to be terribly injured. His skull was fractured in three places and he had also received severe bites in the leg and arm. In addition to these wounds his face was almost torn into shreds, the lid being torn off of one eye and his scalp being terribly lacerated. He was placed in the wagon and taken to Coe's ranch and Dr. Campbell, of this city [Livingston] summoned. The doctor did all in his power to alleviate McCartie's sufferings and after taking 69 stitches in his head and face, dressed the rest of his wounds and left him feeling much better. McCartie is now resting well and the physicians say that if erysipelas does not set in his chances of recovery are first class.

On the morning following the encounter a party went out to finish the bear. Her trail was found and easily followed by the blood, but although they tracked her for a distance of 12 miles, they were compelled to return without killing her. Her tracks measured 11 inches across, and those who saw her trying to demolish McCartie are willing to testify that she is the mother of all the bears.

# An Eye For An Eye

*An Update on A.E. McCartie was given in this news article, as well as a report on another human/bear encounter. A black bear was the attacker in the second story. Shortly after McCartie's accident, Jonas Hedges was prospecting near Livingston, Montana, where he saw a large brown bear. Following the philosophy of his day that the only good bear is a dead bear, Hedges shot it and allowed the wounded animal to flee without pursuing it. Hedges did not think about the next man who might cross the wounded bear's path. Coincidentally, he was the next man, and sure enough, bruin was cranky. Their encounter was published in the August 1, 1892* **Anaconda Standard** *as a special correspondence from Livingston.*

A.E. McCartie, who was nearly killed by a bear in the Crazy mountains a few weeks ago, and who has been in this city [Livingston, Montana] receiving treatment for his injuries, had so far recovered last week as to be able to return to his home on Shield's river. Mr. McCartie's escape was a wonderful one, and although his injuries were very severe his recovery is now assured.

McCartie had hardly been released from the physician's care when word reached Livingston that Jonas Hedges, one of the old-timers of the Lower Yellowstone, had also had an encounter with a bear, which, although of a different species and much smaller than the one that tackled McCartie, was nevertheless of sufficient calibre to use Hedges up in pretty bad shape. The particulars of the encounter, as related by Hedges, are as follows: Last Saturday he and his brother left their home near Stillwater [Montana] on a prospecting tour, and that evening camped on the north fork of the Stillwater. The following morning Jonas took his gun and started out and before long scared up a large brown bear. As soon as he sighted him he fired a bullet into his body and the animal turned and fled into the woods. Hedges had not gone out after any large game and cheerfully let the bear get away. After waiting a short time he shouldered his rifle and started on and a few hours later came to a spring, and being thirsty laid his gun down and knelt down to get a drink. While he was thus engaged the bear made a sneak on him, and when he started to rise to his feet he was confronted by the bear he had wounded a few hours before. Before Hedges had time to lay out any plans for a fight the bear was upon him and, grabbing him by the leg, took off a good sized section of flesh. Hedges realized that his only chance was to play possum, and keeling over he lay on his back, hardly daring to breathe. After smelling around a second or so the bear turned and started off and Hedges, thinking it was a good time to have revenge, made a grab for his gun. In an instant the bear was upon him again and this time finished the job by taking a chunk out of his right arm and breaking both bones of the left arm. This time Hedges played possum in dead earnest, and so successfully did he carry out the part which circumstances had so suddenly forced upon him, that the bear finally concluded he had finished him and trotted off into the timber. As soon as he was sure the animal would not return Hedges got up and went to camp and was driven to Stillwater, where he took the train for Big Timber [Montana]. His injuries were dressed by Dr. Moore, after which he took the train for Livingston. On arriving here he was taken to the residence of his brother, E.V. Hedges, where he will remain until his wounds heal.

# Hunter Takes a Tumble

*One of the West's most successful bear hunters, Vic Smith, a former Indian fighter and scout, had a close call with a grizzly in what is now known as the Anaconda-Pintlers in Montana. Although Smith was notorious for bringing down many bruin as well as every other kind of wild game, he was taken by surprise one day while hunting. Upon noticing large bear tracks, Smith secured his rifle; but in a flash a large silvertip appeared and knocked both the hunter and his horse off a ledge. Mr. Smith related his close encounter to reporters from the* **Anaconda Standard***, September 7, 1902.*

"The most satisfactory way, from a self-preservation point, to shoot a bear is to first find a comfortable seat on a limb of a well developed tree," remarked "Vic" Smith yesterday when asked regarding the proper method to pursue when hunting Bruin. "I find that when the hunter is up a tree and has sighted a good-sized bear all conditions prove more satisfactory for the man behind the gun. Of course, the real clever hunter is not frightened to death when he spots a bear, but the bears you are likely to encounter over in the Big Hole country are big fellows and they have an unusual amount of strength and vitality. Why, you can plug one of those fellows square in the heart and he'll run fully 200 feet before dropping. I've known them to do this even after their heart has been literally torn to pieces. When the hunter is sure the bear will come his way soon he knows that if he remains on the ground the brute will scent him a long distance away. If he is up a tree the wind blows over Bruin's head and he gets no clew." [sic]

Montana's unique scout, Indian fighter and hunter knows whereof he speaks, for he has hunted buffalo, bear and the other large game of the West for many years. He climbed over the mountainous peaks of the Big Hole range before a piece of ground was broken by the footprints of man or domestic animal. He knows the cliffs, the ravines, the valleys and the gorges of the mountains for 50 miles about this country like a book. "Vic" Smith is not a hunter who likes to tell of his experiences or of the big game he has brought down in his time. His manner when speaking of the many thrilling adventures in which he had taken an active part is more the style of a modest country school boy. He delights to hunt, but he doesn't consider that he has moved the world in its position when his gun brings down a fine, antlered deer, a mountain sheep or a savage silver-tip bear.

So it was yesterday, when relating to the Standard representative the experience he had during last week in which Bruin got the drop on the hunter and not only killed his horse, but brought about the fall from a cliff which nearly cost Mr. Smith his life.

In relating the story Mr. Smith said:

"I went out Thursday a week ago. My purpose for making a trip into the mountains was to bring down a big bear which had been killing off the cattle at the Walker ranch in the Big Hole country. A good reward had been offered for the brute's death, and I concluded to try my luck. On the 1st of the month I camped on Fish Trap creek, about 35 miles south from Anaconda [Montana], on the Big Hole river. On that day it occurred to me to go after game and I climbed to Goat's peak, some distance above timber line. That particular locality is not at all an inviting place, for it is infrequently visited by man and consequently the wild game abounds there. The point visited by me is the summit of the Rockies and affords considerable sport for the hunter. I managed to kill three mountain goats and two deer and returned to camp well pleased with my trip into the peaks. On the following morning I took saddle and pack animal and started again to the mountains, expecting to bring my game to camp. I had reached a high altitude and was walking leisurely along leading my saddle horse with the pack animal following when I noticed exceptionally large bear tracks on the ground ahead. Securing my rifle from the pack saddle I continued on my way. Shortly our path led over the top of a rugged peak. The path was hardly four feet wide and continued to wind around the mountain top. On my left were innumerable natural caves here and there in the mountainous wall.

"When I had proceeded some 50 feet along this treacherous pathway my saddle horse snorted and pulled hard on the rein fastened over my shoulder. I quickly turned my head and saw standing erect on his haunches, with outstretched paws, a big silver tip bear. The animal was in the act of striking the horse. I jumped, as did the saddle horse, while my pack animal turned and ran back. Bruin's paw struck the saddle, and as the horse winced the claws of the savage brute scratched along the seat of the saddle. The blow, however, was sufficient to knock the horse from his footing, and he tumbled over the ledge, pulling me with him. My gun went spinning down the mountain, and horse and man fell in a conglomerate mass some 25 feet below. The animal struck on my right leg and severely bruised it. Besides this injury my left hand and arm sustained bruises and cuts. I managed to secure a hold on a projecting rock, after I had gone some 50 feet further in sliding rock. The horse found itself unable to stop, and soon was bounding and bumping, like a boulder, down the steep incline. At times the horse shot into the air 50 or 75 feet, and then it would strike against a rock and go on further down, bumping and rolling. Strange to say, the animal could not straighten out, or it might have been saved considerable of the fall. When it went over the cliff it struck head first, and that's the way it continued down the mountain for fully half a mile.

"I looked up as soon as I saw that there could be nothing done to save my horse, and there was the bear calmly looking over the ledge. I had neither gun nor knife, as both found their way from my grasp and tumbled to the depths below. Bruin looked savage enough to jump from the cliff after me, but soon he pulled his head back and was gone. I concluded to save the pack horse at any rate, and after no little difficulty got back to the path by a circuitous route. My horse was standing about 100 yards distant, and securing him I continued on to where I had left my sheep [goats] and deer the day before. The sight that met my eyes demonstrated why the bear had not made a greater effort to kill one of the horses or me. Both deer had been attacked by the brute, while one of the goats was partially eaten. Bruin had feasted on my game and was doubtless in his cave asleep when I passed along the path with the horses. Thanks to the deer and goats, I was saved a fiercier [sic] struggle with the bear single-handed and unarmed.

"I managed to get back to camp by riding the pack animal, and later I was overtaken by Councilman Luxton and his party of friends. They kindly assisted me and made matters comfortable, and yesterday I returned to Anaconda."

The hunter had some badly bruised limbs as evidence of the rough and tumble experience. He said he had no intention of going back for the silver tip bear that has raised such havoc with him, but those who know him best say "Vic" will get that bear or the bear will get him before the winter sets in.

# A Mother's Revenge

*In 1907, the following gruesome bear encounter of Doctor Charles B. Penrose was widely reported because he was the brother of U.S. Senator Bois Penrose. Doctor Penrose angered a mother grizzly by shooting one of her cubs. He had shot impulsively without thinking that the cub's mother could be close. As a result, the doctor nearly lost his life. In addition to receiving widespread press coverage, Penrose wrote about his horrifying experience in the book Hunting and Conservation, edited by George Bird Grinnell. However, the account appearing below was written by Arthur Alvord Stiles, the man who accompanied Penrose at the time of the tragedy and who was responsible for saving his life. His article titled "A Bear Hunt in Montana" appeared in the National Geographic Magazine, February 1908; pp. 149-154.*[4]

With the end of the hunting season in the Far West there comes to light a true and exciting bear story—one that well might have made the bravest hunter look to his safety, or even have thrilled the sportsman spirit of President [Theodore] Roosevelt himself.

The incident occurred last September [1907] in the forest of northwestern Montana. The party consisted of Dr Charles B. Penrose, a well-known physician of Philadelphia, the victim of bruin's ferocious attack, and his two brothers, Spencer Penrose, of Colorado Springs, and Senator Bois Penrose, of Pennsylvania, now in Washington [D.C.]. The party had spent the early part of the season exploring a section of the Lewis and Clark Forest Reserve, where trails were to be found and where travel with the pack-horses was comparatively easy. Toward the end of the summer, however, Senator Penrose desired to see a part of the country hitherto unsurveyed and without trails or passways of any kind. It is a section of high and rugged mountain peaks, snowfields, and living glaciers, wholly uninhabited except by the wild animals, and wellnigh inaccessible save in the dead of winter, when some adventurous soul of doubtful judgment might make his way thither on snowshoes.

As it happened, a small party of topographical surveyors of the U.S. Geological Survey was then penetrating into this God-forsaken region, carrying with them their pack-train of mules, camp equipment, and map-making instruments. This was the first pack outfit of any kind to enter into the territory. Senator Penrose and his brothers joined the government party, and by them were conducted well up among the snow-capped peaks of the range.

Continued bad weather having stopped the work of the surveyors and made all mapping impossible, the writer, who was chief of the government party, offered to take Senator Penrose out for a hunt. The Senator and his younger brother, however, were tired out with the long and difficult journey to the government camp, so Dr. Penrose, who had endured the hard climb better than his brothers, volunteered to accompany me to a distant glacier basin, where they expected to find big game. The saddle horses were left at the head of this basin, and, little knowing of the fate that awaited them, the two men separated.

I had just sighted a fine buck deer and was on the point of creeping away from it so that Dr Penrose might come and kill it, when I heard three shots in rapid succession. I gave no special heed to the reports, which came from the other side of the ridge, and was about turning to shoot the deer myself, when I heard two more shots; a moment more and another report rang out. Immediately becoming alarmed, I ran back in the direction from whence the shots came. I suppose I reached the doctor in about five or ten minutes. As I came around a mass of broken boulders I saw Dr Penrose wandering aimlessly around in the canyon bed. He had no gun. His hat was gone, his coat torn off, and his trousers rent. Blood poured from his head and neck, and he gripped his left arm in his crimson right hand. When I reached him he murmured piteously, "Water, water." I ran and brought water in my big sombrero from the other side of the rocks. He drank it like a thirsty horse, and I thought I saw part of it run out through a gash in his cheek. Then he said: "Stiles, I am all in; I have had a fight with a bear."

With signal cloth I hurriedly began to tie up the worst of his wounds, and as I did so the picture and the bleeding man told me the story. A few rods down the gulch lay a grizzly cub, so large as to appear full-grown, except to the careful observer. Near by was the huge carcass of a mother grizzly, and near her the doctor's Mauser rifle, cast aside and empty. All was plain now. In his excitement Dr Penrose had not noted that the bear which his first three shots had so promptly slain was yet a young cub, whose grief-stricken and enraged mother might then be making her way from the rocks and brush to avenge the death of her offspring. Going down to examine his prize, he placed his rifle on a rock, fortunately not far away.

He was stooping over the dead cub when there came from behind a rush and an awful cry. He turned and saw the mother bear coming upon him, then not sixty feet away. With almost superhuman presence of mind Dr Penrose caught up his Mauser again and fired two shots into the enraged beast. Instantly he took from his pocket his last remaining cartridge, worked it into the rifle, and sent a third steel-jacketed bullet into the on-rushing bear. Swift and sure as were the little bullets, the bear's fury was not checked in time. With one stroke of her paw she sent him into the gulch, eight feet below. She sprang down after him and caught him in her mouth and shook him as a cat might shake a mouse. She dropped him. Again she caught him up, his face between her glistening tusks. She tore his scalp; his eyes narrowly escaped. A tusk penetrated into his mouth from the side of his cheek; another tore open his throat. There were five gaping wounds in his chest. His thigh bore an awful, irregular tear, and the flesh hung in ragged pieces from the wound, half as wide as your hand. His left wrist was twisted and broken, and the bones stuck out through the quivering flesh. The bear tried once more to shake her half-dead victim, but she sickened with her own awful wounds, and, staggering, fell dead at his feet.

The little Mauser bullets, fired a moment before, had finally had their deadly effect, and by his steady nerve and accurate aim Dr Penrose had saved his own life. Had the beast lasted another half minute the doctor would have been with his fathers, and the little cub's death would have been avenged. But the heroic mother had fought to the last, and now, with her dead baby, lay quiet and still forever.

Recovering sufficiently, the bleeding man sat up and began to take stock. As he meditated thus, there came a new adversary. In actual fact, or in the suffering man's delir[i]ous fancy—I have never known which—a third bear bounded out of the brush from another direction. The doctor's heart sank; he could make no resistance now; he hoped that death might come quickly. The new enemy approached to close quarters, and, walking around, snarled and growled savagely, yet evidently undecided what to do. Then, with a cry of mingled rage and fright, it dashed off down the gulch and was lost in the forest.

The journey back to camp was difficult and dangerous, but the suffering doctor, who now began to realize his frightful condition, was bearing up bravely. Wrapping my big cow-boy slicker around him, I managed to get him on my horse, and we turned back to camp, where we had left the Penrose party. My faithful horse did his duty nobly, as we climbed and stumbled along for two hours without trail, at last reaching the teepees at nightfall. The unexpected sight of the wounded and bleeding doctor somewhat demoralized the group of waiting men, and after some delay a pine-knot camp-fire was made for light, and with the patient lying at full length on the ground I began my surgical operations, assisted by such much-needed instruction as the doctor, in his awful pain, could give me while the work progressed. I applied antiseptics and placed bandages, all of which happily he had with him in a small emergency case. Finally the broken wrist was reached. It was agreed that I should remove the protruding bones, the nervy patient thinking he could endure the pain of the operation without anesthetics. I disinfected the little knives and appliances and the last operation began. The pain was awful. With one agonized groan the man gave up for the first time. We held a hurried conference. The wrist would have to be left as it was, and we bound it up once more in signal cloth. It was one o'clock in the morning when I finished my amateur surgery. Thoroughly distracted by the sight of their brother's suffering, Senator Penrose and Spencer withdrew to another tent, and I lay down near Dr Penrose to wait for dawn.

My life on the frontier has been full of trying episodes, but oh, that night! How would we get Dr Penrose out of the mountains? I dare not guess how many times I asked myself that question. As the gloomy hours dragged by I listened to the heavy breathing of the man whose nerve and fortitude I had already come to admire, now asleep and groggy with the morphine injected to stop his unbearable suffering.

To go back the way we came up would mean two days and a 600-foot climb on foot. He could not last. By the second day we would be packing out a dead body. Yet there was no other route. The situation was desperate. In the lonely flickering of that camp-fire I meditated, and my sympathies went out to that wounded man. As the case presented itself at that moment success in guiding the party to the railroad meant the doctor's life, if not his comfort; failure meant death, simply. Before that welcome dawn had come I decided to run a hazard. We would take Dr Penrose to the railroad by an unheard of route. Providence might point the way.

At dawn the little caravan started. Again the big black horse carried the almost helpless doctor, Senator Penrose and Spencer walking on either side to steady their brother through the tight places. The faithful guide, Bill Hague, lead the extra "packs," and two young men from the Survey party, Malcolm Force, of Montclair, New Jersey, and Billy Kemeys, of Washington, D.C., worked as axemen. Thus, for eleven hours, we climbed down, down, down, five miles through the forest and jungle, cutting our way as we went. At dark we dropped through to the railroad, completely exhausted, but safe. Our route had proved successful. I could not have cut another tree or broken another brush, and my two Survey boys had stood by me like men.

Quickly we conducted Dr Penrose to a lonely section-house two miles down the track, where the Great Northern Limited was flagged, and he was taken away to Minnesota, where, three days later, he was operated upon by the surgeons at the Mayo Hospital. Since then he has retired to his country home near Philadelphia. Though his recovery is not yet complete, his progress has been very remarkable.

As a memento of the encounter with the bear, Dr Penrose has presented the writer with a beautiful Mauser rifle, imported from the Krupp works at Essen, Germany. In the stock of the rifle is set a little silver nameplate which bears the simple inscription: "Arthur Stiles, from C.B. Penrose."

# How "Old Two Toes" Got His Name

*L. W. (Gay) Randall, son of one of Montana's first dude ranchers, Dick Randall, told of three fatal maulings by a grizzly dubbed "Old Two Toes" in his book* **Footprints Along the Yellowstone***. The first account involved Johnny Graham, an experienced hunter who set out to trap a giant grizzly north of Gardiner, Montana, in the early 1900s. Unfortunately, Graham's efforts failed and he was killed. Three bloody toes were left in the trap; thus the bear acquired the name "Old Two Toes." The following excerpt was taken from the chapter titled "Bear Hunting Parties—Old "Two Toes"—A Trip On the Hell Roaring River," pp. 139-143 of Randall's book, published by the Naylor Publishing Company in San Antonio; copyright 1961.*

After a hard Montana winter, spring is usually late. It was mid-April. The deep snow was mostly melted. The ground was saturated and soggy. Johnny Graham, old prospector and miner, walked briskly from his log cabin high on the side of Crevasse [Crevice] Mountain, in the Jardine mining area just north of Gardiner. Johnny was going to his mining claim a half-mile around the side of the mountain. He was tired of the inactivity of the long winter, and wanted to get working on his mining claim as soon as possible. Hageman and Brown, the other claim owners, were his only neighbors on the mountain. He was even tired of seeing them every week or so.

About halfway to the mine, the tracks of a big bear angled down the steep slope, following along Johnny's trail to the mine. The prints were plainly outlined in the damp soggy earth. Johnny could hardly believe his own eyes. These were the biggest bear tracks he had ever seen, long and wide. The straight claw marks made it plain that this was a grizzly. Johnny stepped in one of the plain prints carefully with his heel to the bear's heel imprint. The bear's foot was longer than his, well over a foot long. The track was fairly fresh, but there was no way of telling just how long ago it had been made, certainly though, not more than a day.

Johnny hurried back to his cabin to get his rifle. There was no feed available for bears at this time of year, except an ant hill or a leftover cache of pine squirrel's pinion nuts. Johnny reasoned that this monster bear had scented the carcass of his old pack horse beyond the mine tunnel, that he had shot in the late fall when he had broken his leg. Johnny hurried back along the trail in the hopes of catching this monster bear feeding on the carcass. His experience as a hunter made him cautious in approaching the remains lying partially concealed in the edge of a clump of scrubby pine timber. Some magpies fluttered away as he approached and he knew immediately that only birds were feeding on the old horse.

A close-up inspection revealed that the big bear had been there and gorged himself on a very large portion of the half-rotted horse meat, which was probably his first meal after coming out from hibernation.

The chance of getting this old monster was good. Johnny reasoned that he would return within a day or so at most for another feed, although he now probably had the belly ache and scours from his big feed. There was hardly a chance of catching him feeding at the bait during the daytime. He immediately returned to his cabin to get the sixty-pound, Newhouse bear trap that had caught him many a bear on this same mountain, but never one with a foot like this one.

The labor of lugging the big trap three-quarters of a mile, and making a perfect natural set, was offset with excited expectation of catching what he was sure was the largest grizzly that had ever roamed the area. After finishing the set, he decided he wanted to tell his neighbor prospector about the big bear, so he walked another mile along the mountain side to Hageman's cabin. Johnny and Hageman visited and talked, Johnny telling him of the foregoing details, otherwise, the complete story about Johnny Graham's last trapping experience would never have been known.

The next morning Hageman was purposely puttering around outside his cabin. Johnny's trap set was within gunshot hearing distance and Hageman knew that Johnny would go to look at his trap the first thing. He listened expectantly until after ten o'clock. There were no shots, so he surmised that the old bear had not come back to the bait the night before.

On the following morning it was different. Before nine o'clock Hageman heard the unmistakable boom of Johnny's old 45-90, and a few seconds later another shot echoed down into the Bear Creek Canyon. Hageman knew that Johnny was an experienced hunter, with steady nerves and a good shot. "I was just about as excited as if it was my bear, and immediately decided to go help Johnny skin him," Hageman told me later.

When Hageman arrived at Johnny's trap set a half-hour later there was no response to his call. He followed the heavy clog drag marks down the hill a couple of hundred yards. There he found Johnny, torn and mangled, moaning out his last breath of life, too far gone to talk or explain anything. There was no bear to be seen. There was nothing he could do for Johnny—he was gasping his last agonies of a terrible death from mutilation. The monster killer was gone.

Hageman hastily sized up the scene of battle. Johnny's gun was leaning against a tree thirty yards away. The bark was scarred and torn on the tree nearby with teeth marks and claw scratches. Between two fallen logs lay the big-toothed jawed trap with its heavy eight-foot clog of green pine log jammed tight between the fallen logs. In the trap jaws were three bloody toes with four inch claws.

There was only one conclusion at which to arrive. Johnny had come to the bait that morning to find that the trap was gone. Following it down the hill a couple of hundred yards, he spotted his monster bear tangled up in the windfall, accounting for the two shots. The bear was stunned, although Johnny mistook him for dead, leaned his gun against a tree, then walked down to start the skinning job. The bear suddenly came to and lunged out of the trap and tore Johnny up.

Hageman high-tailed it into Gardiner on foot as fast as he could, making record time for eight miles of rocky up-and-down-hill going. He hurriedly told his story, and immediately Dad [Dick Randall] and a couple of men volunteered to go back with Hagemen and a pack horse to bring in Johnny's body.

That night there was much talk around the saloons. A hunt for the killer grizzly was organized for next day. A local guide named Dock Shores, had a pack of lion dogs, blood hounds, and wolf hounds that were good trailers, so it was decided they could follow the trail easily from the blood that this old brute would leave.

I had a good grain-fed horse that was used to rough mountain going, so I horned in on the party for the excitement of it. Before nine o'clock the next day we were at the site of the killing of Johnny Graham. Dock set his half-dozen hounds loose on the trail. The various toned voices of their barking and baying echoed down into Bear Creek Canyon with a continuous vibration. As they took to the trail the excitement of the chase of tracking down a man killer was on.

The going was tough through sparsely-timbered country, rough and rocky underfoot, with so many rocky ledges that we had to pick an easier way around than the trail that the dogs were traveling. Sometimes the dogs headed into the more densely timbered Crevass [Crevice] Basin making a circle in the heavy timber, then streaked out down the slope towards the Yellowstone River. We were handicapped by the rough terrain, following as fast as we could in the general direction of the baying hounds. Finally these sounds became fainter and we had only the general direction to follow, stopping to listen occasionally as the barking grew fainter. After a couple of hours' chase, with our clothing torn from low hanging limbs, bleeding and scratched hands and faces, we came to the Yellowstone River. The dogs had stopped here, losing the trail scent. They were barking and sniffing the ground, whimpering for another trail scent. On the loose sand bar of the river bank, there were enough clear footprints of the big killer to determine that he had taken to the river.

We all knew that this was the end of the chase. We were inside the boundary lines of Yellowstone Park nearly two miles, with dogs and unsealed firearms, which was unlawful. We did not tarry long. Dock Shores hastily led the way up Crevasse [Crevice] Creek on an old game trail that would take us back across the boundary line in the least possible time.

The park was then patrolled by U.S. Cavalry troops stationed at Fort Yellowstone, at Mammoth Hot Springs. Guides operating in the area were particularly anxious to keep in the good graces of the gruff army major who was Park Superintendent.

Although we were trying to capture a man killer, the army and park rules undoubtedly would grant no leniency for men with loose dogs and firearms within the boundaries, but would confiscate our outfits, and mete out a stiff fine and a term in the guard house.

It was there, where we had to quit the trail of this monster killer, that we tagged him "Old Two Toes" while he retreated to the sanctuary of the interior of Yellowstone Park, where he was undoubtedly born. Little did I suspect that I would ever see this killer and, least of all, that I would meet him face to face in close quarters in the near future.[5]

# "Two Toes" Kills Again

*Randall related another story about a second victim who died from wounds sustained in an encounter with "Old Two Toes," on pp. 148-150 of his book. According to Randall's account, freight driver Pat Welsh (or Welch) died after being mauled while he slept under his food-filled freight wagon in Yellowstone Park. A September 12, 1916 news article in* **The Livingston Enterprise** *reported a similar story but said the victim was Frank Welch of Corwin Springs, Montana.*

Word came in from the park [Yellowstone] that Pat Welsh, a freighter, had been almost torn to pieces by a bear at Soda Butte, on the Gardiner-Cooke City Road inside the park. Pat had been taken in to the hospital at Mammoth Hot Springs and was not expected to live.

The details, pieced together later by Pat and Buff Anderson, another freighter, of the gruesome hand-to-hand encounter proved it had been Old Two Toes and his second victim.

The mining town of Cooke City is sixty miles east of Gardiner and just north of the Yellowstone Park boundary line, laying snowbound and practically isolated most of the winter. Supplies for its some seventy-five residents must be freighted in over the road through the park before the roads became choked with the heavy snow. Pat Welch [sic] and Buff Anderson were two of the husky freighters who liked to get their heavy hauling done before the unimproved dirt road became soft from the equinoctial storm which usually struck in September.

This was their first main trip of the fall, their freight wagon with a trail wagon loaded with the usual staple supplies for a mining community, was pulled by six horse teams.

Pat's wagons were loaded with sugar, flour, and crates of cured ham and bacon. As usual, they camped at their regular spot at Soda Butte Creek. The weather was clear and they unrolled their bedrolls under their respective wagons, as was their habit in fair weather. Along about midnight, Buff Anderson was awakened by Pat's husky voice and the clatter of pans, at his wagon about fifty yards away. Buff called to ask what the trouble was. Pat replied that a bear was tearing his load to pieces. By the time Buff slipped on his trousers, Pat was yelling for help. When he came near Pat's wagon, he could distinguish Pat's body in the pale moonlight writhing on the ground with the bear growling over him. They had no firearms for defense, as they were inside the park boundaries. Immediately, Buff thought of the Roman candles they carried for the purpose of running persistent bears from their camp. By the time he located and lighted one of the Roman candles and it was shooting balls of fire in the general direction, Pat was moaning in dreadful agony. The massive frame of fur, mauling and tearing at Pat's body, rose to its full height on hind feet. Buff shook the fire-spitting candle furiously, with the balls of fire landing full in the chest of the killer that looked as big as one of his Percheron freight horses. Even in the dim light Buff was sure that this was the biggest bear that he had ever seen, and that it was a grizzly. Black and brown bears were frequently bothersome around the freight outfits but this was his first experience with a grizzly, and he was not sure whether the fireballs from the Roman candles would frighten this monster away. The only weapon he could think of was his axe in the jockey box and he realized he would have little chance to get it or use it effectively on a mountain-sized brute like this. The fireballs were confusing the big beast, a half-dozen had landed in his fur before he finally lumbered off into the shadows.

Pat was moaning pitifully on the ground. Buff lighted a kerosene lantern. There was no way of telling how badly Pat was hurt. It was about two miles to the nearest help at the ranger station. Buff hesitated about leaving Pat alone while he went for help, so there was only one thing to do, take a chance. Buff drug Pat's bedroll out from under the wagon and wrapped him in the blankets, built up a fire which he figured might help keep the big killer away, then he went for help.

Crushed, mangled, clawed and bitten, Pat lay for four days in the hospital.

He gave a meager account of the happenings in his moments of consciousness. He said, "I was roused out of a sound sleep by the sound of ripping canvas. I crawled out of my bed from under the wagon. In the dim starlight I could see the big hulk of a bear on top of my trail wagon tearing the tarpaulin cover off my load of crated hams and bacon. I threw my frying pan and cooking kettles at him. He came off the wagon snarling. I yelled for Buff to help. I knew that this bear was going to fight. The only thing I had to defend myself with was my axe. He came at me growling as I picked up the axe and made a swing at him. I hit him once. He knocked the axe out of my hands and was on top of me clawing and tearing; then everything turned black."

The tracks in the road dust were unmistakable. Old Two Toes had killed another man and was again on the loose.

A two-time killer grizzly loose in a community is food for a lot of talk, speculation, and a certain amount of fear. Every guide and hunter in the area knew that this big brute now was not afraid of men, and whoever came across him would have a fight on his hands. Any grizzly, when wounded or surprised in a tight spot, is master of the situation, feared and respected by every animal. He is the monarch of the animal kingdom. Now that he had killed two men, Two Toes would not fear the smell of man whom he could conquer. He would be more cunning than ever, more savage and fearless than an African lion.

# Another "Two Toes" Victim

*The third known victim of "Old Two Toes" was prospector/trapper Joseph "Frenchy" Duret. According to Randall, Duret, or Douret as he spells it, was found dead by a friend several days after he had been missing. However, in an article in the June 9, 1923 **Literary Digest**, another account of Duret's death was reported. In the magazine article, it was written that Duret had told his wife he had caught a large grizzly in one of his traps and that he was going to kill it. When he failed to return home that afternoon his wife sent out a search party. Duret's mangled body was found the next day by a park ranger. According to the magazine article, Duret had apparently crawled 1 1/2 miles after escaping the bear because there was evidence of struggle at that distance. One cartridge had been fired from his Winchester, and the bear escaped with the heavy trap.*

*Below is Randall's account of the tragedy, which was excerpted from **Footprints Along the Yellowstone**, pp. 161-163.*

Then one day the news came to town. Old Two Toes had got his third victim, Frenchy Douret [Duret], a prospector and trapper who was holding down a claim on Slough Creek just outside the park [Yellowstone] boundary line. Frenchy, as was his usual custom, was doing some spring trapping for bears. A neighbor prospector who used to visit with Frenchy frequently, came to Frenchy's cabin. There was no sign of Frenchy about. Inside the cabin he found conditions that indicated that Frenchy had been gone for some days. Unwashed dishes and the leftovers from a meal remained on the usually clean table, the tell-tale piece of smelly, half-spoiled meat, dregs in the coffee cup that had dried up, a residue of dust covering a syrup smeared plate. Also, Frenchy's old 45-70 rifle was gone.

Charley, the neighbor prospector knew that Frenchy had a bear trap set up the creek at the carcass of an old bull elk. The evidence summed up quickly enough by any mountain man was enough to suspect that Frenchy had met with an accident.

At the bait, where Frenchy had his bear trap set, the evidence was clear enough to reconstruct what had happened. The trap was gone from the bait. Following the drag trail of the heavy clog, Charley soon found Frenchy's torn and battered body. Two empty rifle shells were found nearby.

It could only be surmised that Frenchy had come close to the smart old killer and fired; the maddened bear somehow got to him and tore and mauled him to death.

A little party of nearby prospectors took up the trail of Old Two Toes. He was headed toward the park. Within a mile he had been successful in tearing the heavy clog loose from the trap. Following the now cold trail, it was evident that the old killer was traveling on three legs, holding the trap up to clear the ground. Inside the park boundary, he headed for the open country of the La Mar. Here on the bare ridges the trackers gave up, as hopeless, tracking down this cunning old killer whose trail then was a week or more old. From the way he was traveling it seemed that he was not badly handicapped either by bullet wounds or the 60-pound trap.

In talking it over, Dad [Dick Randall] reasoned that Old Two Toes crossed the Buffalo Divide from our bait that fall, to the north slope to hibernate. When spring came, he either forgot about the covered-over, deepfreeze horse, or did not want to make the trip across the divide through the deep snow. Instead he just drifted down the Buffalo Fork to Slough Creek and found Frenchy's bait.

About a year later, the trap was found near the Yellowstone River. There was no clue as to how Old Two Toes got out of it, only the possibility that the foot had rotted off, freeing him of the trap.

For two years or more everyone in the locality kept a sharp lookout for signs of Old Two Toes, the man killer. No one ever reported seeing tracks that would identify him again. Whether or not he died from the wounds of his last encounter with Frenchy, or whether he just died of old age, no one will ever know.

# Tales of Hunting and Trapping Bruin

Western frontiersmen had an unspoken "status symbol" similar to the Indian coup. Many white males measured their own success in terms of bearskins. For each bear a man killed, he rose higher on the scale of heroics. After all, bears of any size, color, sex, age or species were the undisputed ENEMY of man, and each one killed was a victory for civilization.

With this common goal to eradicate bears, men often spent their spare time hunting or trapping the unlovable creatures. Bear hunting wasn't exactly considered a sport because most sports have rules that ensure fair play. However, in the pursuit of bruin, there were no rules other than all should be killed. Even the Boone and Crockett Club, which maintained a particular ethical code for hunting ruminants, failed to protect bears from unrestrained slaughter. Bears were not considered game animals; they were predators.

No, man didn't hunt bears for food or sport as he did for deer or elk. Man hunted and trapped bears because it was his duty to rid the wilderness of these undesirable and dangerous animals. Cubs were just as bad as the big ones, and bringing home a cub pelt was almost as admirable as bringing home its dead mother.

Although some men rendered the fat and sliced off a few steaks, securing the pelt as proof of another dead bear for the bounty and the glory was the main objective of most frontier bear hunters. Sometimes claws or teeth were also taken as souvenirs, but most of the bear meat was left to rot.

Many would-be bear hunters caused themselves or others problems by carelessness or poor marksmanship. Some men would shoot a bear on sight, taking long or poorly aimed shots which only wounded and enraged the bear. There were also those bear hunters who shot at bears and allowed the wounded animals to go unpursued because of their fear or inexperience in tracking. Never was the animal's suffering considered.

Bear hunting has changed somewhat since those frontier days. In those states which still maintain bear populations, bears are now classified as game animals, which gives them some protection against unlimited slaughter. Some hunters today now respect the animals and hunt them fairly or do not hunt them at all. But the ingrained hatred and fear of bears still persists in others who share their forefathers' belief that the only good bear is a dead bear.

# One Bearskin Is Plenty

*Mathias Nash had visions of four bearskin rugs dancing in his head, but to his dismay, the hunter was sharply brought back to reality when the bears decided he was fair game. Mr. Nash's story first appeared in the November 3, 1901 **Anaconda Standard**, but a later version printed in the **Rocky Mountain Husbandman**, September 16, 1937, was more colorful and appears below.*

One day nearly 40 years ago, Mathias Nash, then a resident of Philbrook in central Montana, decided to go bear hunting in the Little Belts. He started out hopefully, of course, but it really seemed that his expedition was to be crowned with unusual success when he jumped four bears right off the bat. He had visions of four bearskin rugs covering the floors of his home and of admiring and interested neighbors gathered about in breathless silence, listening to him tell the story of their origin.

His one fear was that after he had killed the first, the other three would run away, probably in three different directions, and that he would be unable to get more than one or two of them. He decided in fact, that he might as well make up his mind to be satisfied with, say, three of them. The fourth would probably go so far away before he could get on its trail that he might not be able to overtake it.

So after having settled all this in his mind, he whanged away with his rifle and shot and killed the first bear. The others ran, but to his dismay, instead of running away, they ran towards him. They were too close for him to attempt to kill them one at a time, and Nash was not used to killing more than that at one time. So he ran, too.

The pursuit was hot, right from the start. Fleeting glances over his shoulder indicated to him that he wasn't doing so well in the contest, and the thought flashed through his mind that it might be well to climb a tree, in line with the philosophy of an eminent gentleman who once said that discretion was the better part of valor. So he climbed a tree that happened to be convenient to his course, and he did so almost without missing a stride. But he had to discard his rifle in order to do it.

There was solace to the thought, however, that the rifle would be of no use to him whatever if he were dead, but that lying safely on the ground and him alive in a tree, it would be only a matter of time until he could again possess himself of the weapon.

From high in the branches he looked down on the three bears which sat on their haunches at the foot of his perch, licked their chops and growled. Now and then one of them would rise to all four feet and lumber about the tree for a few minutes, only to resume its haunch position.

Mr. Nash sat in silence. The bears stuck on the job. The afternoon shadows began to grow long, and longer. A westerly breeze fanned his cheek. Below him one of the bears pawed at his rifle where he had dropped it in his flight.

When sundown came Nash began to be annoyed. The bears seemed to be prepared to stay all night. The treed hunter's ire rose, and finally he lost all patience. This was no way for bears to act. It was against all rules of the game.

Finally, when he had stood it as long as he could, he gripped his tree limb for one final effort and unloosed at the unsuspecting bruins beneath him a vocabulary enriched by long association with expert mule drivers and bull whackers over rough trails. His vocal effort was entirely successful. It brought him no bear rugs, but it drew the attention of the three chop-licking beasts at the foot of the tree. They looked at him and as he stopped for breath, they looked at each other. When he started in again, they lumbered to their feet and went away.

Nash remained in the tree long enough to assure himself that it wasn't a ruse upon the part of the bears before he slid to the ground. He recovered his rifle and went home. The next day he went back and brought in the one bear skin. He told himself that one was plenty.

# Saved By a Stroke of Genius

*Oregon bear hunter John Griffin told of an exciting encounter he and his trained bear dog had with an angry grizzly. At the time, Griffin was hunting alone and felt compelled to shoot an animal. His friend had recently killed two deer, and Griffin was envious of his luck. Griffin's opportunity came when a grizzly appeared. However, his gun failed and the hunter was forced to drop his gun and climb a tree. While the bear waited at the bottom of the tree, Griffin had to think his way out of his predicament. Ingenuity and his dog Trailor saved Griffin. The veteran bear hunter's unusual experience was published in the September 1921 Forest and Stream on pp. 389-391; 421-424, titled "Trailing the Grizzly In Oregon."*

Some people may think it is all joy to hunt big game in a wild country where you are many miles from civilization, but if you will believe me, there is a good deal of work and genuine hardship mixed up with it.

The hunt I am going to write about occurred many years ago in Oregon. I was accompanied by Riley Hammersly, who has since become a noted hunter himself and has been a game warden in Oregon for many years. This was Riley's first bear hunt and before it was over he realized that he had been up against the real thing.

We took with us on this trip seven good pack horses, only one, however, with provisions and blankets. The others carried empty pack saddles to use to pack our game back and I had my bear dogs, Trailor and Ranger, as we expected to get some bear. Our route lay up Big Butte Creek in Jackson County, Oregon, past Rancharie Prairie, where we camped the first night, and the next day we went to Four Mile Lake and made camp. This lake is situated north of Old Mt. Pitt and is about one-half mile wide and a mile and a half long and is surrounded by open prairie covered with high grass and water cold as ice. There were huckelberries [sic] in every direction from this lake, and in those days there were all kinds of game, such as bear, elk and deer, and grouse by the hundreds in the berry patches.

That evening, after establishing our camp, we went out hunting for meat, as that is about the first thing to do when out on a hunt. We left the dogs in camp and went south towards Mt. Pitt and after traveling perhaps a mile and a half we ran into a big patch of low huckelberry [sic] bushes which were just loaded down with berries, and in a few minutes young, half grown grouse began to fly and light on the trees all around us. Our guns began to crack and we soon had all we wanted and started back to camp. After going a short distance Riley asked me to take the grouse on to camp and said that he would make a little round and see if he could kill a deer for camp meat. Off he went in an easterly direction and I went straight towards camp.

I had gone about half way when I came to a small burn of perhaps two or three acres with some green brush in the middle that the fire had not touched. It struck me that this was a good place for a deer to be lying in at this time of the day, so I approached it cautiously with my gun loaded and ready. I was prepared to drop the grouse quickly and shoot, as I knew that if there were any deer in the brush when they discovered or heard me they would go out mighty lively, and I would have to be quick to get one before he got to the timber a short distance away.

Sure enough, when I got there out went two spike or yearling bucks and away they went, so fast that they were half way to the timber before I could get any kind of a bead on them. As good luck would have it, there was a big log lying right in front of them, and as the one that was behind sprang over it I fired and he was gone out of sight. I went over and took a look and found blood, and after following the trail for forty or fifty yards I found the deer lying dead. I dressed it and putting it on my shoulder, took it to camp and hung it up. Then I cleaned the grouse, built a fire and started supper, expecting Riley to be back in a short time. But he didn't come in until just about dark, and I had finished supper. Although he had not seen a thing to shoot at he had seen a lot of game signs and had found where an old bear had been feeding in a huckelberry [sic] patch recently. This was better luck than I was looking for, as it generally took one day to size the country up and find where the bear were using.

The next morning we were up bright and early, and after another meal of venison, hot bread, butter and coffee we were off. It was about two miles to the berry patch where we saw the bear sign and we lit out for that the first thing. When we got there we found that there had been no bear there during the night and the sign that Riley had seen was too old now for the dogs to track. This was a little bit disappointing, but we went on, however, keeping the same course for awhile, and then I left Riley and turned south towards the Lake of the Woods. Riley said he would keep on east for a while, and then would swing around south and follow the hillside facing towards Pelican Bay.

The country I was passing through was pretty heavily timbered and rather brushy and although I heard deer several times go bouncing off, I never caught sight of any. As I neared the top of the Divide, however, I began to find more open ground, with now and then an open glade that looked more favorable for game. Pretty soon I came to a burn of perhaps eight or ten acres and had the satisfaction of seeing two big bucks just going out on the opposite side. They disappeared before I had time to shoot, so I went on to where I had seen them, and discovered that both tracks were of immense size. This made me pretty anxious to get one or both of them, so I made up my mind to follow them.

Trailor was a wonderful dog to slow track and I put him on the track and put a string on the other dog to keep him back, as I knew he was liable to break at any minute and I could control Trailor without any trouble. The trail led us down the hill a ways and then turned to the right and went out around the side of old Mt. Pitt for probably a half or three-quarters of a mile. It then turned and went down into a basin. I could see all over it, but the brush was so high that I knew there was no use in going down in it for if I got the deer up there would be no chance to see them.

So I concluded to turn Ranger loose and send him down and take chances on getting them as they came out, as the ground was favorable on either side, unless they should happen to go out down hill. I started Ranger on the tracks and, selecting a good place, waited results. He never made a noise, but I could see the bushes shake as he went along, and when he got down in the middle I heard him start to bay and then the brush began to crack and I could see the big horns of the deer as they tore through the high brush. In a few seconds one of them turned down hill and the other, after tearing along for thirty or forty yards, came out into an open rocky place and dropped into a walk, holding his head high up with his big antlers waving back and forth, making a grand sight.

I caught a bead behind his shoulders and fired. He sprang high in the air and flapped his tail down, which was a sure sign that the bullet had passed through his heart. He ran a few yards and fell. Ranger had gone after the other one and in a minute or two I heard him commence to bay. I went on down and there was the deer backed up against a bush and every now and then he would make a vicious lunge at Ranger, who would get out of his way. I kept Trailor with me and made my way down to within fifty yards of the deer and then shot him in the neck, and down he went. He was a big one, having nine points on one horn and ten on the other. The one I had killed first was a six-pointer. Both of them were very fat. All I could do now was to dress them and turn them over on their backs as I couldn't hang them up alone.

I now turned back east again and hunted towards the ridge that Riley was supposed to be on. I passed through some fine hunting ground but saw no more deer until I got to a creek that runs into the Lake of the Woods, called Paradise Creek. Here I ran into a bunch of does and fawns that stood and looked at me until I had counted them and then I walked towards them. This was a great temptation to Ranger and I had to watch him pretty closely and speak pretty sharply to him several times, but he didn't go after them. Trailor looked at them and then looked at me and looked back again, as much as to say: "Aren't you going to shoot those deer?" I said: "Never mind, Trailor, we don't want them." That ended it. He seemed perfectly satisfied and never looked toward them again.

I crossed the creek and went on until I got to the top of the ridge that overlooks Pelican Bay, and here I concluded to blow the horn and see if I could find Hammersly. Sure enough, he answered me away off down the hill towards the Lake of the Woods, and in a few seconds he blew his horn again and this time he gave me the signal to come to him. I lit out down that way and every now and then I would stop and give the horn a toot and he would answer me.

After going perhaps a mile I came up to him and found him sitting on a log waiting for me. He didn't seem to be in any hurry to tell me what he wanted, so I said: "What is the matter with you? What do you want?" He said: "Come here and I'll show you something." So I went down to where he was and he said: "Look there." I looked and saw a n [sic] immense bear track just below the log that he was sitting on. He said he had been following the track for two hours without stopping. While we were talking the dogs jumped over the log and upon discovering the track were off like a shot. We could hear them going down towards the lake making one continual roar, and I knew they were bound to overtake the bear before long, if they kept that up. So we struck out after them and we went pretty lively, too, I can tell you. It wasn't long before we heard them give voice to a different note, and then I knew that the fight was on.

We hurried along as fast as possible and every little while we would stop and listen, and every time they seemed to be in the same place, although they did not bark as though they had treed the bear. I told Riley we would have to be very cautions [sic] and not let the bear know that we were coming or we might have a big chase, so when we got down to within a hundred yards of him we slid along as easily as we could. There was lots of timber but very little brush, so we made sure to keep behind the trees until we got up to within fifty or sixty yards. We moved along very cautiously and all at once I saw the bear; and where do you suppose he was? Neither up a tree or on the ground, but upon a big log walking back and forth and every now and then stopping to strike down at the dogs, as they would rear up with their paws on the log. He was a big one, an old mealy-nosed brown, not dark, but yellow brown.

It certainly was a great sight. He was entirely unsuspicious of our presence, so we could not resist the temptation to watch the performance a few minutes. It was evident that he was going to stay with that log as he had probably already had a taste of what he would get if he got down off of it, as the ground was level and the dogs would surely make it hot for his hindquarters. Once Trailor got upon the small end of the log and came very near getting him by the ham as he was going the other way, and had his eye on Ranger, but he discovered him in time and with a fierce growl swung around and Trailor got off there in a hurry.

We concluded it was about time for us to take a hand, so we each drew a bead behind his shoulders and fired. Over he went, down on the other side of the log out of sight. We could hear the dogs going after him, however, and long before we got to him I think he was dead, for we had shot him squarely through the heart.

It was now away along in the afternoon, as we dressed him and started for camp. We kept upon the right hand side of the creek on our way back and did not see any more big game, although we passed through lots of huckelberries [sic] and saw plenty of grouse.

We soon arrived at camp and after a good dinner turned in for the night.

The next morning we took the horses with us and went to the place where the two big bucks were and tied the horses up there. Then we went on around the side of old Mt. Pitt to hunt a while before we started back to camp. Riley took the lower side and I kept higher up. I had the dogs with me and was on the lookout for any kind of game that showed up. Once two big bucks jumped up right in front of me, not over fifty yards away, and went tearing off down the hill at a terrific rate, but were out of my sight before I had hardly time to get my gun off of my shoulder, let alone get a bead on them.

They kept straight on down the hill and in a few minutes I heard Riley's rifle commence to crack, bang, bang, bang, seven or eight times. I sat down and waited, for I knew if he needed me he would blow his horn. I did not have to wait long, for in a few minutes I heard the horn—one long, loud blast. Then three short ones, toot, toot, toot. I knew what this meant—to come and come quickly. Well, I started for him and the grass did not grow under my feet, either. When I got down to where he was I found him standing over one of my big bucks and he had also wounded the other one.

There was plenty of blood on the track, so I put Ranger on it, and in a few minutes we heard him baying. I told Riley to go on down and finish him and I would stay and take the entrails out of the other one, as there was no need for both of us to go. So off he went and in a little while I heard Ranger going again and I had no doubt about the cause. Riley had been too eager and had not been cautious enough and the deer had discovered he was coming and made a break. I could hear them going down the hill for quite a ways and then he brought him up again. Riley was a little more cautious this time and after a while I heard him fire one shot, and then I knew it was all over.

I finished dressing the old buck which, by the way, had eight points on each horn, and then concluded to go on, as I had not gotten a shot at anything yet. I kept right on around the south side of old Mt. Pitt, working higher all the time, and although I saw any amount of deer sign it seemed as though luck was against me and I could not get sight of a deer to save my life. I kept on, however, and finally I came to a large grassy place on a kind of bench, and here I discovered an elk's track. From the size of it I supposed it to have been made by a cow, and after tracking around awhile I could see that the elk was alone. The track was not fresh and I soon found that Trailor could not follow it, so I circled the edge of the opening and observed where the elk had gone on through the timber around on the west side of the mountain.

It was easy to follow, so I made up my mind to follow it awhile, anyhow, as there was a chance that I might run across another prairie and find it there. I followed along for perhaps a mile and then concluded to give it up and hunt back towards the horses, as I did not know what had become of Riley and could get no answer after blowing the horn. I found out afterward, though, that he had come back to where he had left me, expecting to find me there, but was disappointed, and thinking that I had started back towards the place where we had left the horses he had gone back to where they were and had waited for me there.

When I turned back I kept high upon the hillside, as I did not want to hunt over the same ground. I proceeded along for probably a half or three-quarters of a mile over some pretty rocky ground and finally came into a belt of timber with scarcely any underbrush, with nice soft ground to walk on. This was quite a relief, as I was getting tired and a little bit discouraged, for, to tell you the truth, I wanted to get something to even up with Hammersly, as those two big bucks kept looming up before my vision, and although I really liked to see Riley have good luck, still I would have been mighty well pleased to have gotten them myself, when I first scared them up, and I also felt that he partly owed his good luck to me. I was very anxious to see something to shoot at and was keeping my eyes open for game.

My anxiety was to be relieved sooner than I expected, for upon coming to the edge of the timber, what should I see but a big grizzly coming towards me. He was not over sixty yards away and was walking along slowly over the rocks, with his head down, perfectly oblivious of everything, and especially of the fact that a man with a gun and a dog was so close to him and ready to dispute the way, for in those days I feared nothing that roamed the woods and had no thought other than to open up the fight, even if it was close quarters.

Just as I raised the gun to my shoulder he stopped and raised one paw to the side of his head, apparently to brush off a fly or something, and just then I fired, intending to pour one bullet after another into him as fast as I could work the lever. But alas! my calculations were to be completely upset for the lever of my gun went down but the cartridge bed failed to come up, and I realized I was up against it, as the bear, upon being hit, reared back, gave a growl, bit at the wound and then came straight for me.

Trailor dashed forward when the gun cracked, having discovered the bear just as he reared up, and he met him half way. He made a pass at the dog, but he swung out and above him and Trailor sprang and grabbed him by the ham. This turned him around, but as Trailor got out of the way he came for me again, and now I had to climb. The limbs on the nearest tree hung low and I had no chance to take the gun, so I dropped it at the root of the tree and I went up about as lively as I ever climbed a tree in my boyhood days, when the other boys and I used to climb to see who could get up the quickest. I may have had plenty of time, but I didn't think that I did, and I didn't think I was safe, either, until I had gotten up quite a ways. The bear was at the bottom of the tree, you can rest assured, in less time than it takes to tell about it, in spite of all that Trailor could do, and was rearing up the tree and tearing at the limbs at a great rate. It was enough to make the cold chills run over a fellow, and I confess that I felt almost afraid he would climb up, too, but I knew positively that a grizzly could not climb, on account of his long claws.

Trailor was unaware that I was up there and no doubt was wondering what had become of me. I called to him now to let him know where I was, as I was beginning to feel pretty safe, but at the same time I was thinking mighty fast about what to do. I said: "Go after him, Trailor, go after him." And he did go after him, too. He brought him away from that tree mighty suddenly and swung him round and round, but he soon backed up against it again, and there he stayed. Right there and then I would have given a kingdom for my gun, but how to get it was the question. Trailor could not get at his hams and he seemed to know that I was wondering and wondering what to do.

I did not have much hope of making Hammersly hear the horn, but I decided to try it anyhow. So I blew the horn long and loud, and I could hear it echo and re-echo across the canyons, and it seemed to me it could be heard for miles and miles, but after listening for a long time I got no answer and after trying a few times more I gave it up.

I now urged Trailor again to go after him, but although he came up as close as he dared and barked right up in his face, the bear only struck out at him with his left paw, as the right one was disabled. I studied and studied what to do and thought of different things that had been said about grizzlies and finally happened to think about hearing a man say once that if he was to go out to hunt grizzlies he would take a strong cord and carry it in his pocket and have a hook attached to it, and if he was compelled to climb from a grizzly he would drop his gun at the roots of the tree and drop the hook down and pull up his gun and then he would make it hot for Mr. Bear. This was all nice enough to think about, but I neither had the string nor the hook, and if I had had them how was I going to use them when the bear was sitting on his haunches almost right on the gun?

Another thing I was puzzled about was why the gun failed to work. It was the first time it had ever failed me, and I had been in some pretty close places, too. I knew I had plenty of cartridges in it, for I had not fired a shot since leaving camp until I had shot the bear.

After awhile, I made up my mind to climb down a few feet and see what he would do, so I commenced to come down very slowly and cautiously, for it was a sure shot I wasn't going to get down low enough for him to rear up suddenly and reach me with his paw.

Pretty soon he whirled around and reared up as high as he could reach and I went up higher in a hurry. This manoeuvre [sic] gave Trailor a chance and he dived into the bear so furiously that he dropped back and made a dash for the dog which took him several feet away from the tree. There they had it round and round for several minutes, but did not get far enough away from the tree to give me the ghost of a chance to get down to get my gun. After a while he got back to the same old place again.

This was getting exasperating and I longed for that gun more than I had ever wanted anything in all my life. I thought to myself: "You old reprobate, if I can ever manage to get hold of that gun I'll make it hot for you." I kept thinking of that cord and hook and all at once an idea entered my head what to do, and I wondered that I had not thought of it before. Why not make a string out of my overalls and a hook out of a limb? No one can realize how elated I was when this thought struck my mind, and I immediately went to work to put it into execution.

I took my hunting knife and ripped my pants clear up, so I could tear off long strips, which I tied together, making a long string. Then I cut off a limb and made a hook, and I was ready. I climbed down again and made all the noise I could, and sure enough, the grizzly tried to come up again. Trailor dived into him again, and down he went and made a dash after him for several yards, and when Trailor began to circle around him and get at his hams he backed up against another tree, and there he stayed.

I did not move now for fear he would come back, but I began to let the hook down towards the gun, which was lying there in plain sight with the lever down. Slowly but surely I let the string down to the ground beside the lever. I gave it a little jerk and it seemed to go under the lever, and I pulled up, but it didn't catch. I dropped it again along side of the lever, and this time, as I slowly brought it up, it hooked into the lever, and the reader can perhaps imagine my feelings when I began to see that gun coming up towards me. Once it caught against a limb, but I let it down again and swung it over a little, and I soon had it in my hands.

I will not attempt to tell you how I felt when I got hold of that gun. I was just simply wild. Now the next thing was to see what was the matter with it. I examined it and soon found that the trouble lay in a faulty cartridge. From some cause or other there had not been powder enough put in the shell and the bullet had been pushed too far back, so that when the shell came into the cartridge bed it allowed the next cartridge in the magazine to come down too far, and the cartridge bed couldn't rise. I soon had it out and a fresh cartridge in the chamber, ready for business, and I was just straightening myself out so as to get in a good position to shoot from when the bear came towards the tree again. I thought to myself, "Old fellow, come ahead; I'll fool you this time."

I was considerably lower now and as he reared up and snorted and champed his teeth I let drive right into his open mouth. The bullet passed through the brain and out between his ears and he went over backwards as though he had been hit in the head with a sledge hammer. He lay with his feet stuck straight up in the air for a few moments trembling and then rolled over on his side, dead.

The whole racket had only lasted about two hours, but it seemed to me that I had been up the tree for two days, and I made up my mind that the next bear that put me up a tree would have to go some; but I took good care to look after my cartridges after that.

I had quite a job dressing him and straightening him around, but I got it done after awhile and Trailor and I started for the horses. I had had enough hunting for one day and really did not care whether I saw any more game or not. Riley was there with the horses when I got back and was a little bit out of patience and wanted to know what had kept me so long, but when I told him the reason he seemed to understand. I told him I didn't want him to wound any more deer for Ranger to catch either, for if I had had Ranger the two dogs might have kept the grizzly so busy that I would have had time to fix my gun.

It was so late now that we only had time to get the four bucks in before dark, and the next day we had a big job packing in the two bears.

# Bears Were His Meat

*One day when heading for the hills to hunt, old-timer Pat "Tommy" Tucker encountered an eager young tenderfoot who had bear hunting in his blood. Tucker agreed the lad could tag along, but the young nimrod was not as fearless as he imagined. Author Grace Stone Coates wrote about their amusing hunting trip in Glacier Park in 1878. Her article appeared July 13, 1932, in the* **Dillon Examiner.**[6]

Pat Tucker plans to "raise a cache," this summer, that was planted 54 years ago in what is now Glacier park.

"I got tired of Fort Benton" [Montana], Tucker says, "and wanted to get away from the smell of whiskey and cards and too many people. I wanted to hit the breeze, get into open country, and smell like a man again. This was in October, 1878, and I decided to ride.

"I was in Sullivan's harness shop, getting an outfit ready. Sullivan is still alive, the oldest saddle maker in Montana. He still lives in Fort Benton. I was getting my three pack saddles fixed up, when a stranger came in, [sic] He had long yellow hair, fringed buckskin suit, and wore moccasins instead of boots.

He walked up to me and said, "Is your name Tucker?"

"Why do you want to know?"

"I heard you were looking for a partner to go with you hunting bear."

"Did you ever kill any bear?"

"I'm a pretty good hunter."

"I looked him over and he was too young to have had much experience hunting. Old man Sullivan looked over at me and winked. The boy asked if these packsaddles were my outfit, and I told him 'yes.' I didn't think he was much of a hunter, but I wasn't particularly anxious to be riding alone, so I took him on.

"We headed up north of where Belton [Montana] is now, and came in on Lake McDonald from the north. We fixed up our camp, made ourselves comfortable, and prepared for a good hunt. Every day the boy would come in with an exciting story about how near he came to getting a deer or an elk, or whatever it was he had seen. But he didn't get anything. 'It was gone in a flash,' he would say, 'before I could get a shot.' He was particularly anxious to get a chance at a bear, for according to him, silver-tips were his meat. We had plenty of fresh meat in camp, for the deer didn't get out of my way as fast as they did out of his. One night, I killed a black-tail deer in a little canyon, and gutted it, then packed the carcass to camp and hung it in a tree. The next morning as I was trailing up the canyon, I came on the tracks of a big silver-tip. I could see where he had been feeding and had cleaned up the refuse where I had dressed the deer. I went back to camp and told the boy, and he was all excited, and in a hurry to get out after the bear.

"Like most wild animals, when a bear has eaten till it's full, it is ready to lie down and sleep, go dead to the world. A full animal will stand and fight rather than try to run, while a hungry animal will run—because it can.

"We trailed the bear, and from his tracks I could see he was a big one. The boy followed right along, and his talk was as big as the bear. Finally we could see where the bear had struck across an open park, and into some thick jack pines. The jack pines were so close he could hardly wiggle through them, but we followed him. On the sunny side of the slope stood two big fir trees, and there lay the bear, curled around behind these trees. We couldn't see all of him, but could see the great hairy slope of shoulder and head. I stopped, and nudged my companion, the bear-hunter. 'There he is,' I said. 'See?' and moved aside to let him get sight of the bear.

"One sight was enough."

" 'You know,' he began to stammer. 'I've got a wife and baby back home, and I don't know if I should stay or not. I think I ought to be going.'

"Go right home to your wife and baby," I said, and he sure started.

"He bolted through that scrub timber like a mad buffalo. I expected to see him drop his gun, he was so excited. I looked for it on the trail, afterward, going to camp, for I thought sure he would fling it down.

"I turned my attention to the old silver-tip. I had a 45-90 take-down Winchester, with buckhorn sides [sic], and I knew how to use it. I brought it down on the old fellow and got him squarely between the eyes. He looked like a mountain as he wallowed around in the snow. He came rolling and plunging right toward me.

"When I knew he was through I went up, stuck my knife in him, and got ready to skin him. As I started to skin him, I saw a man coming over the mountain on the opposite side of the coulee. He was a half breed, a nice fellow. He came over and helped me with the bear. I gave him the tallow and some meat. He wanted me to go with him to his camp, but I told him to come to mine.

"I wasn't surprised, when we got to camp to find that Buckskin Joe had kept right on going. My bed was all torn to pieces, and everything was upset where he had grabbed his bedding and whatever he owned, and lit out.

"The half breed told me that his son was sick, and that his wife and boy were at his camp on the other side of the ridge. I agreed to go back with him, and see what I could do. When we got there I could see the boy was in bad shape. He lay wrapped in buffalo skins, and had had a high fever.

"We didn't have much in the way of medicine in those days, but I always carried some "Three H" with me. You could use it inside or out. I put two teaspoons of that in a cup of water, and gave it to the boy, and kept giving him this all night at intervals. The old folks were asleep. After while he felt a little better, and toward morning said he was hungry. There wasn't a bit of bread in camp, but I had seen a buckskin sack by the door, full of pemmican. I made a pot of coffee, poured the boy out a cup of this, steaming hot, broke a piece of pemmican for him and told him to dip it in the hot coffee and eat it. It did him good, and after a sleep he seemed in pretty good shape.

"They wanted me [to] stay around there for a while, to get them fresh meat for camp, so the man agreed to go back to my camp to help me bring over the things I needed. We went back together and packed up some grub and 30 traps that I had brought in with me.

"I stayed at their camp six days, and when I left I left the traps with the halfbreed. I told him just where to cache them, so I could get them when I came back up again. He was a good square fellow, and I am sure he left those traps right where he said he would. When I was in Fort Benton, that winter, his wife told me he had cached them there.

"After we had the camp supplied with meat, and they had dried some and divided with me, I trailed to my own wickiup, and packed up to go to Fort Benton. I wondered how Buckskin Joe had got along.

"When I got to Fort Benton all of my old friends began to exclaim, 'Why Tuck, I thought you were dead! We heard you had got clawed up by a bear!' Buckskin Joe had gone into [Fort] Benton and tried to organize a rescue party for me, telling a terrible story of my being chewed up by a big silver-tip.

"He stayed around Fort Benton only a day or so, and then headed back to Iowa, and that was the last anybody saw of him.

"I know those traps are right where I said to leave them, and it was a good dry place. They'll be as good as new, and I'm going over this summer to see if I can't raise that cache!"

# One For The Money

*While hunting and trapping and trying to make a living in the Rocky Mountains, three men met a grizzly. Because the bear's hide would help them financially, they pursued the animal. However, unlike many men of their day, these men cautiously and strategically approached the bear, which resulted in a thrilling but safe and successful hunt. Percy Selous wrote of their adventure, which was copyrighted by Bacheller, Johnson and Bacheller in 1896. On May 11, 1896, the* **Anaconda Standard** *printed the story.*

Our camp was near headquarters of the Big Horn river, just where Owl creek runs into it—an ideal spot for a shanty, and in every way adopted to a hunter's requirements. We were out on business—trapping for what our furs would bring us in dollars—not merely a pleasure party. Under such circumstances a bear's hide helps to "tote" up the balance and there was plenty of such game in the mountains. "Old Ephraim" ranged here where he pleased—the giant grizzly of the Rockies, about which thrilling stories have been written, some of them probably rather too highly colored. It is the fashion nowadays to accept with incredulity much that travelers and sportsmen write, and to consider it a hunter's privilege to draw the long bow. I don't pretend to deny that some do embellish their narratives so as to make them savor of the miraculous; but those who have themselves hunted can always discern between the truth and the fiction, even where the truth looks for ordinary stay-at-home mortals almost beyond belief.

"That the lion is the king of beasts" seems to us from infancy to be "Q.E.D."[quod erat demonstrandum-which was to be demonstrated], but the lion can't hold a candle to the grizzly bear, either as to courage or tenacity of life. A full-grown grizzly is more than four times as heavy as the finest lion that ever stepped the veldt; and where a lion will more often than not endeavor to escape, who ever heard of a grizzly acting likewise?—I mean if once molested. Of late years the grizzly, in common with other animals, has "tumbled" to the increased efficacy of modern firearms; but it is a respect which demands reciprocity. Hunters and bears agree pretty well nowadays, so long as both go their respective ways. The hunter provides the bear with sundry meals, and in return he is permitted to enjoy himself on "Ephraim's" preserves. Once molest him, however, and there is sure to be trouble.

But I must return to Owl creek, where Gerard, Fawcett and I were hunting and trapping generally. One morning we were all busily engaged in chopping wood. It was before the days of the crosscut saw, and every tree had to be chopped down and chopped up—the delirious pleasure of which work can only be duly appreciated by those who have tried it. I was anathematising [sic] the bluntness of my axe and the necessity of laying in a supply of firing, when a prolonged whistle from Gerard made us both look up; and there, sure enough, stood a huge grizzly in the swamp, some 80 rods from our bit of clearing. Snow had not yet fallen where we were camped, although on the foothills there was plenty and the bear was engaged in munching up what few cranberries remained, for even the carnivorous grizzly enjoys such dainties at times. In fact, where the wild plums grow he will tear down trees to get at the fruit. He had not appeared to pay any attention to the sound of our axes, but when we left our chopping he looked up and raised himself on his hind legs, as though better to take in our position.

"Say, but he has an elegant hide," was Fawcett's remark; which I cut short by bidding him to shut up, or his own hide might become "elegantly" scored. Meanwhile the bear had resumed his normal gait and disappeared into the timber, at the edge of the marsh through which the creek made a bend.

Thinking that in all probability he would not cross the stream, but follow it up towards the mountains, we hastily arranged that I should follow on his trail, which was easy enough to hold, even through the leaves; whilst Gerard was to cut across some distance to the west and head him off. Fawcett, who was never really sure whether he would get "ague" or not even if he came across a fawn, I advised either to stay in camp or else keep some little distance behind me; for in this sort of hunting you certainly carry your life in your hands and the utmost sang froid is necessary. I still used the converted Enfield carbine, which required capping, though a breech-loader; I also had a heavy bulldog six-shooter which took a ball not much less in caliber than that of my military piece. I had not followed our bear far before a young duck [sic] came tearing back on a run-way which crossed the trail I was taking. He went by me like a streak and with the fright he had evidently received before I added to his terror, he was a well-scared deer. Of course, I took no notice of him, but moved carefully on, expecting every moment to come up with the bear.

I was wondering how far west Gerard had gone and was looking for the bark of his old shooting iron every minute, when, as I was climbing over a big cedar which lay directly in my path from the upturned roots of which I was just about to jump, I almost precipitated myself on to the bear. It was only by holding on to one of the limbs like all I knew how, that I just managed to swing myself round into a close shave; but it served me right for being so hasty. "Step once, look twice," the Indians say.

Down beneath me in the moss was the big grizzly, and he was not slow to resent his intrusion on my part. The stump I was perched on was [a] shockingly bad foothold; but as the bear rose on his hind legs and endeavored to scramble up, I gave him a ball in the chest, for I thought myself too low to fire at his head with certainty. The limb he had got hold of gave way at the same moment, and he went to the ground again. Instantly reloading, I was lucky enough to get a cap out in time, for he was up and at me in a bigger fury than ever. I don't believe I shall ever forget the expression of that particular bear, he was so close to me I certainly had little leisure for making observations, but the huge jaws, all sputtering with blood and foam, were within a few feet of me. I lost no time in giving him another bullet, but although I knew it had gone true, he took about as much notice of it as he would of a saloon.

As I leaped back I caught sight of Gerard coming up in the distance, and I knew he had taken in the situation. The bear had reached my vacated position, and I may be thankful that I was light compared with my huge antagonist. By jumping from one fallen log to another I managed to keep afoot pretty well; whereas the bear crashed through everything like so much match wood—and you may imagine I led into the places most likely to bother him. Then Gerard came up and gave him the contents of his gun without any apparent effect. I had no chance to reload; it was as much as I could do to keep on my feet, not always successful at that; but I kept on letting him have the contents of my revolver, which, from any impression, it appeared to make upon him, I might just as well have left alone—unless, indeed, I wished to make him more furious, which was quite superfluous. All at once he came to a stand; and as he paused I also halted, loading as I did so with all speed. He appeared to be sinking down, at least I thought so as I fired at his eye. Gerard plugged him from behind at the same moment. At the shots he collapsed entirely, and the huge creature, which but a minute before had "raising tarnation" all around, settled down as gently as if he had gone to sleep. I had, of course, loaded up again, but any more shooting was unnecessary as far as he was concerned. We both got up together, Gerard and I, to find that my last shot had struck him full in the eye as was intended.

It had been a pretty lively dance for me, and it was only the nature of the ground, which was all cedar swamp, that saved me. The immense weight of the bear, something like 1,500 pounds, made it impossible for him to get through the soft places without getting mired, whereas I could run along most of the logs without breaking through. As it was, I was all torn up as far as clothing went. Fawcett now came along, and all three of us sat down on the bear. After resting a bit we soon got the skin off and saw that there was one cartridge left in my six-shooter; for, candidly, I had not been able to keep count of the number of times I had fired it off, though I knew I had fired three times out of my carbine. Well, we found that every shot fired had taken effect some way or other—10 altogether, and all except Gerard's two, which were buried in his back, at very short range. My five 45- caliber pistol balls were distributed about his chest and neck, and plenty deep enough, too, and besides the brain shot, my two, heavy army bullets were embedded in his lungs.

As he lay there, before we skinned him, he looked the grand old fellow he was. You may bet your bottom dollar that if you have anything to do with a grizzly bear, you will have all your work cut out. He never turns tail and dies game under all circumstances; nor will you ever hear any word but one of respect for his fighting qualities, if you ask the opinion of every hunter in the Rocky mountains.

# A Remarkable Performance

*In the following story, a grizzly bear caught in a 45-pound trap dragged the entire works for nearly 15 miles over rugged terrain before the trappers found it. This remarkable trapping tale appeared July 5, 1900, in the **Libby News**.*

Jake Teeter and Chas. Drew have returned from a three months' trip into the mountains east of Kalispell [Montana] about 60 miles. They have been trapping bear and brought back with them nine fine pelts and a good bear story. They are probably two of the finest trappers in the hills and it is said of them that they can get bear where there are none. But of course this is coming it strong, as Bret Hart says about the 24 packs of cards in the celebrated poker game with the festive celestial. However, the story is a good one.

It seems that they had about fifty miles of bear traps and it kept them pretty busy going from one end of the line to the other and they were unable to visit each trap every day. In one trap, which weighed 45 pounds, they succeeded in trapping a bear one day and when they got around to that place in the line the trap was gone. In addition to weighing 45 pounds it had been anchored to a pole about nine feet long and this pole was about nine inches through at the big end. They at once started to trace the animal and it took them three days before they could locate him. In that time he had probably gone about 15 miles, through windfalls, over mountains and rocks, all the time carrying the trap and the pole with him. At places he would get caught on trees and snags and at these places he would either chew them off or break them down, until he arrived at the top of a ridge of rocks way up high on the mountains and on the north side of the mountain these rocks shot down in an almost perpendicular jump for about 3,000 yards[7] [feet], and this distance was covered with deep snow which was soft from the warm sun.

The bear apparently never hesitated, for his track could be plainly seen as far as the eye could trace it down this toboggan slide, the trap and the pole plowing up a furrow several feet wide and as many deep. Teeter went one way to get around the bottom of this slide and Drew went the other. Near the bottom they found the bear. He had got tangled up with a green sapling and was busy chewing it off when he was shot by Teeter. He was a large grizzly. Mr. Teeter considers this one of the most remarkable cases of the vitality of a bear in his wide range of experience and it is certainly a remarkable performance. In addition to this they have one other grizzly, the rest being black and brown bear.

# The "Terror of the Hills"

*Two bear stories appeared in the June 23, 1904 Western News. The first story related the capture and killing of a "monster" grizzly which had eluded and terrified hunters and trappers in the Cabinet Mountains for years. One man believed the bear was "charmed" because the hunter had tried to shoot a total of 39 cartridges at the 1500-pound animal during two different encounters, to no avail. The second story involved an encounter with an infuriated black bear, which was shot in the nick of time.*

Two bear stories are added to the list this week. Of course, both are carefully vouched for. Thos. Fleetwood fathers one of them and A.B. Johnston stands sponsor for the other. This newspaper has implicit confidence in each of the relators and would recommend a patient hearing at the hands of our readers. On account of dimensions the Johnston bear story will be told first. And Mr. Johnston has the hide to show for it—it is hanging in his office now. At least he pointed to a hide hanging on the wall and said that was it. The story is as follows:

For years there has been known to exist in the Cabinet range back of Troy and Libby [Montana] a mammoth grizzly bear. He has been seen numerous times by trappers and hunters and on account of his size and the wonderful feats attributed to his prowess, together with the apparent fact that he was impervious to the power of powder and shot and too wily to be caught in any trap set for him, he became known as the "Terror of the Hills."

With each recurring season of late years it has been the ambition of hunter and trapper alike to get this monster. With each recurring failure the prize has become a more valuable one and the most careful inquiry was made of all who came from the mountains if anything was known of the big grizzly, for that is what the animal is, and as has been said the hide is here as the best evidence.

The most wonderful stories are told of this animal. One is that when caught in the trap in which he met his death a few days ago his bellowing was heard for over 10 miles and he kept it up for 3 days and nights and old hunters and trappers who happened to be in that section and heard him verify the statement that none ever heard such awful noises. And at night as the roaring of the infuriated animal reverberated through the stillness of the snowcapped Cabinets these men, accustomed as they are to the solitudes of the mountains, admit having felt at times a succession of shudders chase each other up and down the spinal column, and they were not at all sorry when morning came.

Another story is that one night several years ago he came out of the mountains near Troy and broke into a pig pen of a rancher living near the place. During the night he killed over 20 full grown hogs out of some 36 in the pen and of these he carried off into the mountains 14. And the most remarkable thing about it is that although his trail could be followed for several miles into the hills no one ever found where he cached all that pork.

One hunter relates that he met this animal twice and each time the circumstances attending the meeting would tend to the belief that his was a charmed life. On one occasion he saw the animal standing on a reef of rocks not to exceed 40 yards away. The hunter says he fired 23 times, all the cartridges he had, at the animal, who stood perfectly still during the fusil[l]ade, never making an effort to get away. None of the shots took effect, though the man is counted one of the best marksmen in the camp. On the other occasion he suddenly came onto Mr. Terror of the Hills when the latter was knawing [sic] at the carcass of a dead animal and he was not over 60 feet from him. Leaning against a tree he took a careful aim and pulled the trigger. The cartridge failed to go off. Another shell and another, until 16, again all he had with him, were tried and none of them would go off. While not superstitious this hunter thinks things are not what they might be when dealing with the big bear.

And so on. There are many stories, enough to fill columns of space were they printed, connected with this animal. However, he is now no more among the living. He was caught in a monster trap about two weeks ago in the mountains back of Troy and Libby by Frank Gerrad. As big as the trap was the captured animal had almost succeeded in gnawing it to pieces and in this endeavor he had broken nearly all of his teeth. He weighed about 1500 or 1600 pounds, his hide is about 12 feet long by eight and a half wide and the claws are over five inches in length.

The hide is valued at a hundred dollars by Mr. Johnston. It should be bought by some society or club, to the end that it be preserved and that many people could see it.

The other bear story, that for which Thos. Fleetwood assumes all responsibility, is as follows; the hide for this one will probably be here in a short time:

While hunting on Miller creek, about 25 miles south of Libby a couple of weeks ago, Mike Wallace saw a black bear. Taking aim he succeeded in wounding the animal. While generally a black bear will not attack a man, yet when wounded it is said they put up a vicious fight. Upon being hit the bear turned and came for Mike. The distance between them was about 150 yards. Another shot and another was fired at the animal until but one shell remained in the gun.

All this time the animal was coming straight for the hunter. Mike was on one side of a big log and firing across it. The bear succeeded in getting right up against the log when the last shot was fired and he rolled over dead, not to exceed six feet from the man behind the gun. The muzzle of the gun was not over a foot from the animal's head when he pulled the trigger which ended the contest. It was a close call.

# Bears, Bugs and Sharks

*Two men looking for adventure in 1903 hired a cook and a guide to accompany them grizzly hunting on Alaska's Admiralty Island, located just off the coast of Juneau. The men traveled by canoe and stayed on the island for five weeks. Even today, Admiralty Island is known for its large bear population, so the men certainly chose the right area to hunt. At first the hunters had personnel problems, having to hire several different guides. Overall, however, the hunters had an interesting and successful trip, including an unusual experience with sharks. Andre Champollion wrote about their adventure for* Forest and Stream. *His article titled "Hunting the Alaskan Grizzly" appeared in the May 2, 1908 issue on pp. 688-690.*

About the middle of July, 1903, Dr. Phelps and myself landed from a canoe on the east coast of Admiralty Island, Alaska. An inspection of the map of Alaska will show Admiralty to be one of the large mountainous islands which lie along the coast of the southeastern Alaskan strip about eight miles as the crow flies from the prosperous town of Juneau, which is situated on the mainland. Admiralty is about the same shape and size as Long Island. Conditions there may have changed somewhat since the above-mentioned date, but at that time there was an extraordinarily dense population of wild animals. The most important of these from our point of view were the grizzly bears, tracks of which we saw less than ten minutes after landing. The island is covered from end to end by a range of mountains, on the summits of which snow lingers practically all summer.

Near the salt water and up to a height of a thousand feet are forests of magnificent hemlock, fir and balsam trees, which have never yet been touched by the lumberman's destructive ax. Creeks and trout streams abound, and at the time of year we are speaking of the salmon were leaving the salt water and beginning to run up these streams by the hundreds of thousands for the purpose of spawning. Bald eagles, ravens and crows as tame as sparrows sat around on the lofty treetops, eyeing us inquisitively as we pushed our canoe ashore, while hundreds of sea gulls arose from the beach and soared about, uttering cries of disturbed quietude.

There were two other men in our party besides ourselves whom we had hired, the one to act as guide, the other to cook and do camp chores. The first three weeks of our residence on Admiralty were uneventful because our guide soon proved himself to be thoroughly incompetent, although he said that he had killed some bears the previous year. We could not get him up before nine o'clock in the morning. He was a rather heavy, fleshy man, and after walking a couple of miles, he would complain of sore feet, remove his shoes and lie down to rest for an indefinite length of time. An Indian whom we hired to take his place, though a good hunter, was afraid of the bears, and our impression was that he rather sought to avoid them; in fact, the grizzly bear has a well-deserved reputation for irascibility and vindictiveness, not only among the aborigines, but also among the white men, most of whom are prospectors and therefore continually exposed to danger of attack from *Ursus horribilis*. She-bears with cubs are especially to be feared. We heard one man sum up his feelings in the terse phrase, "You many never need a gun, but when you do, you need it badly!" Several western authorities have asserted that a grizzly bear will not attack a human being unprovoked, and one writer in a communication to the New York Sun not long ago declared that he never will under any circumstances. This is true probably of localities where these animals have been extensively hunted and the fear of men and guns has been so thoroughly inculcated in them that their only idea is to beat a hasty retreat whether wounded or not. That this does not hold true in Alaska, I think the reputation the grizzly has gained there, and the present narrative will help to prove.

In summer the bears are in the habit of coming to the creeks as soon as the salmon begin running. They gorge themselves with fish and then return to the depths of the forest. The best way therefore to get a shot is to lie in wait for them where salmon are plentiful, especially early in the morning and toward sunset.

As already stated luck had been against us, and the spell was not broken till some prospectors whom we had met in Juneau invited us to join them in their hut in the mountains above timber line. Being uncertain as the advisability of such a move, we decided that one of us should accept the invitation and the other should stay and hunt the creeks for a few more days. We drew lots and I followed the miners.

The country up there was absolutely superb. You could look around for a radius of seventy-five or a hundred miles at endless chains of snow-covered peaks. Way below was the salt water cut up into innumerable bays, channels and inlets. Nowhere was there a sign of civilization. One might have thought oneself on the earth before the appearance of man. I spent three or four days wandering amid these enchanting surroundings with gun and field glass. Here and there were patches of grass and cowslips which had been very recently beaten down and bore the marks of bear tracks and beds. Some of these beds looked big enough to have been made by a cow or horse, but no bears showed themselves till the fifth or sixth day.

I had been sitting in observation from a point of vantage, when away below me half a mile distant I observed a curious round speck which did not at first appear to me as anything unusual, and I gave it little thought. Looking in that direction a few minutes later, I noticed that the speck from round had assumed an oblong shape. On examining it with my field glass, my heart leaped into my mouth with excitement, when I espied two good-sized grizzlies rolling around in the grass playfully "swatting" each other with their large paws. It must be confessed that I faced the idea of attacking those animals alone with a good deal of apprehension, but knew that on returning to camp it would be impossible for me to refrain from speaking of what I had seen, and that the men would then ask what I had done. I could already see myself sheepishly acknowledging that I had done nothing, and the whole mining camp roaring, so I chose danger as an evil less to be feared than ridicule, and started down the mountain toward the bears. They disappeared from view for fully twenty minutes while I circled a lofty crag and finally got within five hundred yards of the spot where I had first seen them. The bears were no longer playing together. One of them stood facing in my direction, while the other, who was much larger than his companion, lay flat on his belly in the tall grass. All that could be seen of him was his head bobbing up and down as he fed off a blueberry bush. In endeavoring to get nearer I lost my footing and slid about fifty yards on a steep slope covered with heather. I supposed when I looked again that the bears would be in full flight, but to my great surprise and relief they had seen nothing, the wind blew cross-wise, and everything was favorable.

In order to get a good open shot at close range, I was obliged to crawl through a growth of stunted timber about sixty yards wide, the trees of which were not more than four feet high. When I arrived on the other side of these bushes the bears were about eighty yards from me. The smaller one now stood quartering away and the other was still nearly entirely hidden by shrubs and long grass. I therefore decided to dispose of the smaller one first. My .45-70 rifle was loaded with ten cartridges, when I opened fire. As the bullet struck him, the bear reared on his hind legs, viciously pawing the air and biting at his wound. He uttered a series of low growls, which sounded a good deal like two mastiffs fighting. He seemed to be trying to get at an enemy which he supposed must be within reach. As I was hidden behind one of the small pine bushes, he could not see me, and the idea evidently never entered his head that something had been hurled at him from a distance; the report of the rifle meant nothing to him.

Perceiving that he could not find his enemy, he took to his heels and went off diagonally at a mad gallop, howling with pain and rage, while another one of my bullets hit the face of nature somewhere in his vicinity. By this time the bigger bear was on his feet, uttering low growls, jumping and plunging through the long grass. Now and then he would rear up on his hind legs for a few seconds to peer around inquiringly. Just as he did so for the third or fourth time one of my bullets took him somewhere behind the fore shoulder, and after tearing madly around as the first bear had done, he also began to bolt. Fearing that I should likewise lose him, I threw all caution to the winds and stood up in plain sight, at the same time firing another shot. This shot was also caught by mother earth, but it accomplished its purpose in attracting the bear's attention, for instead of running away, he wheeled about and charged.

The nearer he came the easier he was to hit, of course, but my shooting had become decidedly erratic after so much excitement, and though hit several times, the bear had not checked his speed a particle when he was only fifteen feet away. My knees began to quake, but I stood my ground nevertheless for one more shot. To reach the place where I was standing, the bear had to jump into a slight depression of the ground, and as he did so he exposed his spine. I fired a parting salute at the middle of his back and turned without waiting to see the result. Being in the pink of condition and in a decidedly panicky frame of mind, I made the dust fly at a rate of speed that I had heretofore not considered myself capable of. I jammed two or three more shells into the magazine of my gun as I fled, then after covering some thirty or forty yards, abruptly faced about confidently, expecting to see the bear reaching for my heels. But he was done for. The last shot had hit him in the spine and he lay flat on his belly. He was a fine specimen and must have weighed between five and six hundred pounds. To my great regret I was never able to find the first bear.

The next day Phelps joined me, and after hunting deer a few days for fresh meat and unsuccessfully trying to get a shot at more bears, we went back to the salmon creeks. We had hired another Indian guide, who proved to be worth his weight in gold, for in a week we managed to get four more bears. By this time the creeks presented a really extraordinary spectacle. They were literally packed with hump-backed and dog salmon. It was impossible to wade across without stepping on the fish. Many of them were decaying alive and dying and a nauseous stench filled the air. Add to this the incessant attacks of black flies and mosquitoes and the surroundings were far from being as agreeable as they had been while we enjoyed the hospitality of the miners.

The next encounter with a bear was when Phelps got his first shot at one. We had been hunting a certain creek unsuccessfully for a couple of days. The wind seemed to be possessed of a very devil and blew on our backs no matter which way we turned. On two occasions we lost what might have been an excellent opportunity for a shot at big bears, had they not been made aware of our presence by the wind. One day at noon we returned to the creek to examine a huge bear trap we had set the night before. Most of our hunting, as already stated, was done either early in the morning or late in the afternoon or evening, and we did not expect to meet any bears roaming around at that time of day. As we approached the creek, Phelps, who was walking ahead, suddenly motioned to us to drop on our bellies. We did so and he crawled forward for a few paces, took aim and fired. At the crack of the rifle a series of formidable growls arose from the creek, and as we jumped to our feet we saw a large brown bear wounded making desperate efforts to get away. One more shot finished him, and he dropped in the waters of the creek. This animal weighed between four and five hundred pounds.

The day after, we removed our camp to another section of the island. Most of our traveling was done in a large Indian dug-out made of one piece of timber, which belonged to our guide. In this we carried everything we needed. We pitched our camp on the beach a few hundred yards from the creek we intended to hunt on. It must be understood that though we were on salt water, the coast line of the island is so irregular, so cut up by bays and inlets, that the water was most of the time as smooth as on a lake or pond.

We had not been at our next camping ground fifteen minutes and were still unloading our provisions and belongings from the canoe, when we noticed a smallish grizzly bear some two hundred yards away, walking along the beach holding a salmon in his mouth. We decided to try for a shot at closer range by means of the canoe. We therefore all embarked and pushed our craft very noiselessly in his direction. He arose on his hind legs and eyed the canoe suspiciously, but the wind was in our faces, besides which we were going so slowly, and bears are so near-sighted that he was not in the least alarmed. When he resumed his four feet, I shot at him, my bullet breaking his hips. We immediately paddled ashore, and the wounded bear for such a small one (he could not have weighed more than 150 pounds) displayed a most extraordinary amount of vitality. I shot him repeatedly through the body, but my .45-70 bullets seemed to have as little effect on him as if they had been peas. His hind legs were completely paralyzed from the effects of the first shot, and yet he made desperate efforts to attack us with his teeth and front paws. However, his struggles gradually subsided, and Phelps, to make sure, drew his hunting knife and stabbed him in the ribs. The bear in a last paroxysm of agony and rage made a lunge at my companion's face, and the latter, stupefied with astonishment at this sudden revival of pugnacity on the part of an animal he had deemed as good as dead, dropped his knife, tripped and fell over backward while the rest of us lay on the ground splitting our sides with laughter.

That same evening we had spent two fearful hours on the creek, neither seeing nor hearing any bears, but being slowly devoured by the black flies and mosquitoes. When the sun began to set we left our post and returned to our canoe, which was anchored in the salt water. Before flowing into the salt water, this particular creek ran through a large delta covered with long grass yet free from timber. We had just emerged from the woods and were walking in single file along the right hand bank of the creek, when two hundred yards away on the other side, coming out of the forest at a lumbering gallop, we saw a large bear. He was headed directly our way, and we all crouched low and waited. In a minute or so the grass and weeds on the opposite side of the creek parted and a handsome silver-tip grizzly hove in sight. He immediately rose on his hind legs and sniffed the air inquiringly, as if to say, "Where are they?" A bullet in the brain from Phelps' rifle was the reply and bruin fell on his side like a sack of potatoes. This bear had got our wind and was evidently looking for trouble. We had never seen him before, neither had we molested nor provoked him in the least, and yet he came right for us. His motives might not have been hostile, some will say. As to that, I leave the reader to draw his own conclusions.

On the following evening we shot the biggest bear that it was our good fortune to secure. We had been hunting the same creek for an hour, and we were coming out on the delta, when about five hundred yards away we saw what appeared to be an unusually large bear standing on a branch of the creek swallowing a salmon. We crouched low and jumped into the canoe. After paddling along the beach for a few minutes we got to within two hundred yards of where he stood. It was my turn to shoot, and I decided to make sure of him by crawling in his direction for another hundred yards. My gun had a hair trigger and I very carelessly went along with it at full cock. Before I was aware of what had happened, my gun fired off in the grass and the big bear was up on his hind legs to see where that queer noise came from. I immediately threw in another cartridge and shot at the animal just as he dropped on all fours. He ran off diagonally and I fired again while the other men who were watching proceedings from the canoe opened up a regular fusil[l]ade. The bear dropped dead after running forty yards. My first intentional shot had hit him in the heart and, ranging back, had pierced one lung and the intestines. My second shot broke one hind leg. Two or three shots from the canoe struck him in the belly and haunches and yet he managed to go thirty or forty yards. He was a beautiful old silver-tip and weighed in the neighborhood of seven hundred pounds. The Indian filled the animal's lungs with air by means of a small reed which he stuck into his wind pipe, thus inflating the lungs as we would a football. This caused the dead animal to float, and we towed him along behind the canoe to our camp. In the morning we photographed our bears and removed their hides, throwing the carcasses into the salt water. That night we were aroused by a tremendous splashing along the beach in front of our tent. There was a bright moon and we could distinguish the fins of two or three huge sharks as they fought for the carcasses. By morning everything had disappeared. This was a novel sight; grizzly bears being devoured by sharks!

Our Indian now refused to guide us any longer unless we increased his pay, alleging that where we had been hunting was a "much danger creek." It must be admitted that some of the tracks we had seen were enough to command the respect of the most hardened bear hunter. Besides this the long grass on the delta was beaten down as if a herd of buffalo had been there. We were using the Indian's canoe, and he imagined that we could not possibly get along without him or his craft. But we refused to be bullied by this petty blackmailing scheme, which, by the way, is common among the Alaska Indians in their dealings with white men. We therefore returned to Juneau, hired another canoe and started back to Admiralty Island the next day without a guide. When he saw that we were not going to give in, our Indian begged to be taken back at the original price, but we refused. We returned to "much danger creek," but hunted there in vain for two days. Not a hair did we see because the place had been entirely "queered" by our shooting. We then christened it No-Danger Creek, and moved to a new spot where Phelps shot one more silver-tip of moderate proportions, the demise of which was not marked by any extraordinary circumstances.

Our bag now amounted to three silver-tip grizzlies, two bald-face grizzlies, so called because they are gray-colored in the face as contrasted with their bodies, which are a russet brown hue, and one cinnamon bear. Our stay on the island had covered a period of five weeks, during which we saw eight or ten bears besides the six we actually bagged.

Some of the adventures here related may seem exaggerated perhaps, but it must be borne in mind that we were hunting in a country that had practically never been disturbed. Besides being numerous, the bears, as already hinted, were reckless and courageous in the extreme on account of their unfamiliarity with men and guns. The animals we hunted were grizzlies pure and simple, except the cinnamon bear, which is a variety of the black bear. They had nothing to do with the famous Kadiak [sic] bears which inhabit an entirely different section of Alaska and are of a different species.

# This Guy Wasn't Mourning

*In 1932, two hunters had an interesting experience with two black bears while hunting near Missoula, Montana. They found a male black bear at the "grave" of another black bear and erroneously assumed that the live bear was guarding the grave of its mate; whereas, bruin was most likely standing guard over his next meal. Cannibalism was misidentified as faithfulness. It is interesting to see how such myths developed regarding bears before they were formally studied. The following article appeared in the* Rocky Mountain Husbandman, *January 30, 1936, with the headline "Black Bear Meets Death at Grave of Mate It Guarded."*

Chandler J. Jensen, Butte [Montana] district forest ranger, told the story of a weird burial in the animal kingdom recently. It was an interment that ended in tragedy for the chief mourner.

While attending the State university, Jensen, in company with Sergeant Maywood Kirkwood, attached to the R.O.T.C. there, trekked into the woods near Missoula [Montana] to hunt bear in the fall of 1932.

They had hunted all day when, about sunset, Sergeant Kirkwood sighted a black bear. He fired once, apparently wounding the bruin, which ambled with that peculiarly rapid, awkward and lopsided lope of his kind into the trees surrounding the open plot.

The trail of the bleeding bruin was soon lost and the hunters gave up the pursuit. The following week, Kirkwood and his companion returned to the territory to hunt. About a mile from the spot where the bear had been wounded the week before, they came upon another. They fired almost simultaneously and the black bruin pitched sideways and lay dead.

As they walked cautiously toward the spot where the bear lay, Kirkwood noticed a leaf-filled depression. From under the blanket of leaves the head of another bear protruded.

"Carefully uncovering the body of the bear in the hole, we discovered that the bear, a female, had been shot in the chest, apparently dying from the wound. We believe it was the one Kirkwood wounded the week previous," Jensen said.

Paw marks around the hole indicated that a large animal, presumably the one that had just been killed, had scraped leaves and dirt upon its dead mate. The female had either crawled into the shallow dip to die or the male had pushed it in the hole before covering the body.

Then he stood guard over the gunshot victim. Faithfulness in death had brought about his own doom.

# Hunting Old Ephraim In Idaho

*Charles H. Crandon told about a bear hunting trip he went on in the Sawtooth Range in Idaho in the 1920s. Crandon's party was pursuing a sheep-eating grizzly. They found the bear and a frightened unarmed man who happened to encounter Old Ephraim when he was out for a stroll. Crandon's tale was published on pp. 15-17; 44-45 in the January 1929 issue of* **Forest and Stream.**

*Following is an excerpt from that article, which was titled "With Old Ephraim In The Sawtooths."*

The journey from South Florida to Idaho is a long one. Whether or not a hunting trip is worth it depends entirely upon what the hunter gets out of it; his love of the wild rugged country to be found out there; his companions on the trip and the amount of wild game that abounds.

My companion on this trip was Shelby Constant, of Buhl, Idaho. He has been one of my closest friends ever since the World War, at which time we were "buddies" in the 66th Balloon Company. Our last trip was in the Montana Rockies in 1926. This year we agreed upon the Sawtooth Range.

Arriving in Buhl on September 23rd, I found "Sheb," as he is known to his friends, with everything ready for the trip. He had a 12x14 wall tent and a dandy camp stove with small oven. The latter he had borrowed from a sheepherder up on the Snake River, who had it made for his own use when out on the range.

Sheb had a small radio outfit with ear phones that he insisted we take along. I protested on account of having to take everything in on horses, but that was one thing Sheb held out on and it went in on the back of a big "blue" mule.

Early on the morning of the 24th, we crossed the divide at Galena Summit, dropping down into the wonderfully beautiful Sawtooth Valley flanked by majestic peaks. Here are the head-waters of the famous Salmon River. A whole book could be written on the scenic beauties of this valley. White frost had visited the section several times already this fall, and painted the aspens and other trees in crimson, red and gold. A broad valley stretching away as far as the eye can see, with floor and mountain slopes wearing a garment of gorgeous colors. To give an adequate description would, as T. [Theodore] Roosevelt remarked, "bankrupt the English language."

Up through Bear Valley and Pen Basin, we arrived on the evening of the second day at a place called Yellow Pine, so named because of the abundance of this beautiful tree. You won't find Yellow Pine in a railroad time table, for it is sixty-five miles from the nearest railroad. Some idea of its isolation can be had from the fact that from November to April the roads into this place are closed on account of deep snow. A dog sled brings in the first class mail (letters) only, once a week when possible. Five families winter in here. There are three children to attend "public school."

Clark Cox does not live in Yellow Pine "proper," but about ten miles out on a ranch. His is one of Yellow Pine's "five families," and furnishes one of the school children. For thirteen years he has run his own cattle in Bear Valley. Cox has a fine caviya of horses and acts as guide and packer to hunters going into the mountains. In winter he traps and hunts. There is one other person who makes a visit to this little mountain home something to be remembered, and that is Mrs. Cox. A delightful personality and a real culinary artist. It is worth the trip to Yellow Pine to eat her bread and biscuits made with bear lard.

Cox is a real mountain man, strong, self-reliant, accustomed to the hardships in the mountains, eager to throw his right leg over the wildest "bucker" that can be found, and a dead shot. Buckers have, at one time or another, broken both his legs, his left arm and shoulder, and splintered bones which had to be removed from his lungs. Yet I saw him high up on a mountain ridge, get under a two-hundred-and-forty pound buck I shot, and ease him onto the back of a big red mule, which he had first blindfolded with his green wool shirt. And he did it in about three shakes of a lamb's tail!

Now about blindfolding the mule. I said to Cox, "Why do you tie your shirt over his head?" He stopped humming his favorite tune, "Ole Man River," long enough to remark, "After I get this critter tied on with a diamond hitch, so'z we won't have buck-meat scattered all over these hills, maybe you'll see." Then he added, "He's been feeding on this here wild elk grass and might have peculiar notions."

After properly tying the buck on, Cox stepped up and took the lead-line, saying, "Now, you fellers, just step back a bit and I'll shake loose this head gear." As he pulled his shirt off, the mule turned his head around to see what all this dead weight might be. And right then he did his level best to get from under that buck. It looked for a time like the mule and Cox would pull up all the bunch grass on that slope. But Cox stayed with the mule and so did the buck, and that meat was brought into camp in record time.

Later on we were to learn that this man would lead us onto rock and snow slides that would make our hair stand on end. I have ridden western horses for many years, and was under the impression that I was a pretty fair rider, but when Cox turned his dogs loose on a bear track, he left me like a train does a tramp. Riding the prairie and hills is one thing; riding into those mountain basins filled with fallen timber full of snags, swamp holes and brush, is something else. When

Cox ran into a fallen log that set three or four feet off the ground, he "lifted his horse over," as he termed it, with his spurs.

Cox and his horses were mountain born and bred. Rock and snow slides were every day occurrences to him. Had we used prairie-bred horses, neither the horses nor ourselves would have come out alive.

About six-thirty one morning just as we had finished breakfast and were sitting around the kitchen stove enjoying a smoke, the telephone rang and Cox answered it. (Cox has this telephone by courtesy of the Government Ranger Station. There are no public telephones up there.) In a few minutes he returned, saying, "Boys, hop to it and help me throw saddles on a couple of mavericks. Old man Clem Bessinger tells me he has a big bear down there. Clem was telling me about this bear a couple of weeks ago. He says this bear has been killing his sheep and raisin' h_____ in general for a long spell. I told him to telephone me the next time the bear cut in on his band. That was him just phoned. Wants me to come right down with the dogs and trail him down. It's about four miles down on the South Fork. Let's go."

While we were throwing on the saddles, Cox said that Bessinger had told him that this bear had the peculiar habit of eating what he wanted and covering the carcass up with leaves, brush, etc. Cox said he never heard of a bear doing this, but knew that cougars did, and thought this must be a cougar. He so expressed himself to the old man, who said, "Well, if this is a cougar, he is being followed by a h_____ of a big bear, for I have seen his tracks."

Cox had given Sheb a fine little gray mare by the name of Lydia. Mine was a big black; a green horse shod for the first time about two weeks before and powerfully frisky. Cox said they hadn't named him yet, "We just call him the big new black." Well, Sheb had Lydia, so I named mine E. Pinkham. In a short time we were going down the road right out straight, Cox in the lead and Lydia and E. Pinkham close behind.

Two or three days previous to this, a cousin of "old man Bessinger's" by the name of Gabe Wiggins, dropped in to make him a visit at the chuck-wagon out there in the hills. Gabe lived in Ola, Idaho. Bookkeeper for a packing plant down there. He was a big red-headed fellow about forty years old, and weighing one hundred and eighty. "A city chap from Ola," Cox remarked.

After the telephone conversation referred to, old man Bessinger started out to investigate and see how many sheep had been killed. They found where fifteen sheep had been driven up a small gulch, five killed and a sixth about two-thirds eaten. Bessinger suggested that they stroll about a bit and see if they could locate the direction the bear took, so that when Cox arrived, they could tell him. The old man started up the ridge while Gabe kept to the bottom, with the two sheep dogs running on ahead.

Gabe had gone about half a mile when he heard the dogs growling and snapping. He hurried on. Coming out of the thick brush, he observed just ahead of him a big clump of willows with a large yellow pine on the edge. Backed up against the tree was "Old Ephraim," as the trappers call the grizzly. The dogs would dart in now and then and come out with a mouthful of hair.

The dogs hadn't hurt the bear any, but they had made him powerful peeved. Gabe hove in sight about seventy-five feet from where this activity was taking place. Old Ephraim was thoroughly riled by this time. Taking a good look at the newcomer, he promptly lost interest in the dogs, and started for the red-headed gentleman from Ola. And according to Gabe, said bear made remarkable time right from the jump.

Gabe had no rifle. Fact is, he did not own one. The old man had suggested they take a stroll, but this was anything else but. Gabe had seen bears before, but later admitted he had never seen one before in the wilds. Certainly never had one tried to get this familiar before. But instinct told him this was one time when he must make a quick decision. He did. There was a small yellow pine near by, but not any too near. Gabe struck out for it with a will and purpose as unbending as a boarding-house biscuit.

Gabe was forty years old and hadn't shinned a tree for thirty years. This was a pretty small tree for a hundred-and-eighty-pound man to go climbing up on, but it was the only life-saver in sight. That is, it was the only one Gabe figured he could reach before the bear did. He circled the butt of that pine in less time than it takes to tell it. Up he went, but none too soon. The tree was getting smaller and smaller as he neared the top, but every time he looked down into the gaping maw of the beast below, he moved up a little higher.

Now old silver-tip will not climb a tree. The browns and blacks will unless they get too big and heavy. It all means the same to Gabe, however, as he neither had the time nor knowledge to classify the brute. But one thing was sure, there was a heap of bear headed in his direction, and for no peaceful purpose.

It seemed to Gabe he would soon be in a mighty bad fix. He knew the bear would climb that tree for two reasons. He would be getting rid of the dogs, for one thing, and then he had shown, just as plainly as a bear knew how, that he had designs on Gabe. And Gabe knew that tree was not strong enough to hold them both, and he had gone up just as far as he could go. The bear had his front claws on the tree and his snout was curled back revealing the terrible fangs beneath. Gabe tried to holler, but it seemed to him he could only emit a miserable squeak. It took all his strength, what he hadn't used climbing up, to hold on. And the Lord only knew where Bessinger had gone to.

The dogs continued to worry the bear, Gabe giving them every encouragement he could from his slender perch above. Old Ephraim didn't come up, but neither did he go away. Seemed like he was going to sit it out until Gabe, who was getting weaker and weaker, would drop right down there among those teeth and claws. After what seemed an age to Gabe, the bear turned on the dogs and started for the swamp with the dogs biting at his heels.

Gabe waited a while. He was thankful for the opportunity. It would be sometime before he would be himself again. After several minutes, he slipped down. He decided right then and there that this was enough of that sort of thing, and headed back for the chuck-wagon. The bear, the dogs, and even the old man could go to thunder; he was going to light out of there. And that was that.

About this time Cox, who was considerably in the lead of Sheb and I, was plunging through the willows, which were eight to ten feet high and very thick. He heard the dogs on ahead and was headed for them. He was coming directly in front, but a little to the right of the retreating Gabe. He was coming hard and crashing timber. Gabe heard the racket and at the same time caught a glimpse of something coming his way. Something black. Another bear!

If Gabe was quick before, he was even quicker this time. Without taking a second glance, or giving the matter a second thought, he sprang for the nearest pine and did his stuff.

The nimble Gabe later confessed, "I sure thought it was another bear. I was feeling right nervous at that particular time, anyhow, and when I got a slant of something black coming my way—oh, boy, it went all over me like an old-fashion smelling bottle. I thought the woods were full of bears!"

This time, having had recent experience, Gabe not only made better time, but higher altitude. Cox rushed by on his big black not fifteen feet away, without even seeing Gabe. By the time I got along there he had started down, but was in a very disagreeable frame of mind.

I had never met this chap they called Gabe, but when I spied him up there, I pulled up. He was on his way down, but seemed to hesitate about it. He later explained that he had hopes we would pass him by, as Cox had done, without seeing him.

I had never met old man Bessinger, either. But I knew he was supposed to be around here somewhere. Perhaps this was he. It flashed across my mind that this man had something to do with the bear hunt, although I could not imagine what it could be. So I inquired, innocently, "What you doing up there?" He glared down at me. One thing was sure, he was darned unfriendly. It was several seconds before he blurted out, "Oh, I'm cuttin' down cones for the chipmunks; whaderyer think I'm doin'?"

Just then I heard a shot, followed by a second and a third. I knew Cox had located the bear, so I put the spurs to E. Pinkham and left this disagreeable bird. Anyhow, I couldn't see any percentage in carrying on a conversation like that.

The bear was again up against a tree, as they so often do when attacked by dogs, and was fighting the dogs. Old Stranger, Cox's bear dog, was now at him. As I came in sight I saw old Stranger jump in. The wise old fellow had become too courageous for once. The bear reached him with his left foot, catching the dog with his powerful claws just in front of his hind legs. Stranger grabbed the bear by the nose and hung on. The bear was trying to squeeze him, but Cox had broken the bear's right front leg with the third shot. The second shot had broken his lower jaw, while the first shot had passed through the bear's body just in back of his shoulders, but a little high.

The three dogs jumping around the bear made it very difficult for Cox to get a good shot. He had to be very careful not to hit one of the dogs. He had now fired the last cartridge in his rifle, a .30-30 Carbine. He knew, too, that old Stranger was a dead dog if the bear ever got him where he could squeeze him with his powerful left leg. And Cox thinks the world of that dog. Without hesitating a second, Cox rushed in and brought the butt of his rifle down across the bear's nose. The bear loosened his grip on Stranger and the dog sprang away.

When Cox hit the bear he split the butt of his rifle and badly bent the lever, so that when he went to throw another cartridge into the chamber he could not do so. There was no time to lose. I was off my horse and ready to take action if Cox got in trouble. I knew better than butt in, unless it was absolutely necessary. Cox saw at a glance what the trouble was with his rifle, and slipped a shell into the chamber and fired. This time the bullet entered the right eye and passed through the brain. This ended the fight.

Cox knew, as every experienced hunter knows, that the thing to do is to knock the bear down with the first shot and keep him down. That's the thing, keep him down. A wounded bear is no plaything, and especially a grizzly. They are the hardest to kill of any animal on this continent, and the meanest fighters.

And another thing that even many hunters do not know, and that is that a bear can outrun a good horse for a hundred yards or so. But this bear was never knocked down. He was a whopping big fellow and tough as a pine knot. Even after the last shot was fired, he stretched out his huge front legs as if he was going to lie down, and sprawled out on his belly.

This old grizzly weighed nearly five hundred pounds. Mrs. Cox rendered, or "tried out," as she termed it, over thirty quarts of lard. The hide now decorates the cabin floor.

Bessinger and Gabe had now joined us. The old man was much pleased to see that critter lying there. He had killed many of his sheep. Gabe, too, wore an expression of full and complete approbation. He turned to old Bessinger and said, "Well, we've got him." "We got him?" blurted out Bessinger. "What do you mean by WE? The last time I saw you, Gabe, and I saw the whole fracas from up yonder on that ridge, you was jumping the butt of that pine like a parched pea in a March wind." Gabe was busy rubbing his legs where the rough bark had rubbed off much skin. He straightened up pronto, and shot back, "The h_____ I was. I may have circled that tree once, I don't remember. You can make wise cracks, for you was all comfortable up there on the ridge. But I know this, the seat of my pants was only about three jumps ahead of that big devil. Say, Lem, over in France I went over the top more than once, and you know it. And I ain't braggin' about it either. But what I mean is, this is the first time in my life that I ever felt gone beaver. I s'pose you being so smart, would have throwed a hackamore and a pair of hobbles on him. I found him, which was more'n you done. You make me sick!"

Well, our trip had started off with a bang. That afternoon we pulled out for the back country, a two-days['] pack. Three riding horses, five pack mules and three dogs. . . .

We were now in a section of the country where few white men had ever been. For several miles south Indian Creek flowed through a boxed canyon, with almost perpendicular walls. We decided to explore it on horses. We had to swim deep pools, jump fallen timber and climb over boulders, following the river bed every foot of the way. It was hard going.

Being under the impression that we were trail-makers in this section, you can imagine our surprise when, coming around a bend in the river, we saw ahead of us on the bank of the stream, a tent. We stopped, looked at the tent, and then at one another. How and when did this outfit get in here? It surely took a stout heart and no end of courage to undertake packing that outfit in a place like this.

We drew up in front of the camp. None of us spoke. We were studying the situation. The tent was a 12x14 wall tent and a new one, when put up about a year before. Porcupines had gnawed the base, but it was in otherwise good condition. From cuts on the trees about, and the ash pile, it was evident that no one had lived here for about a year. Not a piece of fire-wood, or the chips from cutting any, were about. Whoever had made this camp had lived here but a short time.

I knew what Cox was thinking. Presently he said, "Boys, this gets me. Let's go in and see if there is a dead man inside."

But no corpse was found. There was the bedding, the kitchen utensils, two axes, both with razor edges, and one with a protector over the blade; a knife, fork and spoon. The fork had been whittled out of green willow. Everything was orderly and just as it had been left a year before. We looked for a message, but found none.

The question now in the minds of all of us was, why had a man taken all this risk and trouble, for there had been plenty of both, to pack in here and then desert the camp in a few days.

Cox was a mountain man. His deductions were those of a man who had spent his whole life in the hills. He reasoned the thing out as a hunter or trapper would. "Boys," he said, "this bird was no trapper nor no hunter. Trappers are dirty cusses. If there'd er been one here you'd see the bones of skinned animals all about this camp. There ain't a bone. And a hunter don't tote an outfit like this here one. And a hunter wouldn't pitch camp in a place like this, anyhow. No, this bird was a green-horn. Probably lost his horse out in the hills, where he went looking for feed, and then lost hisself out there. Let's leave everything just as they be, boys, 'cept this fork, Charlie," handing it over to me, "you might like to keep that."

No knowing how long that camp will remain there before someone else finds it. The mystery will no doubt remain locked up in those big hills.

# Beware of Them Big B'ars Out Thar

$M$any people maintain an irrational fear of bears and regard them as blood-thirsty killers because of a few maulings. It doesn't matter that most bears have an instinctive fear of humans and flee at the slightest indication of a human's presence; many people will only remember the horror stories. But bears, like humans, are individuals.

Nowadays people who harbor deep fears of bears are often those individuals who will not likely encounter a bear outside a zoo or automobile. Yet, this ancient superstitious fear remains. Pioneers regarded bears as symbols of untamed nature, and nature was something that needed to be subdued.

The following chapter includes some amusing stories showing people's unreasonable bear paranoia. Often times, people scared themselves by crying "bear" unnecessarily. They perceived danger where there was none. However, in some cases, people had good reason to fear bruin because they wounded or frightened it, making it defensive. Fear was justified then. In his book *Tough Trip Through Paradise,* Andrew Garcia eloquently portrays the terror inspired by an enraged grizzly.

## He Growled Something Terrible

*Martha Edgerton Plassmann, daughter of Sidney Edgerton, Montana's first territorial governor, told an amusing anecdote about some aristocractic eastern hunters who came to Glacier National Park to hunt. One man who desired a grizzly hide persuaded the guide to take him bear hunting. However, upon hearing a terrible growl, the would-be bear hunter decided a bearskin wasn't necessary after all. His terror convinced the rest of the party to forget about bear hunting. Mrs. Plassmann's story appeared in the Judith Basin County Press in 1926.*

When the Great Northern first crossed the Rockies on its way to Puget Sound, it traversed in the neighborhood of Glacier National Park, a comparatively unknown region. It possessed little to attract the farmer or stockman, and for this reason remained an almost unbroken wilderness, a large part of it belonging to the Piegan Reservation.

To better advertise the railroad, and possibly with a view to the national playground to be established there, every effort was made to advertise this section. The hunting grounds of the nation were rapidly being turned into farms, and Nature in its primitive moods, was rarely to be seen outside of private game preserves belonging to the wealthy, and it is doubtful whether primitive moods would be tolerated there. Out here was a hunter's paradise, where wild animals were plentiful, and there was a chance for more enlivening sport than following the hounds on the trail of an anise bag.

So it came about that influential men of an adventurous spirit, were brought here, and given a summer's outing in charge of trusty guides, who could be relied upon to return them safely to Midvale Station, after their hunt ended.

This story is of such a party, a small company of Down East millionaires who were tired of manipulating the financial market, and desired a change of surroundings and amusements. They found themselves in due time at Midvale (now Glacier Park), and leaving the train outfitted there for a hunting trip in the mountains. That is to say, they outfitted to a limited extent, for they had brought with them all the luxuries such pampered darlings of Fortune, come to regard as necessities. They also secured the services of an excellent guide.

They were agreeable gentlemen, who even won the approbation of their guide, whom they treated like a fellow man, and not as a servant. Having selected a suitable location far in the mountains, they went into camp for a few days, making that the central point from which they went in pursuit of game.

One of their number, when out alone with the guide ran across a grizzly, and shot it in the foot, when the guide dispatched it, taking very good care to let the gentleman continue to cherish the pleasing illusion that it was he who fired the fatal shot. As the guide later reported, "The fellow was tick[l]ed to death to think he had killed a grizzly, and boasted of the exploit, as was quite natural, on his return to camp."

This inspired one of his friends to go and do likewise. He made the guide promise to take him into the grizzly country the next day, and the following morning they set out, but not in the direction where the guide believed they would find grizzlies. A guide took a long chance who, on rousing a grizzly, was forced to let the other fellow fire first. In this instance, the guide was none too sure of his companion's skill as a hunter. Although he was not anxious to disturb a bear, strange as it may seem, he soon ran across the trace of one, and announced the fact to the prospective grizzly killer.

"How do you know a bear is near?" inquired the man.

"I can see where he went into the clump of underbrush down there," the guide replied, pointing to the place where he thought the bear was hidden.

"Why not you then go in and drive him out?" suggested the hunter.

"We don't hunt that way," responded the guide. "If I went in there, I would probably be the one driven out. We'll wait here until he shows himself, and if he's hungry, it would be well to have your gun ready."

Unconvinced, but reluctant to take the initiative in the hunt, the gentleman seated himself on the mountainside, and waited for the bear to make the first move. He had with him a pedigreed dog of some aristocratic breed, that he valued at $5,000, and sit[t]ing there, he bethought himself that the animal might be suffering from thirst. There was a stream below, but the way to it led by the covert of the grizzly. It was unthinkable that the dog should be permitted to run such a gauntlet. Turning to theguide [sic], the man said:

"I wish you'd go down there and fetch some water for my dog. I think he's thirsty."

The guide looked at the dog, which lay panting at his feet, and then glanced apprehensively at the thicket which sheltered the grizzly. He knew from long experience that these animals were apt to be irritable when suddenly aroused from slumber. To go to the stream was a task not lightly to be undertaken. He did not care to refuse, however, and gain the reputation of being afraid, yet he was determined to safeguard both his person and his reputation for courage, and he was resourceful, as will be seen.

Taking the pail they had brought with them, he started down hill, when in some perfectly unaccountable manner, he stumbled and fell headlong, and in so doing growled ferociously like a bear. At the fearful sound, the man seated on the mountainside above, hastily rose, and followed by his prize dog, made a rapid bee line for camp. Unfortunately, the going was rough, his foot caught, and down he went, hurting himself so badly that he was unable to go on, until the guide came to assist him.

"Did you get a shot at the bear?" asked the man.

"No, I didn't see him," answered the guide.

"Neither did I," the man said, "But I heard him growl something terrible— close at hand. I thought it was time for me to get out of there, so I went."

"I see you did," retorted the guide, and you went so quickly that you left your gun, and here it is," he added, as handing the weapon to the would-be bear hunter, he supported the latter back to camp. After this experience, none of the party expressed any longing for an encounter with a grizzly, being fully satisfied with smaller game.

# Not What It Seemed

*The following story telling how Mr. J.P. Hansen "killed his bear" appeared September 5, 1901, in the Anaconda Standard. A party of professional pranksters took the city slicker camping in the Flint Range in Montana and played a practical joke on him that worked so well that it was worth reporting in the local newpaper.*

Bears? Don't talk of them to J.P. Hansen. Mr. Hansen is a pleasant young gentleman who has been a resident of Anaconda [Montana] for several months as a representative of the Nordberg company of Milwaukee, superintending the erection of machinery in the new works. Only the other day did he find time to go for an outing, and on that trip came his bear experience—one he will remember for many years.

With a party of friends he went out to the vicinity of Mt. Powell to camp for a few days. In the party were the usual professional joshers. Mr. Hansen, being wise in the ways of the kind, was not trapped until the last day in camp, but when caught the catching was so well executed that the story has traveled far out of the little circle that witnessed its incidents.

It was late in the afternoon. Mr. Hansen had come in tired and worn out from his long ramble over the hills, and found the conversation taken up entirely by the subject of grouse. Grouse, according to the men in camp, were thick up the slope about half a mile away. They would furnish excellent sport, only every one was too tired to go.

"You said you wanted shooting, Hansen," said one of the party, "and you would get it there, but I wouldn't advise you to go. You look as if you were beat. My, but you must be tired. And you didn't go very far, did you? Well, city life does take the starch out of a man."

The ruse worked. Indignantly Mr. Hansen denied that he was at all wearied and insisted on going at once after the grouse.

"But you might run across a bear," some one suggested.

"That doesn't make any difference," said Mr. Hansen, "and, anyhow, there aren't any bears there."

With that he seized a shotgun and started up the hill. Consternation at his choice of weapon was seen on every face.

"Hold on, there," called the quick-witted one, "you aren't going to shoot grouse with a shotgun, are you?"

"Why not?" demanded Mr. Hansen.

"Oh, nothing," was the careless reply, "only I thought you were such a good shot that you would take a rifle. All the boys said that you were the only man in the party who could hit a bird with a rifle."

Mr. Hansen frowned, but he traded the shotgun for a rifle and struck out again.

Minutes passed, and then came the expected sound of rifle shooting far up the hill. Shot after shot at brief intervals rang out, and as each one was heard the party, rushing up the hill, paused to laugh.

All hands arrived on the spot just as Mr. Hansen ran forward, hunting knife in hand, to pounce upon his prey. Flushed with the joy of the hunt, he sprang upon the prostrate mass of fur and then, amazed, sprang back. A shout from the crowd told him he had been victimized.

Silently and gloomily he stalked down the hill, while the boys gathered up the remains. They shook the grass out of the old dogskin robe that was one of the comforts of the camp and examined it with care.

"It's lucky we kept him from taking the shotgun," the wise one remarked. "He'd have blown the old robe into bits. He's got six holes in it as it is."

# | "Look At Him Run"

*Some Bitterroot area hunters had a thrilling experience while bear hunting, or at least one member of the party did. Two of the men pursued a bear with dogs. Bruin, becoming annoyed at the ordeal, turned around and charged Frank Martin, who happened to be the closest hunter. Martin quickly recognized the danger at hand and headed toward town, with bruin close behind. It seems that the bear just wanted to lead the race, but Martin didn't know it. The account reported in the August 17, 1922* **Western News** *" 'Better to Lose Trousers Than Life' Is Moral Drawn From Bear Hunt."*

A two year old black [bear] was killed Sunday morning by Earl Moore about three miles from the mouth of Sawtooth canyon.

Early Sunday morning Earl Moore, Jim Cole, Frank Martin and Alexander Dietrick of this city [Hamilton, Montana] decided to go bear hunting. After borrowing dogs from Lloyd Thompson the quartet left for the wilds of Sawtooth. After progressing about two miles up the canyon the dogs struck a hot trail and soon from their cries it was apparent that the game was at bay. The sanguine hunters hurried forward to put an end to the game—a bear!

Moore and Martin were in the lead of the other two hunters when they came to a thicket in which the bear had taken refuge. The bear infuriated and aggravated beyond belief by the dogs suddenly rushed from the thicket and bore down upon Martin, the closest of the two hunters. Martin decided it would be better to have his friends say, "look at him run" than "don't he look natural!" so he hurled his gun to the wayside and was off with a flying start for the valley three miles distant.

As Martin started down the canyon beating strategic [sic] retreat, the bear followed, closely pursued by the dogs. Martin had the right of way but the bear wanted him to get out of its way and let somebody run that could run so as it overtook the flying Eagle baseball player, it rudely pawed the hunter a blow on the rearmost part of his anatomy, felling him and cleaving his trousers from him at a blow. Had not Jack, one of the air[e]dale dogs belonging to Lloyd Thompson, at this critical moment grabbed the bear Martin would no doubt have been severely injured, Martin took advantage of the lull in orprations [sic] to continue his retreat toward the valley. Earl Moore at this juncture dispatched bruno to the happy hunting grounds with two well directed shots from his rifle. The bear was dead at 11:30 but at 11:31 Martin was no where in sight.

At 11:32 Dr. Herbert Heyward blew out of Darby [Montana] bound for Hamilton with no scheduled stops. At the Grantsdale crossing he reports having seen a dust cloud issuing from Sawtooth canyon. Looking at his watch he noticed it was then 11:34 a.m. At the Skalkaho road crossing he reports having been passed by an unidentified streak bound in the general direction of Hamilton. Tracks left by the streak have been identified as those of one Frank Martin.

The bear weighed about 200 pounds and the four hunters ate their fill of bear steak the evening of the eventful day. No on[e] has reported Martin going bear hunting since last Sunday.

The bear hunt has caused many old timers in this vicinity to enter into considerable argument about the outcome of the hunt. Many openly applaud the action of the bear and none have taken the view that bruno was not entitled to the right of way as yet.

Indeed, public sympathy appears to be wholly with the bear, that if given a fair chance to run might have escaped with its life. Voicing this sentiment a committee headed by A.A. (Power River) Hobbs, proposes taht [sic] a tablet be erected at the site of the killing, inscribed:

"To the memory of one black bear, commonly know as Bruin, who without malice effected a passage at this point."

Also there is agitation for more canyons, or turn outs on trails, better trained bears and other conveniences in the hills.

# Midnight Visitors

*A party of Missoula, Montana, musicians who were camping out for a week had a frightening experience with a "bear" outside their tent one evening. One brave fellow decided he would shoot that bear before the bruin killed them all. The outcome of their amusing story appears below. It came from the September 4, 1902 Daily Missoulian.*

Three local [Missoula] musicians, Messrs. Pollard, Ganke, and Shanklin, as was chronicled in these columns last week, went to the fastnesses of the mountains in the vicinity of Victor [Montana] for a week's outing. They were domiciled in a ten-by-twelve tent and, for the first four nights, all went merry as rag time. On the fifth night, however, there was a commotion in the camp and for the period of time of half an hour, excitement ran high and at least two of the campers lost several pounds in weight by excess of perspiration.

It was all caused, at the hour of midnight, by Shanklin's breathless announcement that there was a bear just outside the tent.

Pollard had falle[n] into "Murphy's arm," the other two remaining awake to talk over the events of the day until their conversation was interrupted by the disturbance of the supposed bear nosing around the cook-stove which was located just outside of the front of the tent.

For several minutes they listened to the commotion, expecting each moment to hear Bruin breaking through the folds of their frail abode.

"Hadn't we better awaken Pollard?" finally queried Ganke, in a whisper.

"Sure," replied Shanklin, "get him up with as little noise as possible and have him dress himself, quick."

Pollard was awakened but, like the Missourian, he wanted to be shown before he crawled from his blankets.

By this time Shanklin had tip-toed about the tent, placed two shells loaded with No. 6 shot, in one shot-gun which constituted the explosive armament of the outfit, and was making his way to the front of the tent.

"You don't expect to kill a bear with that thing, do you?" sleepily queried Pollard.

"Certainly," replied the only brave man of the party, "I've heard of lots of bear being killed, at short range, with bird-shot."

However, Shanklin hesitated and then sat down on his bunk to await further developments. In the meantime the disturbance on the outside of the tent continued and they heard pans, pots and skillets rattling over and from the stove at a lively rate.

Finally, Shanklin jumped up and announced that he "was going to shoot the wild beast before he got into the tent." "We wouldn't stand a ghost of a show with him if he got inside here."

"Cocking the shot-gun and, further arming himself by putting a huge carving knife between his teeth, Shanklin started noiselessly for the front tentflap, Ganke tremblingly following his heels. As they emerged from the front there was a rapid scurrying of heavy hoofs, and a male cow and two heifers scampered away in the moonlight. It was the one exciting feature of the outing, and through it all Pollard remained in his bed. However, this is Pollard's side of the yarn and his two companions may have a different story to tell when they return next Saturday. Pollard returned yesterday and, consequently had the first inning.

# Billy's Bear Hunt

*Old Billy Cowgill was a different breed of mountain man—a coward who was easily lost in the woods. Despite these facts, he was quite a deer hunter. One day while hunting with George Shields, Cowgill told an amusing story about a bear adventure he once had. Shields wrote about Cowgill's tale in his book* **Cruisings in the Cascades and Other Hunting Adventures,** *published by Rand, McNally and Company in Chicago and New York; copyright 1889; pp. 146-152.*

I stopped off at Spokane Falls, on my way home, for a few days' deer hunting, and though that region be not exactly in the Cascades, it is so near that a few points in relation to the sport there may be admissible in connection with the foregoing narrative. I had advised my good friend, Dr. C.S. Penfield, of my coming, and he had kindly planned for me a hunting trip. On the morning after my arrival his brother-in-law, Mr. T.E. Jefferson, took me up behind a pair of good roadsters and drove to Johnston's ranch, eighteen miles from the falls, and near the foot of Mount Carleton, where we hoped to find plenty of deer. We hunted there two days, and though we found signs reasonably plentiful and saw three or four deer we were unable to kill any. Mr. Jefferson burned some powder after a buck and a doe the first morning after our arrival, but it was his first experience in deer hunting, so it is not at all strange that the game should have escaped. Mr. Jefferson was compelled to return home at that time on account of a business engagement, but Mr. Johnston, with characteristic Western hospitality and kindness, said I must not leave without a shot, and so hooked up his team and drove me twenty-five miles farther into the mountains, to a place where he said we would surely find plenty of game. On the way in we picked up old Billy Cowgill, a famous deer hunter in this region, and took him along as guide.

We stopped at Brooks' stage ranch, on the Colville road to rest the team, and the proprietor gave us an amusing account of some experiments he had been making in shooting buckshot from a muzzle-loading shotgun. He had made some little bags of buckskin, just large enough to hold twelve No.2 buckshot, and after filling them had sewed up the ends. He shot a few of them at a tree sixty yards away, but they failed to spread and all went into one hole. Then he tried leaving the front end of the bag open, and still they acted as a solid ball; so he had to abandon the scheme, and loaded the charge loose, as of old. He concluded, however, not to fire this last load at the target, and hung the gun up in its usual place. A few days later he heard the dog barking in the woods a short distance from the house, and supposed it had treed a porcupine. Mr. Brooks' brother, who was visiting at the time, took the gun and went out to kill the game, whatever it might be. On reaching the place, he found a ruffed grouse sitting in a tree, at which he fired. The ranchman said he heard the report, and his brother soon came back, carrying a badly-mutilated bird; he threw it into the kitchen, and put the gun away; then he sat down, looked thoughtful, and kept silent for a long time. Finally he blurted out:

"Say, Tom; that gun got away from me."

"How was that?" queried the ranchman.

"I don't know: but I shot pretty near straight up at the grouse, and somehow the gun slipped off my shoulder and done this." And opening his coat he showed his vest, one side of which was split from top to bottom; he then took out a handful of his watch and held it up—one case was torn off, the crystal smashed, the dial caved in, and the running gear all mixed up. The ranchman said he guessed he had put one of the buckskin bags of shot into that barrel, and forgetting that fact, had added the loose charge. He said he reckoned twenty-four No.2 buckshot made too heavy a load for an eight-pound gun.

We reached "Peavine Jimmy's" mining cabin, which was to be our camp, at three o'clock in the afternoon, and busied ourselves till dark in the usual duties of cooking, eating, and gathering wood. Old Billy proved a very interesting character; he is a simple, quiet, honest, unpretentious old man, and unlike, most backwoodsmen, a veritable coward. He has the rare good sense, however, to admit it frankly, and thus disarms criticism. In fact, his frequent admission of this weakness is amusing. He says that for fear of getting lost he does not like to go off a trail when hunting, unless there is snow on the ground, so that he can track himself back into camp. He rides an old buckskin pony that is as modest and gentle as its master. Billy says he often gets lost when he does venture away from the trail, but in such cases he just gives old Buck the rein, hits him a slap, and tells him to go to camp and he soon gets there. He told us a bear story that night, worthy of repetition. Something was said that reminded him of it, and he mentioned it, but added, modestly, that he didn't know as we cared for any bear stories. But we said we were very fond of them, and urged the recital.

"Well, then," he said, "if you will wait a minute, I'll take a drink of water first and then I'll tell it to you," and he laughed a kind of boyish titter, and began:

"Well, me and three other fellers was up north in the Colville country, huntin', and all the other fellows was crazy to kill a bear. I didn't want to kill no bear, and didn't expect to. I'm as 'feared as death of a bear, and hain't no use for 'em. All I wanted to kill was a deer. The other fellers, they wanted to kill some deer, too, but they wanted bear the worst. So one mornin' we all started out, and the other fellers they took the best huntin' ground, and said I'd better go down along the creek and see if I couldn't kill some grouse, for they didn't believe I could kill anything bigger'n that; and I said, all right, and started off down the creek. Purty soon I come to an old mill that wasn't runnin' then. And when I got purty near to the mill I set down on a log, for I didn't think it was worth while to go any furder, for I didn't think I would find any game down the creek, and I didn't care much whether I did or not. Well, I heard a kind of a racket in the mill, and durned if there wasn't a big black bear right in the mill. And I watched him a little bit, and he started out towards me. And I said to myself, says, I 'Now Billy, here's your chance to kill a bear.'

"I hadn't never killed no bear before, nor never seed one before, and durned if I wasn't skeered nearly to death. But I thought there wasn't no use of runnin', for I knowed he could run faster'n I could, so I took out my knife and commenced cuttin' down the brush in front of me, for I wanted to make a shure shot if I did shoot, if I could. And the bear, he come out of the mill and rared up, and put his paws on a log and looked at me, and I said to myself, says I, 'Now Billy, this is your time to shoot'; but I wasn't ready to shoot yit. They was one more bush I wanted to cut out of the way before I shot, so I cut if [sic] off and laid down my knife, and then I took my gun and tried to take aim at his breast, but doggoned if I didn't shake so I couldn't see the sights at all. And I thought one time I wouldn't shoot, and then I knowed the other fellers would laugh at me if told 'em I seed a bear and didn't shoot at him, and besides I was afraid some of 'em was up on the hillside lookin' at me then. So I just said to myself, says I, 'Now Billy, you're goin' to get eat up if you don't kill him, but you might as well be eat up as to be laughed at.' So I jist took the best aim I could for shakin', an' shet both eyes an' pulled.

"Well, I think the bear must a begin to git down jist as I pulled, for I tore his lower jaw off and shot a big hole through one side of his neck. He howled and roared and rolled around there awhile and then he got still. I got round where I could see him, after he quit kickin', but I was afeared to go up to him, so I shot two more bullets through his head to make sure of him. And then I set down and waited a long while to see if he moved any more; for I was afeard he mightn't be dead yit, and might be playin' possum, jist to get ahold of me. But he didn't move no more, so I went up to him with my gun cocked and pointed at his head, so if he did move I could give him another one right quick. An' then I punched him a little with my gun, but he didn't stir. An' when I found he was real dead I took my knife and cut off one of his claws, an' then I went back to camp, the biggest feelin' old cuss you ever seed.

"Well, arter while the other fellers they all come in, lookin' mighty blue, for they hadn't any of 'em killed a thing, an' when I told 'em I'd killed a bear, they wouldn't believe it till I showed 'em the claw. An' then they wouldn't believe it, neither, for they thought I'd bought the claw of[f] some Injin. And they wouldn't believe it at all till they went out with me and seed the bear and helped skin 'im, and cut 'im up, and pack 'im into camp. An' they was the doggondest disappointedest lot of fellers you ever seed, for we hunted five days longer, an' nary one of 'em got to kill a bear nor even see one. They thought I was the poorest hunter and the biggest coward in lot, but I was the only one that killed a bear that clip."

# Double Trouble

*When* Old-timer Hi Ainsworth *was pro-
specting for a rich float, he encountered a silvertip and impulsively shot at it. While
trying to kill bruin, another bear appeared from behind; then the old man had enough
trouble on his hands for six men. He told his lively story to skeptical reporters in Butte,
Montana, which was published in the October 12, 1891* Anaconda Standard.

A man who gave his name as Hi Ainsworth arrived in the city [Butte] to-day and related particulars of a highly exciting adventure which befell him some days ago in the mountain range beyond the Jefferson [River] and near the line of the National park [Yellowstone]. Ainsworth's story was so startling as to test the powers of credulence [sic] and had it not been for the fact he had proofs of his tale, it is doubtful whether anybody would have believed him. Even as it was, those to whom he told the occurrence made liberal allowance for a very vivid imagination and believed such portions of the story as they considered entitled to credence.

Ainsworth seems to combine the pursuits of hunting and prospecting, and from his appearance and ways it is evident that he is an old mountaineer. He said that a little over a week ago he was climbing up the side of a mountain looking for traces of a lead which evidently was the source of some very rich float that he had picked up near the base. He had already spent several days in the same way, and having seen no traces of any animals more dangerous than a woodchuck, he began to think the locality free from bear and other "varmints," but from force of habit continued to carry his rifle with him whenever he went out from his camp, which was in the valley below. It was well on toward late afternoon, he said, when he was somewhat startled by suddenly hearing a noise a little ahead of him, and at almost the same instant a large silver tip bear appeared in sight. His first impulse was to raise his rifle and shoot the bear. Although usually a dead shot, he said, he missed the bear the first time which then began to advance toward him. Hurriedly slipping another cartridge into the gun he shot again, but only wounded the bear. The last shot, however, had the effect of causing the bear to stop and enabled him to reload his gun. Just as he was in the act of shooting again a crash in the brush behind caused him to look in that direction, and he beheld another bear, even larger than the first, and full of fight. To add to the excitement of the occasion the second bear was making for him and he began to think his end was near. For a second he hesitated, undetermined what to do. In front of him was a wounded bear, and behind him, and drawing dangerously close, was another who was looking for a row. Knowing it was useless to hesitate longer and conscious that whatever he did had to be done quickly, he wheeled and fired at the bear behind him, trusting to luck that the one in front would not advance any nearer and enable him to kill the one in the rear. With this thought he took as good aim as his shaky nerves would permit and fired. A savage growl and a lunge into the air told him his shot had taken effect. In some unaccountable manner he forgot for the moment the presence of the other bear and the excitement under which he was laboring caused him to forget to reload his gun, and this act of thoughtlessness very nearly cost him his life. With a bound the bear he wounded first rushed upon him, and before he could draw a cartridge from his belt and load his rifle the furious animal was so close that he was compelled to use the gun for a club, and with all his might he brought the weapon down upon the bear's head. The blow partly stunned the bear, and it also broke the stock of the rifle off square, leaving only the barrel in Ainsworth's hands. Again the bear advanced and again was struck on the head with what remained of the rifle and rolled over on his side. Well was it for Ainsworth that the last blow had taken such good effect, for the other bear had now partly recovered from the shock of the wound he had received and he, too, was advancing toward the man and was almost onto him before Ainsworth realized his danger. Ainsworth aimed a blow at the bear, who had reared onto his haunches and with a stroke from his paw knocked the descending rifle barrel to one side and with the other paw made a terrific reach for Ainsworth. Fortunately Ainsworth still retained his good hold of the gun barrel and he managed to hit the bear again, but owing to the closeness of the animal, which was now preparing to embrace him, the blow had very little force. Before Ainsworth could raise the we[a]pon a second time the bear had pushed him to the ground and the rifle barrel fell from the man's grasp. Over and over the man and animal rolled, now one on top and then the other, the blood from the bear's wounds streaming over the man and almost blinding him. With his clothing torn and his face and body covered with scratches from the bear's claws and teeth Ainsworth finally managed to release himself from the embrace of the bear, which was growing weaker, and he staggered to where his broken rifle lay. With a last supreme effort he began to shower blows on the animal and then unconsciousness overcame him and he fell to the ground.

It was fully midnight when Ainsworth revived and with much difficulty arose to his feet. At first he thought it had been a terrible dream, but when he saw the two dead bears, the broken rifle and beheld his own horribly torn and lacerated body he knew the fight had been a reality. He dragged himself to his camp, where he was compelled to remain four days before he could move and then was able to go to the camp of another hunter, several miles away, where he received proper care, and to-day arrived in Butte. His face, arms, neck, head and every other visible part of his body is still covered with sores which he said were made by the bear, and the heavy canvass coat and trousers he wore are a mass of patches and shreds, held together by his own rough sewing.

# Problems In The Park

*An Anaconda, Montana, man and his wife visited Yellowstone National Park in the fall of 1902 and returned to town with three interesting bear stories. One story involved the man's own close encounter with a mother bear. The tourist, trying to photograph the sow, failed to realize her cub was nearby until it was almost too late. He escaped, however, and lived to tell about the other park bears who were causing considerable trouble for park workers. These stories appeared in the* **Anaconda Standard,** *October 11, 1902.*

H.R. Warner of 604 West Park street returned Thursday evening from the Yellowstone park, where he and his wife, who accompanied him, spent two weeks seeing the sights of the great western wonderland.

"We made the trip overland," said Mr. Warner yesterday, "and it was a delightful one. Every point of interest in the park was visited by us, and we saw some things for which we were not looking. They were bears. One of the animals came very near getting me, but I outfooted him [her] and escaped. I had previously taken snap shots at five good-sized black ones, but there was one, a huge she, which I desired to photograph. She was in the woods near the Lower Geyser basin. My wife accompanied me into the timber, but remained at a safe distance, possibly 200 yards away, and watched the performance. It did not occur to me that the bear might have cubs, but she had one, and that was where the danger of approach came in. The cub was in the bushes near its mother and I did not see it until after the old one had entered its objections to my presence. When she saw me approaching she raised on her rear feet and growled, and I concluded that it would be necessary for me to push the button of the kodak pretty quick. Just as I trained the muzzle of it on her she started after me on the jump, and I did not get a picture of her. In fact, I did not want one—had no use for it. That bear could go some, but not quite so fast as I could. As I began to run I noticed the cub in front of me, which was the first intimation I had that I was up against the real thing. I had stood between the cub and its mother when trying to get a picture of the old bear, and that is why the latter started after me. She ran only 40 or 50 feet, but I ran farther. While the play was in progress my wife stood back and laughed and wished she had a kodak, too.

"The animals are pretty bad in the park now, but I would not like to see them killed, as some persons have suggested should be done. It is amusing to see them. They tried to enter our tent several times, but I had two good dogs, a pick and an axe for protection against them. The dogs kept them out of the tent. One reason why they are bad now is because the hotels in the park are closed and there is not much food for them.

"While we were there two of the animals had to be killed by a scout, who had instructions from the superintendent at Mammoth Hot springs to do the job. One of the bears killed was a silver tip and weighed 886 pounds. The scout told me he had been in the park 17 years and it was the largest of its species he had ever seen. That bear was a peach. With several others it had its home around the Canyon hotel. The storehouse there contained a quantity of food of divers description and the bears knew it. One night that big silver tip and seven others gathered in front of the house and after a short consultation decided to tackle the storehouse. The big fellow deliberately walked up to the door, a large, heavy one, and with its huge paws smashed it into a thousand pieces in the twinkle of an eye. Then it and the others walked into the house and ate and destroyed $100 worth of goods. The keeper of the place telephoned the superintendent of the park and the latter ordered one of the scouts to shoot the leader of the break, which the scout did while I held a lantern for him to see his mark. The bullet pierced the bear's heart, but the animal lived a few minutes.

"At another place in the park there is a man named Kelly doing some work on a road for the government. The bears are bad near his camp; so bold, in fact, that two of his men are kept on guard every night to keep the animals from eating and destroying the goods. The guards employ a novel method of keeping them away. Shortly before dark they build a fire and gather a lot of pitch pine poles and when the bears come near them during the night they light the ends of the poles and poke the animals with the business end. One of the large bears that had been poked a few times finally got mad, walked up to the fire and with his paws knocked the poles in all directions and ran the guards into the timber. Then all of the bears helped themselves to whatever they could find. The leader of that raid was also killed by order of the superintendent, to whom Kelly reported the matter."

# A Bull—Bear Story

*Foresters also had their own encounters with bears, and many a tale they could tell. E.A. Woods related the following bear story about a smokechaser's experience with a bear. Although the narrator embroiders the account with flowery frontier slang, the story probably contains some degree of truth. His tale appeared in the book* **Rangers of the Shield,** *a collection of stories written by foresters, edited by Ovid Butler and published by the American Forestry Association in 1934.*[8]

"Boys, whenever anybody refers to bears as dear little creatures that mind their own business if you mind yours, they stutter. All th' people that write in th' papers 'bout how you can tickle 'em under th' chin an' scratch their fleas fer 'em is plumb loco."

Immediately around the campfire there was a stir, for when Scotty began to speak about bears the monotony of the evening vanished. The smokechaser was far from being a greenhorn, and frequent were the occasions when he admitted it. He knew all about bears. There was no doubt about it—there could be no doubt. For he had met up with black bears and brown bears, fat bears and skinny bears, large bears and small bears. Yes, Scotty knew bears.

"Yes, sir," Scotty continued, after kicking at the fire, "I used to say hooray for th' grizzlies myself. All this here talk 'bout bears fer pets seemed all right until we run acrost th' O'Brien Springs devil."

"How come, Scotty?" broke in O'Day, a fire guard, who should have known better. "Didn't get your goat, did he?"

"Well, sir, I reckon he did," confessed the smokechaser, throwing a dirty look at the guard. "Would have got your'n, too, if you'd been thar. I don't say he war th' biggest bear I ever seen, an' I reckon he warn't no bigger than a stack of hay, but he war plenty big. Anyhow, I 'lowed he war when I heard him roarin' an' growlin' 'round th' tent."

Scotty paused to look with disdain upon O'Day, the fire guard, before getting to his story. "It war jes this way. Mac, here,"—pointing to Ranger McGill, sitting at his side—' says he to me, 'Scotty, th' country's gettin' powerful dry. I wish you'd take that smokechaser's job at O'Brien Springs.'

" 'You're th' doctor, Mac,' says I, so th' next day we moves up. Before we left, though, Mac gave me th' choice between th' cabin or a tent.

"A tent an' fresh air an' lots of it is what I want all th' time, but you bet your sweet life before I got through I war wishin' I war in a fort with one of these here machine guns.

"Well, we moved up an' got th' tent set up, fine an' dandy. Jes' as Mac war pullin' out, he says to me, 'I notice you ain't got no gun.'

" 'No, I don't want no gun,' I tells him.

" 'Lots of bear 'round here,' says Mac.

" 'That's O.K. Let 'em come.' I tells Mac. 'Half a dozen bear more or less don't make no difference to me one way or another.'

"Well, sir, sure enough, Mac war right. Thar war lots of bear 'round thar. I used to see 'em every evenin' comin' out of th' brush, nosin' 'round camp, pawin' th' slop hole to see what they could find. Every now an' then one of 'em would get kind of sassy an' come pretty close to th' tent after I'd gone to bed. But all I had to do war to hit th' side of th' tent with th' back of my hand an' they would hit fer th' brush like a cyclone.

"But th' night that this fracas that I'm tellin' you 'bout took place, a great ol' she bear with two cubs showed up. She war an ugly actin' ol' sister. A bit mangy 'round th' head. Her coat war kind of rough an' she war sure terrible to look at. I hollered at her once or twice an' threw a rock or two in her direction, but th' 'onery devil didn't pay no more 'tention to them than a rattler does to a lizard. She jes' kinda turned her devilish head sidways an' th' fur on her neck raised straight up. Seems like she had a notion to come toward me, but after a while she saunters off, sorta growlin' an' mumblin' to herself.

"I never gave her 'nother thought. After supper I sat 'round readin' before I rolled in. I called Mac up an' told him what had happened, an' he comes right back with a story 'bout some bear breakin' up a tourist camp at Kilbrennan Lake jes' th' night previous, an' how th' greenhorns roosted on tree limbs all night like a flock of turkey gobblers. 'O.K. Mac,' says I. 'If I need any help I'll holler.'

"Believe me, sir, it warn't long before I war hollerin'.

"By th' ghost of Custer, it war dark that night. Not a star in sight—jes' as black as your ol' hat. After I had been in bed fer a few minutes, I thought I heard a low rumblin' acrost th' meadow. Thinks I to myself, 'I wonder if that ol' sister is figurin' on havin' me roost on a limb tonight?' Not hearin' any more growlin', I rolled over an' went back to sleep.

"All of a sudden like I war wakened. My bed war raised right up in th' air an' thar she war, tryin' to get into th' tent right under me. I had some salt an' canned goods in a box under th' bed, an' I reckon she got a whiff of that. Well, sir, thar ain't no use tellin' you I warn't scared, 'cause I war. I lets out a whoop an' lands in th' middle of th' tent. But thar I war. No gun, no ax, no nothin', an' it war as dark as an' ice cave. Do you reckon I could find a match? I've been smokin' fer forty years an' never once before saw th' time I couldn't find one.

"Finally I had sense enough to fish down in my pocket an' get one, but when I went to light th' candle th' dirty brute started growlin' an' snortin' to beat th' band, an' my nerves failed me. I stood thar shakin' like a loco sheep on a winter night. I don't know what I needed most, a gun or a drink.

"Well, sir, I got th' candle blazin' an' set it on th' table jes' as th' ol' she-devil began rootin' under th' tent again. Th' candle fell an' went out. I don't know to this day whether it war an' hour or a minute, but when I came to my senses I war hollerin' bloody murder an' cursin' worse'n a bull whacker. Cursin', jes' think of it, an' me with one foot in th' grave, so to speak. But anyhow, I had th' satisfaction of hearin' th' dirty brute growl in th' brush 'bout fifty yards away.

"I kinda pulled myself together, which war a sight better than havin' her pull me apart. So I opened th' tent an' slipped to th' phone nailed to a tree close by. In a few minutes I had Mac. 'Get my shotgun an' load it with slugs, an' hurry up,' I tells him, while th' bear war threshin' th' ground an' growlin'.

" 'O.K.,' says Mac, 'I'll be right up. Reckon I'll bring young Baney with me.'

"A good idea, I thought, Th' lad's powerful an' quick as a cat. An' if worst comes to worst, maybe he can get a half Nelson hold on th' she-devil while we beats her brains out with an ax. During th' meantime, while Mac an' th' kid giant war burnin' up th' trail, I keeps hollerin' an' beatin' th' dishpan an' holds th' enemy at bay.

"Now, I'm tellin' you, I war tickled loco when I heard th' ol' Ford gruntin' up th' hill. Sure enough, th' boys war loaded fer bear. Their pockets war bulging with ammunition, an' my ol' shotgun loaded with slugs.

"It didn't take us long to get into battle formation, so to speak. We sat at th' mouth of th' tent awaiting th' enemy. As I have already told you, it war as black out as a stack of black cats. You couldn't begin to take aim at anythin'. But that didn't make no difference. We had lots of ammunition an' three guns, an' I didn't figure a mosquito could get by th' entrance of that tent.

"We didn't have long to wait. We heard th' old girl comin' acrost th [sic] meadow on up th' slope toward th' tent, a mumblin' an' growlin' under her breath. Now I'm tellin' you, you can talk all you please 'bout keepin' cool an' havin' control of your nerves an' all th' rest of that poppycock, but thar wasn't a man in th' tent you couldn't hear his heart poundin'. 'It war intense,' as th' novel says. Closer an' closer she came. As luck would have it she stood in a small openin' in front of th' tent not more'n a hundred feet away. 'Let'er have it,' says I. By th' eternal, mister, you never heard such noise in your life. We all shot at once, an' so did I. I pulled both triggers of that ol' blunderbust at th' same time an' I believe it turned me 'round four times. But this war no time to be foolin' with trifles. Any second we expected th' furious an' wounded critter in our midst, but all war silent fer a minute or so. Then we heard her threshin' th' ground.

" 'We got her! We got her! Light th' lantern! Where's your flash light?' I hollered. 'Now steady, boys, have your guns loaded an' be ready fer any emergency. Follow me.'

"Would you believe it—doggone my picture—but it's th' truth. We had shot Bill Skinner's ol' thoroughbed Jersey bull an' it cost us $32.50 apiece."

# Night of The Grizzly

*In his book* Tough Trip Through Paradise, *Andrew Garcia tells in an amusing manner about an encounter he and his Indian wife had with a grizzly in the Big Hole country around 1878. They had come to the area so that In-who-lise, aka, Susie, his wife, could honor the graves of her dead relatives. Both Garcia and In-who-lise were superstitious and their fears gave them more trouble than the grizzly did. To them, the grizzly was an awful, all-powerful beast that struck terror in their very souls. Garcia masterfully describes the terror inspired by an angry grizzly. This excerpt was taken from part four, pp. 281-293 of* Tough Trip Through Paradise, *edited by Bennett H. Stein, the Comstock edition, published by Houghton Mifflin Company; copyright 1967 by The Rock Foundation.*[9]

Getting our saddle horses, we returned to camp. We got there just in the nick of time. A large silver-tip bear, as much surprised as we were, came bounding out of the tepee. On seeing us, he greets us with a roar of welcome, then tore off down the trail toward the old Nez Perce camp, with our dogs who had been with us up the gulch right at his heels and making the valley resound with their wolfish howls. We found that his "Royal Nibs" had been more than busy. A saddle of venison that In-who-lise had hung on the limb of a tree had been pulled down by the bear and only the bones remained. This gent, after satisfying his appetite on venison, had been satisfying his morbid curiosity. On going into the tepee, we found that the bear had made a roughhouse out of it. Our dried meat was scattered all over, with the ground and everything else white from our sack of flour. Lucky for us, the bear had dumped most of it on the blankets.

Leaving In-who-lise to pick up the dried meat and save what flour she could, I cut down a small tree and fashioned a crude shovel. We made our dinner on some of the dried meat the bear had left. During this time In-who-lise is very quiet. We were soon ready to start back, leaving our dogs this time to watch the camp.

Going back to Red Heart's grave, I scooped out all the dirt wash, but found nothing that might have been interred with him. Unlike the remains of Gray Eagle, no particle of hair was in evidence, indicating that scalping had been done, and that most effectively. I replaced the skeleton the best I could. In-who-lise would not touch anything about the graves. I filled in the earth and, knowing that nothing would disturb the remains, I dug a small pine tree and planted it at the head. Thus we left the brave Red Heart. Going back to the other grave, I cleaned it out and laid the remains of Gray Eagle therein. Kneeling by the grave, I joined In-who-lise, fervently saying all the prayers she knew in Injun. As I filled it in, In-who-lise cried pitifully and there was a welling in my own breast and a dimness came to my eyes. Mounding the earth above all that was mortal of the once stalwart Gray Eagle, I prepared to leave that hauntingly silent gulch. Susie and I stood by the low mound for a time, and after some coaxing I persuaded her to return with me to camp, leaving those two lonely graves with their bones now returned to Mother Earth, In-who-lise softly and reverently said, "In peace at last, now roam happy spirits in the land of the dead."

Going back to camp, we found everything there all right. The bear had not returned, but we were still not feeling any too good with the large grizzly in the vicinity. An hour or so before sundown, I started to round up the horses and drive them up the trail for the night. I told In-who-lise after I drove the horses away, I was going to ride on ahead further up the valley hunting for deer, as the bear had eaten up all our fresh meat. In-who-lise told me not to stay away too long, as she is now afraid to stay alone in camp with that big Sim-a-hi hanging around. She knows he is a bad one and that we have not seen the last of him.

After trying to quiet her fears, I drove the horses up to the mouth of the gulch. The grass was better than in the valley, and I would be sure to find them here in the morning. After turning the horses into the gulch, I rode on ahead still following the old trail the Nez Perce had made in the valley for a mile or more. There were plenty of deer signs, but no deer. I only seen two woodchucks. The air was sultry, not a breath of a breeze could be felt. The heat was oppressive; all is quiet and still as death. Suddenly the sky is overcast with a mighty shadow and I could see far away on the horizon and back in the towering hills, misty black clouds are obscuring the setting sun. When now there came a vivid flash of lightning out of those black clouds accompanied by a distant rumble of thunder, which warned me that a rainstorm was on the way. Disgusted at my hunting luck, I turned my horse around and started back the way I came. Passing the mouth of the gulch, I could see the horses about a hundred yards away, grazing with their heads turned up the gulch and good for all night.

It is a curious though well-known fact that the deer family, including antelope, elk and moose, like the company of horses or cattle, and will come out of their haunts to mingle with them in a friendly way. It was an easy matter for a mounted hunter to ride up close to them. Among the horses I could see three blacktail deer, two large does with young fawns, besides a young doe, a fawn of last year. Sitting as still as a statue in the saddle, I let my horse graze his way till close to the horses. I plugged the young doe in the neck, and the report of my rifle rang out through the gulch. The other two does, with their fawns at their heels, took off up the gulch in wild leaps and bounds. Not waiting to remove the entrails, I threw the young doe up on my saddle horse, and rode into camp holding it in the saddle in front of me.

I was surprised to see that, during my absence, In-who-lise had been working like a good fellow rustling wood, and had enough gathered inside the tepee and outside to last a good week. We were only going to stay for the night, but In-who-lise was thinking that silver-tip is going to pay us another visit before morning.

When she saw the young doe I brought back to camp, she said, "When that grizzly scents that venison in camp, nothing will stop him except a bullet, after he got away with our other venison so easy." She was going to keep a fire burning in the tepee.

I was glad in one way to see the fear of the grizzly hanging around our camp. It made In-who-lise forget, for the time being, all about her father, Gray Eagle. I had been hearing nothing but crying and wailing for her dead people, besides attending Injun funerals every day since we came to the Big Hole battlefield, so that I was now wrought up and nearly as locoed as her. I thought, bad as this is, it will be a change for the better, that is if the grizzly does not claw us up.

In-who-lise prepared her bonfire, all ready to touch off. Since it began to drizzle, she covered the wood pile with saddle blankets. While she was doing this, I cleaned and skinned the deer, giving our dogs their share, and a good-sized chuck to In-who-lise to broil over the coals for our supper. I threw a lariat over a high limb of a tree and hauled the remaining venison up to the limb, thinking if that bear wants that venison, this time he is going to have to climb for it, and grizzlies are too big to climb. It was now dusk and still drizzling. I wrapped the entrails, liver and head in the deer hide, and went up the trail a hundred yards. I bent down a good-sized sapling and fastened the whole works to it as a peace offering to the grizzly. When the sapling sprung up straight, the bundle hung too high for our dogs to reach. Still, it would be easy for the bear to bend down the sapling and get it. I could not decide what to do with my saddle horse. First, I was going to picket him close enough to the tepee. I could cut the lariat and let him go in case of trouble, but I thought that the horse picketed in camp would only be in the way of the dogs and more liable to get shot up than the bear. I did not think the grizzly would tackle the horse on picket outside of camp, so I took him a good seventy-five yards and picketed him extra good so that he couldn't pull the picket pin if he smells that bear.

By the time I got back to the tepee it was dark and heavy rain was beginning to fall; it became a continual downpour, with fierce gusts of wind coming and going. Vicious flashes of lightning cut across the sky and lit up the night like day. The closeness of the terrific thunder claps told us only too well that the lightning had struck nearby. This, with the heavy beating of the rain against the tepee, made us think at least we were lucky not to be out in that storm and had a good stout tepee to keep us warm and dry.

I was hungry and tired, after being on the go since daylight this morning. Susie had finished broiling the venison for our supper and along with it had made coffee and frying-pan bread. The bread contained considerable fine gravel and sand that Susie had raked up with the flour, but I was now used to squaw cooking and it tasted good.

I cleaned both of my rifles, and loaded them and laid them down where I could get them quick and handy. The patter of the rain together with the warmth from the fire in the tepee soon makes one drowsy. Though Susie was nodding from the want of sleep, she is still squatting squaw fashion on the blankets and robes on the bed at my feet, and says she ain't going to bed with that grizzly around and take a chance on the fire dying out. I dropped off to sleep and must have been asleep for some time, when she nudged me. I awoke to find the rain and storm had ceased as quickly as it came. Except for the low half whines and growls coming from our dogs outside, all is quiet. Susie is whispering, "Wake up. Don't you hear the dogs? Like us, they are afraid. They are telling us that Sim-a-hi is coming. Yaw-yaw, we should have camped some other place. Now the dogs will make him mad and he will kill us both." In-who-lise rakes the coals and puts wood on the fire and soon had the tepee lit up as bright as day. Grabbing the carbine, I lifted the tepee flap to look outside. A streak of light from the fire gleams past me into the dark, but all else is darkness. I could see nothing, not even the tree where the venison was hanging; I could see nothing wrong outside. I went back and sat down on the foot of the bed with In-who-lise, and it was not long till either the heat of the fire or the suspense had the sweat rolling off both of us. Then, through the night air comes snorts of terror from my saddle horse, followed by the piercing whistling noise a wild horse makes to warn and call the others for help. And we could hear him plainly as he would stamp the ground with a forefoot, then would dash madly around in a circle the length of the lariat. Trying to pull the picket pin and get away. Susie was nagging me to go outside and start the bonfire near the tepee door. I kept saying maybe the bear won't come; to wait till he did. It would be plenty of time then. Time slowly went by, and the horse on picket was quiet again, but the dogs kept up their low moaning growls, some distance from the tepee, but no bear had showed up.

I began to get brave, and said to In-who-lise that all our scare over that bear was for nothing. I was going back to bed. If the grizzly was going to show up, he would not have taken all this time since the dogs first started to growl; he would have been here long before this. In-who-lise disputes this, saying I can go to bed if I want to, but it won't be for long. That grizzly will come yet. He has been all this time eating the guts I had hung up on the sapling. After he is through, he will want the venison hanging in the camp; a big bear like him eats plenty.

Then, as though to make her words come true, we heard the fierce wolfish snarls and yelps from our dogs. We got the surprise of our lives when three of our younger dogs came bounding through the loose tepee flap as though they had been fired out of a catapult. They were in terror with their tails between their legs, the hair along their backs standing up like porcupine quills as they growl and snarl, looking back the way they came. The sudden appearance of the three young dogs, the way they came bounding into the tepee did not improve my courage any. It sent my heart up in my mouth, and brought the sweat beads of despair out on my temples and forehead. I grasped the loaded carbine, my teeth beginning to chatter, like I was getting the swamp ague. I carefully and cautiously peeked outside, but like before in the pitchy darkness I could see nothing. I whispered to In-who-lise to get me a good live firebrand out of the fire. Still holding the rifle, I crawled outside and pulled the saddle blankets off the pile of wood. I swung the firebrand around till it burst in flames, and stuck it down in the dry leaves and twigs under the pile and quickly dodged back into the tepee. I crouched out of sight, looking out through the tepee flap, carbine in hand, with the buffalo gun lying close to my knees. Everything being wet around the pile of wood, it seemed ages before the kindlings took fire. At first from the pile there only came dense clouds of smoke that hugged the damp ground and rose up to hide even the light that gleamed for a ways outside the tepee fire. But soon there were small flames, and it was with some relief when I seen the whole pile was a crackling burst of flames. As they rose up higher, they lit up the pitchy darkness in a circle of bright light for some distance around.

My joy was short-lived when I could see the tree where the venison was hanging. What I saw under that tree was not encouraging. It must have surprised that bear as much as it did me. Anyway, the grizzly stood under the tree, large as life and twice as natural, and any fool could tell he doesn't like this a little bit. He stood his ground, all humped up ready to scrap, with the hair on his back standing up. He stood gazing and sniffing toward the bonfire, then would utter fierce growls. As In-who-lise and I crouch inside, watching all of this, our terror soon changed to sighs of relief, when, as though he despised us, and as though we were not worthy of his notice any longer, he calmly and deliberately squats his huge bulk down on his haunches. He still faced the bonfire and once in a while would lift up his head and sniff up at the venison hanging on the limb. We could see him plainly, not over seventy-five feet away, and it would have been easy to plug him with the buffalo gun. The only thing that is bothering me now was whether I could lay him out for good the first shot. I did not want to wound him, when in five or six bounds, fire or no fire, we would have a mad grizzly on top of us. I decided to shoot him in the head, but as I started to raise up the gun, In-who-lise pushed the gun down. The grizzly was still sitting contented on his haunches under the tree.

We ought to have known that everything was coming along too good to be true. Suddenly I saw a flash of gray come out of the darkness behind the grizzly. It was so quick I knew it was Spe-lee, the treacherous and vicious wolf-dog, mean and large as any wolf. Spe-lee in her sneaking way fears nothing that has its back turned to her. She had given the grizzly a snapping nip on his rump. The grizzly roared with rage, and at the same time half turning sends his mighty paw with its long claws swishing through the air at her, but is too late as Spe-lee was not there. This was now a busy time for the grizzly. Another wolfish form came springing at him out of the darkness. It is Callo-o-too (Short Tail), another of our Injun dogs with all the sneaking propensities of his wolfish ancestors. Quick as a flash he nips the grizzly on the other side and disappears into the darkness quicker than he came. Spe-lee and him are resenting in their own way the grizzly running them out of camp. With surprising agility, the grizzly springs into action, crunching his teeth in rage. With an active springy motion that was surprising for one so clumsy looking, he hurled himself off into the darkness. It developed into a running fight between our dogs and the grizzly. The grizzly chased the whole bunch around near the tepee; one of the dogs would come dashing in between the bonfire and the tepee and would try to get inside with us. I quickly prodded him, yelping back outside, with my gun barrel. It went this way for some time; we were badly scared. In-who-lise has the carbine and I the buffalo gun, with one of us crouching on each side of the flap, the sweat pouring off us from the heat of the bonfire. To make it worse, we could plainly hear above the howls and snarls of our dogs, the roars of anger from the grizzly every time a dog would nip him. Then would come the crashing and tearing as he chases after the dogs through the willows and brush on each side of the small creek behind our camp. Around and around they went, with us terror-stricken and every minute expecting the dogs and the grizzly to come crashing through the back of the tepee on top of us. We were not sorry when we seen our seven dogs go flying by in a scattered bunch in retreat and take off up the trail toward the old Nez Perce camp, with the grizzly bounding along a few yards behind them in hot pursuit, all disappearing in the darkness.

I whispered to In-who-lise that we were lucky them dogs for once in their lives done what was right, when they did not try to run inside the tepee with us, and that I hoped Sim-a-hi would chase them as far as the Big Hole battlefield. I ought to have known that praising the dogs and grizzly would only bring us bad luck again. My face must have turned a sickly white as I heard yelping draw nearer and nearer, leaving no doubt that the grizzly was after one of the dogs and coming back this way. In-who-lise starts to say something, but the words never left her lips. Now out of the darkness into the circle of murky light leaps one of our young dogs, howling as he came on the dead run, and thirty feet behind him came the grizzly. The dog made a beeline for the bonfire, and with an acrobatic leap clears the bonfire and lands straight as an arrow almost in the tepee door, with one of his sides bleeding badly. Howling in pain and terror, he bounded into the tepee, striking In-who-lise square in the breast, knocking her over on the flat of her back, with her head almost in the fire, her legs going up in the air. In-who-lise, as she was going over, must have pulled the trigger of the carbine. The gun went off with a loud bang, filling the tepee with powder smoke, and worse than that, the bullet came near getting me, singing by close to the back of my neck. The hot powder singed a part of my hair and blackened my cheek. The dog goes by the fire and stands whining and cringing on the bed and robes, with blood dripping down from his side where the bear had ripped him. All I can say was that hell sure broke loose in our house! At the report of the gun, like a clap of thunder close to my face, first I thought I was shot forgetting all about the grizzly outside and letting the gun drop out of my hand, with a howl of terror that put the dog to shame, wildly I clapped my hand up to my tingling ear and cheek to feel if there was blood. By this time In-who-lise had got up on her knees and is furious. She dealt the dog a smashing blow across the ribs with the butt of the carbine that made him howl worse than the raking he got from the grizzly. The dog came crawling up behind me. This only took an instant. Feeling my ear and cheek, I knew that I was not hit. What little nerve I had before this was now gone. A glance outside across the bonfire was enough and brought the slobbers of fear running out both corners of my mouth. I sure had to be thankful to In-who-lise for rustling all that wood, and thinking about building that campfire outside. If that fire was not there, the grizzly would have made sausage meat out of us by now.

I could see him better now; he was not over twenty feet away. He must have weighed nine hundred pounds. He stands there, the incarnation of all that is powerful and terrible, his vicious eyes red, glaring with hatred and venom at us across the fire. The short, pointed ears are flattened back on his broad head. His powerful jaws open and shut, uttering vicious snarls, exposing his long yellow fangs that he crunches and snaps in his furious anger. He throws up his head, sending terrific roars of rage reverberating through the night. His unwieldy-looking body is now animated; it quivers and sways with seething life, making him terrible to behold, a monarch of the brute world in all his mighty strength. He works and braces his hind legs in unison with his powerful front legs as though he is about to spring; his front paws open and shut in their fury, tearing up the grass and ground under them, with his long sharp claws.

The loaded buffalo gun is forgotten, though still on the ground at my knee. I was petrified, as though in some horrible nightmare, unable to resist or help myself. The grizzly's eyes are on mine, gleaming like two vivid coals of fire—compelling, penetrating. Some irresistible force in them draws and holds mine on them. There is a weird uncontrollable fascination for me in them gleaming bloodshot eyes and red-gaping, frothy mouth, with its bared fangs.

The thousand thoughts and acts of a lifetime flashed through my mind in a furious jumble. I do not believe the man lives who could express all of this swift drama of horror. The terror I felt is not to be conveyed by pen or words. I can only say that in those few seconds that seemed ages, I paid with compound interest for all the deviltry that I had ever done.

Time and again I made frantic efforts to lift up the buffalo gun; but my arms shook and my trembling hands are powerless. The gun refuses to budge and seems fastened to the ground. The grizzly has me mesmerized. My lips are now dry and feverish; my tongue refuses to move and is stuck to the roof of my mouth.

In desperation, like a drowning person that clutches at a straw, I thought of In-who-lise. I had forgotten about her, but any fool could see that In-who-lise is a badly scared squaw, as she crouches near my side with the carbine still clutched in her trembling hands. She was now only a woman, scared speechless, with beads of sweat dripping like rain from her nose and temples. Her teeth chatter through her trembling lips. Her eyes are pleading to me to save her.

As before, I failed to lift the gun off the ground. I tried to hide my shame from her accusing eyes, but she sees the terror in my face. For an instant a look of pity swept across her face. Then her breast heaved; her lips curled in contempt as her eyes flash me a look of withering scorn.

This was the hardest blow of all. My woman, now at death's door, despises me—the only one who before this had faith and believed in me. Her accusing eyes bore through me and brought me to my senses. I quickly push the set trigger ahead and cock the hammer.

Slowly but surely I raised the gun up to my shoulder. This time my nerves are iron; the gun does not wobble or tremble while I try to catch the grizzly between the eyes. But the flickering campfire light made the front sight dance. The grizzly, in the moments that seemed a thousand years, is still uttering his roars of rage that seemed to shake the tepee and awake the valley. He kept wagging his head from side to side, still tearing up the ground with his claws. His head was too hard a shot to take a chance on. I lowered the muzzle until the top of the burnished copper front sight gleamed like a small star through the rear sight, catching the grizzly at the base of his neck. Bracing myself and pulling the gun tight against my shoulder, a slight touch on the trigger sent Betsy Jane off with the kick of a mule and a roar that filled the tepee with smoke.

The grizzly staggered backward with a moan that seemed almost human, then rears up on his hind legs, clawing at his bleeding breast for an instant. He plunged forward, then toppled over, falling in a huddled heap, with his nose close to the campfire. His bulky form lies quiet and still across the fire from us.

Slipping in another shell, I cocked Betsy Jane and waited. Except for my heart now beating like a triphammer, everything is still as death, as I gaze exultantly at our fallen enemy. In-who-lise gets impatient; she touches me and whispers to give the grizzly a bullet in the head to make sure he was dead.

Then a slight tremor ran through the grizzly's huddled form, and In-who-lise wrings her hands in terror, screaming, "See, the Sim-a-hi is not dead! Shoot him again!" The grizzly was now moaning and gasping in pain. Slowly at first he feebly struggles, then tries to raise up his huge body off the ground, each time to roll back helpless, only to try it again. Now with a mighty effort, an awful sight to behold, groaning in pain, with the blood spurting out of the gaping bullet hole in his breast, using his front legs, slowly raises part way up on his haunches, swaying as in a drunken stupor, with his hind legs sticking out sideways paralyzed and helpless, as he feebly braces his front legs to keep from falling over. His bulky form now half sits up on his haunches, with his head lying helpless on his breast. Time and again he struggles and tries to raise his head, only for it to fall back on his breast again.

I watched the grizzly with the gun cocked and ready. I could see plainly the death haze beginning to cover his bloodshot eyes, and hear the death rattle in his throat. His fevered breath like steam came wheezing, panting, thick and fast as he gasps and utters low piteous moans of pain, and every time he coughed, a tremor shook his body, with the blood still squirting out of the gaping bullet hole, leaving his breast a crimson red, to come trickling down his front legs and dripping on the ground. The grizzly was a very sick bear.

I slowly raised the buffalo gun until the top of the front sight caught the dying grizzly between the eyes; it was with a feeling more of pity than of triumph. Pressing the trigger, Betsy Jane again went off with a roar. Without a moan, the grizzly rolled over—blood trickling out of a round hole in his forehead. A convulsive tremor ran through his body and legs as he opens and shuts his murderous claws. Then with a long sigh he stretched out in death.

A few minutes after this we stood outside viewing the bulky form. I told In-who-lise, "Here is one grizzly who will never scare the daylights out of us again." Calling the dogs to see if the grizzly had killed any of them, it was some time before they would show up. When they came, I could see that Spe-lee is limping with one side of her face bleeding; besides Callo-o-too and Ku-ton-a-can (Big Head) have more than one long bleeding slash along their sides. None of the dogs would come up to us at the campfire, on account of the dead grizzly lying there. They sat on their haunches at the edge of the light made by the fire, uttering fierce growls and sniffing over toward the dead bear.

We could now see by the grayness of the sky it would soon be daybreak. There was no use in trying to get any sleep. I put more wood on the campfire and went back in the tepee. In-who-lise, after pounding coffee berries in a rag with a rock, starts in to make coffee. She also pounded some of the dried buffalo meat that the grizzly had mauled around in the afternoon. It was as hard and tough as sole leather, but it was good stuff after it had been softened between two rocks. When the coffee was boiling, In-who-lise tries to wash the black burn off my face, but with poor success. The gun had put it in to stay till I wear it off. As she was doing this, her midnight eyes are aflame with love. Her face is wreathed in smiles of pride as she says that now I am an Injun hero. As soon as it is daylight and I go after the horses, she says she is going to cut off the grizzly's front claws so that she can made a hero's necklace out of them for me to wear. When the Injuns see them and she tells them how bravely I killed that grizzly, the Injuns will hold a powwow and christen me Sim-a-hi-chen (Grizzly Bear). Then the men will envy me and the women will be jealous of her, that she has a man who killed a grizzly, a great honor. I had plenty doubts about my being in any hero class, still I did not dispute her. Let her have her sweet dream.

# Young Nimrods and Bear Slayers

When men killed bears on the western frontier their brave deeds often made news headlines. When a youngster killed a bear the remarkable feat received even greater attention. Most of the bear slayers in this chapter were adventurous and daring young boys, but a brash teenage girl was the hero in one account. Some of the boys featured in this chapter were later well-known adults such as William Jackson, famous half-breed scout; Sidney Edgerton, Montana's first territorial governor; and A. Phimister Procter, sculptor.

Some of the bear kills recounted in this chapter could only have been performed by youngsters. For while it was true that undaunted nerve was needed in several of these escapades, an equal amount of youthful folly was required. Many of these inexperienced bear slayers took risky chances that grown men of mature judgment would not have attempted.

## Look Before Firing

*William Jackson, former Custer scout, related an exciting grizzly encounter he and his older brother Robert had as youths, to writer James Willard Schultz. The boys had sneaked away from their grandfather, Hugh Monroe, alias Rising Wolf, who was marking a tree to notify wandering Blackfeet of his presence. Before long, Robert spotted a dark object he thought was a buffalo and shot it without positively identifying the animal. It turned out to be a grizzly, and the enraged, wounded bear charged the boys. This exciting account was taken from pp. 13-19 of Schultz' book* **William Jackson—Indian Scout,** *published by the Riverside Press—Houghton Mifflin Company in Cambridge; copyright 1926.*[10]

We left camp on foot, followed the well-worn trail down across the big prairie at the foot of the lake, and stopped in a narrow strip of pines and cottonwoods that bordered a small stream running from the mountains down into the river. There Rising Wolf scalped the trunk of a tree with his big, Hudson's Bay Company knife, and with pieces of shining black coals from a sackful of them that he had gathered from around his lodge fire, painted quickly his man-and-wolf sign upon the white wood. This sign would save us from surprise attacks by wandering war parties of our tribe. After the first one had been painted, we went down across a narrow strip of prairie and into another little grove, and when our grandfather stopped to bark and paint another tree, Robert signed to me to go down the trail with him, and, unnoticed, we stole away.

We found fresh tracks of deer and elk, and side by side, with ready rifles, we stole on, eagerly looking for the animals, Robert whispering to me: 'Whichever of us first sees a deer or elk is to have the shot at it.'

'Yes. Of course,' I replied.

We passed through the grove, and were half-way across a small grassy park, when we saw that the thick brush at its lower end was quivering as if an animal of some kind pressed through it, going up the valley. We faced that way, and after a moment, as the brush ceased quivering, Robert hissed to me: 'Do you see it?'

'No.'

'I do, just a part of its body, dark like that of a buffalo. It is a buffalo! I am going to shoot!'

He fired, and with the report there burst upon our ears a frightful, hoarse roar of pain and anger, and out from the brush leaped a monstrous bear, seemingly as big as a buffalo bull. Clearing the brush, it stopped and sat up, a huge grizzly bear.

I wanted to turn and run, but there flashed through my mind the assertions of the old trappers at the fort, that it was useless to attempt to run from a grizzly, that the one thing to do was to stand and try to kill the animal as it came on. And at that, I took careful aim at the side of its body, just at the edge of the ribs, as I had so often heard was the most vital place. I fired, saw the bear flinch and with terrible roaring clap a paw against its side, and with long, bouncing leaps come at us. Then I did run. I saw Robert running—and lost sight of him. I was sure that the bear was gaining upon me, though I could not see him: I dared not take time to look back, and I had the dreadful feeling that every forward step that I took would be my last one.

'Rising Wolf! Rising Wolf! Help!' I shouted.

I was running back up the trail—heading for the grove in which we had left our grandfather. I could not resist the urge to look back to see if the bear really was after me. He was, and coming fast, bloody foam oozing from his partly open mouth. I was now quite near the grove, and saw with sickening despair that, even if I could reach it before the bear could overtake me, its high cottonwoods were unclimbable.

Again I shouted: 'Rising Wolf—' but my breath was going; I could no more than gasp the other word, 'Help!'

And then I noticed that one of the great trees, on the left of the trail, had a sturdy and very long limb that arched toward the ground, and that by a high jump I might possibly grasp it near its outer end and swing up onto it and climb above reach of the bear. I dropped my empty and useless rifle and made for the limb, sprang and seized it with both hands. Just as I was raising up onto it, the bear lunged up and struck at me, one of its claws ripping my right trouser leg from the back of the knee down, and cutting into the flesh. The downward force of the blow caused me to lose my right hand grip of the limb, and for an instant I swung suspended by but one hand; but with a last upstrain I managed to renew my hold, tried to raise up onto the limb, and found that I hadn't sufficient strength. I looked down and saw the bear turning about to spring at me again: 'He will get me this time,' was my despairing thought. But right then the bear suddenly sank quivering to the ground as, close by, my grandfather's rifle gave a thunderous boom! I dropped to the ground and, too weak to get upon my feet, stared at the dying animal.

'What does this mean? What have you boys been doing?' cried my grandfather, as, hastily reloading, he came and stood over me, his blue eyes bright with anger. I saw my brother running toward us, and he came before I could get breath to answer the question, and exclaimed: 'Oh, what a whopper of a bear! We got him, didn't we!'

'Yes, and he all but got your brother! Come, quick now, let me hear all about it!'

'The bear was going through the brush, down there; we could see it shaking; and then I saw just a little of its body and thought that it was a buffalo, and when I fired, it came jumping out into the open and sat up, and then brother fired, and it came for us,' Robert replied.

'I've a good mind to give you a real switching! Both of you!' the old man exclaimed. And then, after a moment: 'Well, you had a narrow escape. Let this be your lesson that you must never shoot at anything that you cannot see plainly. Why, that might have been me, or one of your uncles moving through the brush! And another thing: you boys are not to go off by yourselves to hunt, and if you again sneak away from me when I take you out, I will put your rifles where you can't get them again this summer. There! Do you understand that?'

'Yes. And now let's skin the bear. I want to see where my bullet struck it,' Robert quickly replied. Myself, I could no more than nod my head. There was a gone feeling in the pit of my stomach.

But after a time, I managed to get up and help in the skinning of the great bear that weighed, Rising Wolf said, all of a thousand pounds. His shot had broken its neck. Robert had shot it well back, and my bullet had pierced the end of one lung, from the effect of which it would soon have died, had not my grandfather so opportunely snuffed out its life.

Having finished skinning the bear, we hurried back to camp, and got an old horse that was not afraid of bears, upon which to pack in the heavy hide. Then, when we dropped it upon the ground in front of the lodges, the women made loud protest against its being put there, and declared that they would not flesh, nor peg it out to dry, as they were not Sun Women—that is, sacred women, women who had, with vows, and fasting and prayer, taken part in the building of the annual great lodge, the so-called medicine lodge in honor of the god.

But just then our Aunt Lizzie came from the river with a bucket of water, and after listening to them for a moment, she set the bucket down, and said to us: 'Even if the bear is a man-animal, I am not afraid of it; and though I am not a sacred lodge woman, I will flesh this hide, and dry it, and tan it for a bed robe for my brave young nephews!'

'Good! Good! I'm glad that I have anyhow one child who is not a coward!' Rising Wolf exclaimed.

'To fear the shadows (souls, or spirits, or ghosts) of bears, as capable of harming us as are the shadows of Crows, Assiniboin[e]s, or any other enemies, is not cowardly,' my grandmother told him.

'We will not argue about it. Our daughter will tan the hide. She will not be harmed by doing it—'

'Not if my prayers can protect her!'

I did not hear the rest of the argument, for Aunt Lizzie was calling to Robert and me to help her with the hide. Before sundown we had it pegged out upon the ground, its flesh side as smooth and white as a piece of paper.

# Rising Wolf Rescues Another

*As a teenager, Rising Wolf (Hugh Monroe) also had a close call with a charging grizzly near St. Mary's Lakes. Young Monroe had been commissioned by the Hudson Bay Company to travel with the Blackfeet Indians to learn their language and to see how far West the company's rival, the American Fur Company, had gone. Lone Walker, the tribe's chief, looked after the young white explorer while he traveled with the Indians. Rising Wolf befriended two of the chief's children, Mink Woman and Red Crow, and the three of them often hunted together. One day when the three youths were returning from a goat hunt, they were charged by an angry grizzly. Their exciting encounter was excerpted from pp. 77-84 of* **Rising Wolf—The White Blackfoot** *by James Willard Schultz, published by the Riverside Press—Houghton Mifflin Company in Cambridge; copyright 1919.*[11]

The sun had set when we crossed the river and the big prairie at the foot of the upper lake, and started on the trail along the lower lake. It was almost dark when, hurrying along at a good lope, we crossed the park opposite the island, and entered a quaking aspen grove. And then, without warning, Red Crow's horse gave a sudden sideways leap and threw him, and went snorting and tearing off to the right, and Mink Woman's and my horses took after him, plunging and kicking with fright, and try as we would we could not stop them. I saw the girl knocked from her horse by a projecting, low bough of a cottonwood tree. Behind us Red Crow was shouting "Kyai-yo! Kyai-yo! Spom-ok-it!" (A bear! A bear! Help!)

As I could not stop my horse I sprang off him, holding fast to my gun, passed Mink Woman struggling to her feet, and ran to assist my friend, his continued cries for help almost drowned by the terrible roars of an angry bear. Never had I heard anything so terrible. It struck fear to my heart. I wanted to turn and run from it, but I just couldn't! And there close behind me came the girl, crying, "Spom-os! Spom-os!" (Help him! Help him!) I just gritted my teeth and kept on.

I went but a little way through the brush when, in the dim light, I saw Red Crow clinging with both hands to a slender, swaying, quaking aspen, and jerking up his feet from the up-reaching swipes of a big bear's claws. He could find no lodgment for his feet and could climb no higher; as it was, the little tree threatened to snap in two at any moment. It was bending more and more to the right, and directly over the bear, and he was lifting his legs higher and higher. There was no time to be lost! Scared though I was, I raised my gun, took careful sight for a heart shot at the big animal, and pulled the trigger. Whoom! And the bear gave a louder roar than ever, fell and clawed at its side, then rose and came after me, and as I turned to run I saw the little tree snap in two and Red Crow drop to the ground.

I turned only to bump heavily into Mink Woman, and we fell, both yelling, and sprang up and ran for our lives, expecting that every jump would be our last. But we had gone only a short way when it struck me that we were not being pursued, and then, oh, how can I describe the relief I felt when I heard Red Crow shout to us: "Puk-si-put! Ahk-ai-ni!" (Come! He is dead!)

Well, when I heard that my strength seemed suddenly to go from me, and I guess that the girl felt the same way. We turned back, hand in hand, wabbly on our legs, and gasping as we recovered our breath. Again and again Red Crow called to us, and at last I got enough wind into me to answer him, and he came to meet us, and led us back to the bear.

I had not thought that a grizzly could be as big as it was. It lay there on its side as big bodied as a buffalo cow. The big mouth was open, exposing upper and lower yellow fangs as long as my forefinger. I lifted up one huge forefoot and saw that the claws were four inches and more in length. Lastly, I saw that there was an arrow deep in its breast. Then, as we stood there, Red Crow made me understand that when his horse threw him and he got to his feet, he found the bear standing erect facing him, and he had fired an arrow into it and taken to the nearest tree. I knew the rest. I saw that the arrow had pierced the bear's lungs; that it would have bled to death anyhow. But my shot had been a heart shot, and just in time, for the little tree was bending, breaking even as I fired, and the bear would have had Red Crow had it not started in pursuit of us.

"The claws, you take them!" Red Crow now signed to me. But I refused. I knew how highly they were valued for necklace ornaments, and I wanted no necklace. Nor did I want the great hide, for its new coat was short, and the old winter coat still clung to it in faded yellow patches. Red Crow quickly unjointed the long fore claws, and we hunted around and found our ibex hides, which had come to the ground with us, and resumed our way in the gathering night. The horses had, of course, gone on, and would never stop until they found the band in which they belonged.

After the experience we had had, we went on with fear in our hearts, imagining that every animal we heard moving was a bear. There was no moon, and in the thick groves we had to just feel our way. But at last we passed the foot of the lake and saw the yellow gleaming of the hundreds of lodges of the camp on the far side of the river. The ford was too deep, the water too swift for us to cross it on foot, so we called for help, and several who heard came over on horseback and took us up behind, and across to the camp, where we found Lone Walker was gathering a party to go in search for us.

What a welcome we got! The women hugged and kissed Red Crow and his sister, and me too, just as if I were another son, and Lone Walker patted us on the shoulder and followed us into the lodge, and fussed at the women to hurry and set food before us. We ate, and let Mink Woman tell the story of the day, which she did between bites, and oh, how her eyes flashed and the words poured out as she described with telling gestures our experience with the bear! A crowd of chiefs and warriors had come into the lodge when word went around that we had killed a big bear, and listened to her story with close attention and many exclamations of surprise and approval; and when she ended, and Red Crow had exhibited the huge claws, Lone Walker made a little speech to me. I understood enough of it, with his signs, to know that he praised me for my bravery in going to his son's rescue and giving the bear its death shot.

Let me say here that in those days, with only bow and arrows, or a flintlock gun, the bravest of hunters generally let the grizzly alone if he would only let them alone. The trouble was that the grizzly, sure of his terrible strength, only too often charged the hunter at sight and without the slightest provocation. I have recently read Lewis and Clark's "Journal," and find that they agree with me that the grizzly, or as they called it, the white bear, was a most ferocious and dangerous animal.

# As Brave As They Come

*Another youthful bear story written by James Willard Schultz involved trapper and trader Thomas Fox. Fox had planned to publish his own frontier adventures but died before he was able to complete the task. Schultz was asked to finish the work for him.*

*In the fall of 1860, young Fox and an Indian boy named Pitamakan, son of a Blackfeet chief, decided to go off by themselves to trap beaver. Their adventure trip turned into a harsh test of survival. First they were attacked by Kootenai Indians who stole all their belongings except the clothes they were wearing. Then a sudden snowstorm came, leaving them stranded in the mountains for the winter. For a while they took refuge in a bear's den, and throughout their ordeal, Pitamakan not only showed manly courage but also adept ability to improvise. Although he had been influenced by the white man's modern tools and techniques, he could recall his people's stories of how Indians lived long ago before flint, steel, guns and other conveniences.*

*Below is an episode of their adventures in which the boys killed a bear with clubs because they desperately needed its sinew to make cords for bows. The account was excerpted from pp. 121-133 of Schultz' book* **With the Indians in the Rockies,** *published by The Riverside Press—Houghton Mifflin Company in Cambridge; copyright 1912.*[12]

Well, we took up the dim trail on the farther side of the river and followed it through the timber toward the cave at the foot of the cliff, but I, for my part, was not at all anxious to reach the end of it. Midway up the slope I called to Pitamakan to halt.

"Let's talk this over and plan just what we will do at the cave," I proposed.

"I don't know what there is to plan," he answered, turning and facing me. "We walk up to the cave, stoop down, and shout, 'Sticky-mouth, come out of there!' Out he comes, terribly scared, and we stand on each side of the entrance with raised clubs, and whack him on the base of the nose as hard as we can. Down he falls. We hit him a few more times, and he dies."

"Yes?" said I. "Yes?"

I was trying to remember all the bear stories that I had heard the company men and the Indians tell, but I could call to mind no story of their attacking a bear with clubs.

"Yes? Yes what? Why did you stop? Go on and finish what you started to say."

"We may be running a big risk," I replied. "I have always heard that any animal will fight when it is cornered."

"But we are not going to corner this bear. We stand on each side of the entrance; it comes out; there is the big wide slope and the thick forest before it, and plenty of room to run. We will be in great luck if, with the one blow that we each will have time for, we succeed in knocking it down. Remember this:

We have to hit it and hit hard with one swing of the club, for it will be going so fast that there will be no chance for a second blow."

We went on. I felt somewhat reassured, and was now anxious to have the adventure over as soon as possible. All our future depended on getting the bear. I wondered whether, if we failed to stop the animal with our clubs, Pitamakan would venture to defy his dream, cut off a braid of his hair, and make a bow-cord.

Passing the last of the trees, we began to climb the short, bare slope before the cave, when suddenly we made a discovery that was sickening. About twenty yards from the cave the trail we were following turned sharply to the left and went quartering back into the timber. We stared at it for a moment in silence. Then Pitamakan said, dully:—

"Here ends our bear hunt! He was afraid to go to his den because our scent was still there. He has gone far off to some other place that he knows."

The outlook was certainly black. There was but one chance for us now, I thought, and that was for me to persuade this red brother of mine to disregard his dream and cut off some of his hair for a bow-cord. But turning round and idly looking the other way, I saw something that instantly drove this thought from my mind. It was a dim trail along the foot of the cliff to the right of the cave. I grabbed Pitamakan by the arm, yanked him round, and silently pointed at it. His quick eyes instantly discovered it, and he grinned, and danced a couple of steps.

"Aha! That is why this one turned and went away!" he exclaimed. "Another bear was there already, had stolen his home and bed, and he was afraid to fight for them. Come on! Come on!"

We went but a few steps, however, before he stopped short and stood in deep thought. Finally he turned and looked at me queerly, as if I were a stranger and he were trying to learn by my appearance what manner of boy I was. It is not pleasant to be stared at in that way. I stood it as long as I could, and then asked, perhaps a little impatiently, why he did so. The answer I got was unexpected:—

"I am thinking that the bear there in the cave may be a grizzly. How is it? Shall we go on and take the chances, or turn back to camp? If you are afraid, there is no use of our trying to do anything up there."

Of course I was afraid, but I was also desperate; and I felt, too, that I must be just as brave as my partner. "Go on!" I said, and my voice sounded strangely hollow to me. "Go on! I will be right with you."

We climbed the remainder of the slope and stood before the cave. Its low entrance was buried in snow, all except a narrow space in the centre, through which the bear had ploughed its way in, and which, since its passing, had partly filled. The trail was so old that we could not determine whether a black or a grizzly bear had made it.

But of one thing there could be no doubt: the animal was right there in the dark hole, only a few feet from us, as was shown by the faint wisps of congealed breath floating out of it into the cold air. Pitamakan, silently stationing me on the right of the entrance, took his place at the left side, and motioning me to raise my club, shouted, *"Pahk-si-kwo-yi, sak-sit!"* (Sticky-mouth, come out!)

Nothing came; nor could we hear any movement, any stir of the leaves inside. Again he shouted; and again and again, without result. Then, motioning me to follow, he went down the slope. "We'll have to get a pole and jab him," he said, when we came to the timber. "Look round for a good one."

We soon found a slender dead pine, snapped it at the base where it had rotted, and knocked off the few scrawny limbs. It was fully twenty feet long, and very light.

"Now I am the stronger," said Pitamakan, as we went back, "so do you handle the pole, and I will stand ready to hit a big blow with my club. You keep your club in your right hand, and work the pole into the cave with your left. In that way maybe you will have time to strike, too."

When we came to the cave, I found that his plan would not work. I could not force the pole through the pile of snow at the entrance with one hand, so standing the club where I could quickly reach it, I used both hands. At every thrust the pole went in deeper, and in the excitement of the moment I drove it harder and harder, with the result that it unexpectedly went clear through the obstructing snow and on, and I fell headlong.

At the instant I went down something struck the far end of the pole such a rap that I could feel the jar of it clear back through the snow, and a muffled, raucous, angry yowl set all my strained nerves a-quiver. As I was gathering myself to rise, the dreadful yowl was repeated right over my head, and down the bear came on me, clawing and squirming. Its sharp nails cut right into my legs. I squirmed as best I could under its weight, and no doubt went through the motions of yelling; but my face was buried in the snow, and for the moment I could make no sound.

Although I was sure that a grizzly was upon me and that my time had come, I continued to wiggle, and to my great surprise, I suddenly slipped free from the weight, rose up, and toppled over backward, catching, as I went, just a glimpse of Pitamakan fiercely striking a blow with his club. I was on my feet in no time, and what I saw caused me to yell with delight as I sprang for my club. The bear was kicking and writhing in the snow, and my partner was showering blows on its head. I delivered a blow or two myself before it ceased to struggle.

Then I saw that it was not a grizzly, but a black bear of no great size. Had it been a grizzly, I certainly, and probably Pitamakan, too, would have been killed right there.

It was some little time before we could settle down to the work in hand. Pitamakan had to describe how he had stood ready, and hit the bear a terrific blow on the nose as it came leaping out, and how he had followed it up with more blows as fast as he could swing his club. Then I tried to tell how I had felt, crushed under the bear and expecting every instant to be bitten and clawed to death. But words failed me, and, moreover, a stinging sensation in my legs demanded my attention; there were several gashes in them from which blood was trickling, and my trousers were badly ripped. I rubbed the wounds a bit with snow, and found that they were not so serious as they looked.

The bear, a male, was very fat, and was quite too heavy for us to carry; probably it weighed two hundred pounds. But we could drag it, and taking hold of its fore paws, we started home. It was easy to pull it down the slope and across the ice, but from there to camp, across the level valley, dragging it was very hard work. Night had fallen when we arrived, and cold as the air was, we were covered with perspiration.

Luckily, we had a good supply of wood on hand. Pitamakan, opening the ash-heap, raked out a mass of live coals and started a good fire. Then we rested and broiled some rabbit meat before attacking the bear. Never were there two happier boys than we, as we sat before our fire in that great wilderness, munched our insipid rabbit meat and gloated over our prize.

The prehistoric people no doubt considered obsidian knives most excellent tools; but to us, who were accustomed only to sharp steel, they seemed anything but excellent; they severely tried our muscles, our patience, and our temper. They proved, however, to be not such bad flaying instruments. Still, we were a long time ripping the bear's skin from the tip of the jaw down along the belly to the tail, and from the tail down the inside of the legs to and round the base of the feet. There were fully two inches of fat on the carcass, and when we finally got the hide off, we looked as if we had actually wallowed in it. By that time, according to the Big Dipper, it was past midnight, but Pitamakan would not rest until he had the back sinews safe out of the carcass and drying before the fire for early use.

It is commonly believed that the Indians used the leg tendons of animals for bow-cords, thread, and wrappings, but this is a mistake; the only ones they took were the back sinews. These lie like ribbons on the outside of the flesh along the backbone, and vary in length and thickness according to the size of the animal. Those of a buffalo bull, for instance, are nearly three feet long, three or four inches wide, and a quarter of an inch thick. When dry, they are easily shredded into threads of any desired size.

Those that we now took from the bear were not two feet long, but were more than sufficient for a couple of bow-cords. As soon as we had them free, we pressed them against a smooth length of dry wood, where they stuck; and laying this well back from the fire, we began our intermittent night's sleep, for as I have said, we had to get up frequently to replenish the fire.

The next morning, expecting to have a fine feast, I broiled some of the bear meat over the coals, but it was so rank that one mouthful was more than enough; so I helped Pitamakan finish the last of the rabbit meat. He would have starved rather than eat the meat of a bear, for to the Blackfeet the bear is "medicine," a sacred animal, near kin to man, and therefore not to be used for food.

Killing a grizzly was considered as great a feat as killing a Sioux, or other enemy. But the successful hunter took no part of the animal except the claws, unless he were a medicine-man. The medicine-man, with many prayers and sacrifices to the gods, would occasionally take a strip of the fur to wrap round the roll containing his sacred pipe.

Pitamakan himself was somewhat averse to our making any use of the black bear's hide, but when I offered to do all the work of scraping off the fat meat and of drying it, he consented to sleep on it once with me, as an experiment, and if his dreams were good, to continue to use it.

I went at my task with good will, and was half the morning getting the hide clean and in shape to stretch and dry. Pitamakan meanwhile made two bow-cords of the bear sinew. First he raveled them into a mass of fine threads, and then hand-spun them into a twisted cord of the desired length; and he made a very good job of it, too. When he had stretched the cords to dry before the fire, he sharpened a twig of dry birch for an awl, and with the rest of the sinew, repaired our badly ripped moccasins. At noon we started out to hunt, and on the way dragged the bear carcass back to the river and across it into the big timber, where later on we hoped to use it for bait.

# An Audacious and Accurate Aim

*A bold teenage girl embarrassed a man by displaying no fear of shooting a grizzly with only one shell in a rifle. The bear was most likely a yearling since it was still able to climb a tree. Besides shooting the bear, the girl bravely approached a mother grizzly to return her cub, which the teenager had captured the day before. This story appeared June 18, 1898, in the **Anaconda Standard**.*

Bears of all sizes, ages and varieties are coming down into the Musselshell valley this winter, says a correspondent of the New York Sun, writing from Key Handle Ranch, Montana. The mildness of the weather is the cause of their leaving their places of hibernation in the Snowy and Bull mountains. They are fat and saucy, and as the mercury has seldom been as low as zero in this locality, they are not sluggish. It is possible, and sometimes painful, to learn a little more about bears, even after one is certain one knows all about them. This story illustrates that fact:

"Having been to the postoffice," said the man who told it, "I stopped at the 'Flying V' ranch to give them their letters. There the daughter of the family proudly exhibited a young cub weighing about 20 pounds, which she herself had caught and carried home the day before. She was proud of her conquest, and naively suggested that the cub's mamma might be somewhere close. It was almost a foregone conclusion that she was. Having had some experience in trampling on the feelings of an angry mother of a missing cub, I directed the conversation to an entirely different subject. Shortly after luncheon I caught my cayuse and set out for home.

"I had just reached the top of the hill when my horse started to bolt, but, throwing the bridle rein over his head, which is the signal to a cayuse to stop, I swung out of the saddle and found myself between the frightened horse and a little ball-faced grizzly, whose hostile intentions could have been interpreted by the most casual observer. Suspense is worse than battle, so I picked up a stone and threw it at the bear. The action precipitated a riot. The bear and the horse danced around me in bewildering confusion. Having kept hold of the bridle reins I soon got back in the saddle, and was soon a hundred yards away. This action seemed to puzzle the bear, who had probably seen horses and men apart, but had never seen a man on a horse. When one has killed a real grizzly one hates to be imposed upon by a bad-tempered lil[l]iputian edition, so I turned my cayuse and charged the bear.

"When my cayuse stampeded he had run past the cabins at the 'Flying V' ranch. My yells and the riderless horse informed them that something was wrong, and when the daughter of the family, a girl of 16, came close enough to hear I told her I had a bear up a tree and asked her to get a gun quick. Thereupon she ran back to the house, and when she reappeared she was followed by the queerest procession I have ever seen come out to kill a bear. First came the girl with a Marlin 44-40 repeater. Then came her mother carrying in her arms a 2-months-old baby. A boy of 7 pulling the unwilling captive cub near with a pug dog barking at his heels completed the force.

" 'There is only one cartridge in the gun,' said the girl, as she handed it to me.

"The remark was made in a matter-of-fact way that appalled me. If the young woman expected me to attempt to shoot a ball-faced grizzly whose temper I had tested, I would much rather she and her mother and all except the fat pug dog would go back to the house. There was only six square inches of bear visible, but I knew there was several hundred pounds of bear up that tree. The family refused to accept my advice to retire while I massacred the bear, and, therefore, I declined to shoot. The last time I had seen that ball-faced grizzly's countenance it had the expression of a fiend that was perfectly capable of devouring the entire family, pug dog and all.

"I handed the gun back to the girl and told her to go to the house and fill the magazine with cartridges. She smiled contemptuously and then, before I could prevent it, raised the rifle and fired. The bear fell with a thud and was dead before he reached the ground, but coming directly toward us with open jaws and red tongue, I saw another bear, that even in that exciting moment I had no difficulty in identifying as the mother of the captive cub.

"The family ran, that is, all except the girl, the pug and the cub. I thought the girl was too much scared to run. I wanted to, but could not very well stampede and leave her. The pug did not have sense enough to run, and the cub had no reason to. Opening a big claspknife, I waited for the onslaught. Bruin is always a boxer, and it behooves an antagonist to guard well the solar plexus and other vulnerable points. I saw a huge form rise before me, and while ineffectually trying to sink the knife in her body, I felt my arms pinioned to my side with a grip so terrible that it seemed to paralyze the action of my muscles. Her hot breath almost suffocated me. There was no room for hope. A quick death was the only boon I could consistently crave. Time is merely a measure of events, and I now know that the criminal who is hanged, from the time the rope falls until he reaches the end of the rope, lives longer than any man who is now alive. I spent a short eternity in the arms of that bear.

"Voluntarily old Bruin let me go. I fancied I had almost scented the noisome zephrys [sic] of the Styx and had caught a glimpse of Old Charon's face, and I am yet considerably humiliated because I can recollect nothing resembling a chinook breeze from Paradise. I am yet surprised the bear let go, but a girl of 16 had had sufficient presence of mind to speculate on the chances of establishing the identity of the true heir-at-law of my tormentor. So she gathered up the little cub bear, despite his squeals, scratches and other protestations, and taken him to his mamma.''

# Monster Bears and Young Boys

*Frank Metzel related two amusing bear stories that happened during his youth in southwestern Montana. One was about his first "big" bear kill, and the second described how another lad "escaped" from a bear by climbing a tree too small to hold him. These entertaining tales appeared November 19, 1906, in the* **Anaconda Standard***.*

Frank Metzel, the former postmaster of Puller Springs, who has just returned home after a few days' visit in Butte, is one of the champion bear hunters of the West, and in the days when bear were plentiful in Southern Montana bowled over many of the varmints who made life miserable for the stockmen. Mr. Metzel was in a reminiscent mood when seen by a reporter of the Standard at the Butte [sic] the other night, and the talk naturally drifted to bears.

"I remember the first bear I ever killed as well as if it were yesterday," he said. "It was a little while after I got my first rifle, and I was scarcely in my teens. I went hunting up in the hills along Jack creek, and I was looking for bear. Pretty soon I saw one coming down the ridge, and judging from the direction in which he was heading, he intended passing close to me. Then I ran down into a gulch and picked a tree which would be easily climbed and waited. After a time I again sneaked up on the ridge and caught a glimpse of the bear. He was about half a mile nearer and jogging along contentedly. Again I sought the foot of the tree and waited, and after what seemed an hour or two more the bear came trotting along over the brow of the hill and directly towards me. He looked as big as a house, and I took a good shot and fetched him. He doubled up and howled in agony and stampeded towards a brush heap. I was exultant, but was wise enough not to follow bruin into the brush, so I hurried to my saddle horse and in a few minutes I was at the ranch, flushed with victory.

"'I have shot the biggest bear in the Jack creek hills,' I yelled when I got within hearing distance, and the entire family came out, my father, Alexander Metzel, being in the lead.

"'What do you think he will weigh, Frank?' the old gentleman asked.

"'At least 650 pounds,' I answered, thinking I had cut the weight at least in two. And then we all went up to the clump of brush into which I had seen the bear crawl, and the blood on the trail told them I had made a good shot. Presently one of the boys, Charley, got a good look into the willows and located the bear. I saw him go in and yelled in dismay, for I was afraid the monster would turn on him and eat him alive. Presently we heard Charley laughing, and soon he came backing out of the brush carrying my bear as if it were a jack rabbit. 'Here's your 650-pound bear,' he laughed in derision, and he threw it down the hill at my feet. To say I was disappointed was drawing it mild. The bear was a hungry-looking cub, and it must have been an orphan, for it would not have weighed 40 pounds the fattest day it ever saw.

"But I had the laugh on Charley a little later," continued Mr. Metzel. "Just a day or two after we were going up to Red Rock to look after the cattle which were ranging there. We had saddle horses and a pack horse, and when night came we went into camp on Coal creek. I was fixing the camp and Charley was looking after the horses, and the first thing I knew Charley came running into camp as fast as his legs would carry him, yelling at the top of his voice that a bear was coming down the creek. I had considerable difficulty in getting my rifle unpacked, as it stuck in the scabbard. By this time the bear was getting dangerously close and it was too dark to shoot real good. Anyway, I took a breast shot and bowled the bear over. He picked himself up in a minute and, bawling at the top of his voice, came direct for our camp. With a yell of terror Charley stampeded to the top of a little quaking asp[en], which promptly bent double with him after he had climbed up 15 or 20 feet. I was too interested in getting another shot at the bear to pay much attention to him until I heard him yell, 'Hurry up, Frank: there's plenty of room up here!' And then I saw him dangling, his feet within three inches of the ground. I laughed so heartily that the bear plunged by our camp and got away, and I can tell you it was a long time before Charley heard the last of that tree-climbing episode."

# Ropes Can Be Handy

*Two young New Mexico cowboys encountered a female bear one morning on their way to a roundup and attacked her without any firearms. Their weapons consisted of a couple of ropes and a knife. The boys' adventure was reported in the October 23, 1901* **Missoulian.**

Hook Ludson's two boys, Hugh, aged eighteen, and Pierce, who is fourteen, had an experience lately which illustrates well their handiness with the rope and ability to take care of themselves. The two boys were working with the roundup in the Naeglin Cidon country, in the Mogollon mountain region, and started one morning to join another roundup outfit that was working about eight miles away. Their course took them down a deep canyon for several miles and then over a steep ridge into another narrow valley.

About three miles down the canyon made an abrupt bend, the walls being several hundred feet high. As the two boys came around this bend they almost ran into a large she bear, who was feasting on a freshly killed calf. Both had left camp without buckling on their six shooters and belts of cartridges; but, angered at the sight of the dead calf, both charged at the bear, ropes swinging in readiness for a throw.

The bear fled down the canyon. The speed of an old, lean she bear is remarkable, and for a quarter of a mile neither boy was able to get close enough to land his rope. Brush, trees and bowlders made it a difficult task to cast a fifty foot rope with certainty, but Hugh at last managed to drop a loop over the bear's head and left foreleg, and swerving his horse to the right, the bear went on one side of a scrub oak and the horse on the other. When the rope tightened, the horse was nearly thrown from his feet, and the bear turned a somersault.

The younger boy was going at such speed that he nearly ran over the bear as she rose to her feet, but this did not prevent him from dropping a loop over her head as he went by. By this time Hugh's rope had slipped down around the bear's body, and as Pierce tightened his rope Hugh's caught around both hind feet. The bear was again thrown to the ground by a jerk from Pierce's rope, and Hugh, hastily throwing several turns of his rope around the horn of the saddle, jumped to the ground and started toward the bear, pulling out his knife and opening it as he went. Watching his chance, he stabbed the bear several times in the region of the heart and then slashed her throat. In a few moments the bear ceased struggling. After scalping the bear for the bounty the boys cut off a few pounds of meat and went on their way.

# Sidney's Secret Sin

*Martha Edgerton Plassmann, daughter of Montana's first territorial governor, told how her father, Sidney Edgerton, killed a black bear when he was a boy. The bear was a pet belonging to his brother-in-law, Richard Darling. Sidney accidently killed the bear but failed to have the courage to tell Richard how it happened until years later. His Puritan conscience bothered him all those years because he had told a cowardly lie. However, there may be more to this story than is told. It appeared May 14, 1936, in the Rocky Mountain Husbandman.*

My father, Sidney Edgerton, was born in 1818 at Cazenovia, New York. His birth took place shortly after his father's death, and so sure were those in attendance on his mother that he could not live, preparations were made for his burial, which did not take place until 82 years later.

After her husband's death, my grandmother Edgerton found it difficult to support her family, of whom Sidney was the youngest. In those days few occupations were open to women; but Mrs. Edgerton had no choice in the matter, willingly undertaking any task that would feed and clothe her children. She seems to have been a woman of versatile talents, although denied the education she craved and that had been given [to] her brothers. She spun and wove, as did most of the women of her day; helped to make the clothes of her neighbors; was the one always selected to make the election cake for training days, or other great occasions; and solved the mathematical problems the village schoolmaster found too hard for him. Added to this, my uncle told me how far in the night he frequently wakened, to see her seated at the loom, weaving cloth for others, or for her own family.

This work often took her from home for indefinite periods, when her youngest child stayed with his sister, the wife of Richard Darling, who owned a farm not far away.

One spring, when about six years old, Sidney was with the Darlings. On the day of which I am writing, Richard started plowing, telling Sidney he might go along. This delighted the little fellow, who gladly followed his brother-in-law to the field. On the way there he unconsciously noted how everything about him rejoiced at the coming of spring—all except Richard's bear he had reared from a cub. It was now full grown, and almost ceaselessly tugged at his chain, pacing round and round the stout pole that checked his efforts to break loose.

Sidney did not like the bear, who gave every indication that the feeling was reciprocated. The boy had been warned to keep well out of the brute's reach.

On arriving at the field Sidney decided to stay outside, where he could watch Richard, and dig in the soft earth on the edge of a tiny stream. He had no toy spade like the children of today; his sole implement was a stick he picked up from under a neighboring tree. It answered the purpose, however, and he was soon busy turning up the moist soil, while talking to himself, as was his custom when alone.

He fancied himself plowing: the stick being the plow, and the horses drawing it creatures of his vivid imagination. Frequently he paused to watch Richard steadily going back and forth over the field, leaving behind him long furrows of fragrant earth to mark his progress.

While thus engaged, the boy stopped talking and could hear sounds about him. Plainly came the clank of the bear's chain, seemingly close at hand. Turning quickly he discovered the huge beast almost upon him, and evidently in a vicious mood. To call for help was useless. Richard, at the further side of the field could not hear him. Instinctively, with the stick he held, the child struck the bear full in the face, with all his puny strength. To his amazement it fell over and lay strangely still.

Wondering, Sidney approached it; thrust at it with his stick; then finding it would not move, knew it was dead, and he suddenly realized that something he dreaded more than the bear's threatened attack confronted him. He must tell Richard his pet was dead, and he, Sidney, killed him. Laying down his stick, the little fellow crawled through the rail fence, to follow Richard, who, intent upon his task, paid no attention to the child at his heels, wearily stumbling along the furrow, trying to muster up enough courage to impart the dreadful news, while surmising what Richard might say; fearing what Richard might do.

Sidney had always known Richard, yet never, until that day was he greatly impressed by the size of his brother-in-law. Now, as he looked at him, the man towered above him like a giant. And what was stranger, his size seemed to increase the longer the boy regarded him. His shoulders, also, were so broad, suggesting reserve strength that filled Sidney with sinister forebodings when he thought of the news he brought.

By this time they had reached the further side of the field, when Richard turned the horses and the plow for the parallel furrow. It was then, for the first time, he caught sight of the child.

"Hello, Bub! Where did you come from?" he asked. "I thought you were over the fence, playing in the mud."

"I was." Then bravely added, "The bear's dead."

"Is it? How'd he die?"

This was the crucial moment for the boy. No one can understand what it meant who has not had the Puritan upbringing like these two. Sidney rapidly considered the matter with his brother-in-law growing larger every minute before his very eyes. Richard loved the bear—it was his pet. Now he knew it was dead; but what would happen when he heard how it had been killed! Sidney swallowed hard as in a thin voice he replied, looking down, and kicking aside a lump of earth with his bare foot, "I don't know."

It was out at last. For better or- worse—he trusted for better—Sidney deliberately lied; one of the worst sins in the Puritan category. Then, to his confusion and surprise, what was Richard saying: "Well, I'm glad he's dead. He was growing cross and dangerous."

If he had confessed that he was the slayer, Sidney suddenly realized he would not have been punished; but if Richard ever discovered he had told a lie about it, there could be but one result. Nothing could save him from paying the full penalty for his unforgivable cowardice.

The critical age had not then arrived, and many things were implicitly believed by intelligent men and women, that today are regarded as myths—or worse. Into almost every Puritan household came the New England Primer, and from it the children often learned their alphabet, for it was thought disgraceful to enter school without knowing it. Together with their knowledge of the ABC's they gained from the Primer much Biblical lore, beginning with:

"In Adam's fall We sinned all,"
and ending with
"Zaccheus he Did climb a tree His Lord to see,"
to which the irreverent added the lines considered very shocking,
"The limb did break And he did fall, And did not see his Lord at all."

Another unfailing stimulus to veracity was the story, still current, of George Washington, his hatchet, the fallen cherry tree, and the never-to-be forgotten assertion of the accused small boy, "Father, I cannot tell a lie."

Confronted with a similar situation, Sidney proved himself no hero, he not only could, but did lie shamelessly as we have seen, and what made his sin the worse, he thoroughly understood the enormity of his offense. Had Richard cared to investigate the mystery, it would not have required a Sherlock Holmes to reveal who killed the bear. Thanks to his lack of curiosity, however, he was content to know it was dead.

Once relating the story of his childhood to a group of his fellow lawyers, my father said, "Richard never knew of my part in the affair until I became a man. His sole comment on my confession being, "I always wondered how that bear happened to die."

"Admitting my guilt, however, failed to relieve my conscience, and now, after 60 years have passed, I bitterly regret that I did not possess enough moral courage to tell Richard the truth."

# Beginner's Luck

*Incredible luck befell a young Colorado teenager one day when he took off hunting by himself. With a malfunctioning gun, the inexperienced nimrod managed to bring down a big bull elk and a grizzly bear within a short time. His adventure, which was written down years later, appeared on pp. 55-56 of* **The Literary Digest,** *April 26, 1919.*

The astounding feat of big-game hunting related in *The Oregon Journal* (Portland) as a youthful exploit of A. Phimister Procter, the sculptor, could have been performed only by a boy. No man would have dared tackle it. The future sculptor was then a slight youth of sixteen and small for his age. The episode, as told to Fred Lockley, of the Portland paper, took place in Colorado when that State was young and more of a wilderness than it is to-day. Young Procter was camping with his father and elder brother in one of the wildest and most inaccessible sections. Being considered too young to do any real hunting, it had not been thought necessary to furnish the boy with a gun of his own, but he had picked up a decrepit old 50-70 Winchester which had once been thrown away as having outworn its usefulness. Boylike, he tinkered up this weapon and finally got it to where he could sight and fire it, but the ejector refused to work. He hit upon the happy expedient of putting a 30-caliber bullet into the barrel of the gun after firing, and thus, by shaking it up and down vigorously, jarring out the empty shell. One day the brother and a companion had planned to make an extensive trip into the mountains to hunt big game. The younger brother was exceedingly anxious to accompany them, but was told in that tolerant and irritating way in which elder brothers sometimes speak to their juniors, that it was out of the question; that they were going on a long and dangerous expedition and could not be bothered with little boys. What happened after that is thus set forth:

It was a wonderful day for hunting big game, as there was just enough soft snow on the ground for tracking. I stuck around camp till nine o'clock, and the longer I waited the more rebellious I felt at being left and told that I was too young to go along.

Finally I filled my pockets with cartridges and decided to strike out by myself and see if I could get a deer or an elk. I walked back into the hills for several hours without seeing anything. In the afternoon, somewhere about three o'clock, I decided to call it a day and go back to camp. I was sitting on a fallen tree taking a rest after my long jaunt when I heard something walking leisurely through the brush near by. In an instant I was alert. A moment or so later a herd of elk walked out in the clearing. I can't begin to tell you the thrill I felt as I sat there and watched those elk walk across the hillside, utterly unconscious of my presence. In the lead was a splendid bull elk. He had magnificent antlers. Ever since I was five I had been sketching, and he appealed to my artistic sense as well as to the hunting instinct in me. I took careful aim, but just as I fired he took alarm and leapt. Instead of hitting him just back of the foreleg I broke a hind leg. There was a crash as the elk bounded away. I forgot my weariness and the fact that I was hungry, and ran after them. I had no difficulty in following the trail of blood on the snow. The rest of the herd had taken a different direction from that of the wounded leader.

Presently I came upon the wounded bull, lying down. I ran up to cut his throat, but he had a different idea about the matter. The minute he caught sight of me he struggled to his feet and charged. He had been lying in a patch of small dead timber. Too late I discovered it was rotten timber. I jumped back of a dead tree six inches or so in diameter. The bull elk charged, and hitting the rotten trunk head on, it snapt [sic] off and sent me sprawling. I got up and took refuge behind another, to have that also snapt [sic] off when he hit it with his massive horns. He was bawling and fighting mad. I saw a large uprooted tree and scurried beneath its upturned roots. The elk tried to paw me or get at me with his horns, and they didn't miss me far.

My hands were trembling so I could hardly get my 38-caliber bullet out of my pocket, but I managed to drop it down the barrel of my Winchester and shake it up and down till the empty shell was ejected. I threw in another shell, and putting the muzzle of my gun between the roots I prest [sic] it against the elk's throat and fired. He fell in a heap and kicked for a minute or so, and then lay still.

I crawled out, a very shaken but proud small boy. I wanted to take that head back to camp. It took me nearly till dusk to cut the head off at the shoulders. I swung it over my back, holding it by the prongs of the antlers. I was small and tired. It weighed nearly one hundred pounds. I started for camp, which was nearly four miles away. I would carry it a while and then sit down and rest. It was just about all I could do to stagger along with it. I came to a ravine across which a tree had fallen, forming a natural bridge. It was the shortest way, so I started to walk across. The bark was old and loose. When I was about half-way across the bark slipt [sic] off and down I went into the gulch with the heavy head and horns on top of me. In falling I gave my back a bad wrench, so for a few minutes I thought I couldn't walk.

The adventures the boy had already gone through would have been considered about enough for one day by almost any adult person. Not so with this youthful Nimrod, however. Even wilder and more hair-raising experiences were in store for him. The account continues:

While I was in the ravine, dreading to tackle the job of walking back to camp, I heard a peculiar shuffling sound not far away. I wondered what it was, and decided to investigate. I crawled out of the ravine, and not far away was the biggest thing on four legs I had ever seen. It was a huge grizzly bear. It was turning rotten logs and stones over to eat the grubs under them. It was so intent on its supper that it had neither seen nor heard me. With my crippled back and my crippled gun I decided that if I was going to kill it I had better do the job with the first shot. Think of the folly and audacity of a boy with a defective gun starting trouble with a grizzly bear. It never occurred to me not to try to kill him. I had heard an old hunter say never to fire at a grizzly when he is looking in your direction, for he will charge the place where the shot comes from, so I waited till the bear was broadside on, and then fired. He gave a roar that seemed to shake the ground. He turned his head around and began biting himself savagely where the bullet had hit him. I slipt [sic] my small-sized bullet into the barrel of my gun, shook it up and down till I had knocked the empty shell out, threw another shell in, and waited for a chance for another shot. He continued to roar and bite the place where he was wounded. I shot again, but this time he saw the smoke from my gun and charged. I tried my ejector. It worked, and threw out the empty shell. I got in another shot, and again he stopt [sic] and roared savagely while he bit the place where I had hit him. As I dodged to a better place I managed to get the empty shell out and throw a fresh one in. He was getting too close to me to be comfortable. I had hit him, but he kept on coming, and I thought it was all off with me. I worked my ejector, threw out the empty shell, threw the lever up, putting in a new shell, and fired when he was only a few yards from me. He went down, tried to get up, but couldn't make it, and began tearing the ground up with his powerful forepaws. Pretty soon he was struggling less and less, and finally he lay still.

I struck out for camp, as it was getting dark. I was about all in when I finally caught sight of our camp-fire. I walked into the light from the snapping pine boughs and my father caught sight of me. He said kindly: "Well, son, what luck?" I said: "Pretty fair; I killed a bull elk and a grizzly." They wouldn't believe me at first. I told them that after I had eaten supper I would guide them to the place so they could bring in the meat. My father and brother, Judge Westcott, and Antelope Jack got up the pack-horses while I was eating, and saddled them, and we struck out to where I had left the body of the bull elk. We cut him up and loaded him on the pack-horses, and then went to where I had left the elk head in the ravine where I had fallen. We found it safe and sound and the grizzly near the edge of the ravine. I had fired at it five times and hit it four times. I still have one of the claws of my first grizzly.

I have hunted all over the country, both in my own country and in the Canadian Rockies and the Selkirks. I have bagged big-horn [sheep] and mountain goats, elk and grizzly, cougar and deer, but I never felt so proud as I did that night when I came in and reported I had got an elk and a grizzly. My brother and Wild Horse Jackson had been out all day and hadn't got a thing, which

helped take the sting from their remark about me being too young and inexperienced to go hunting with grown men.


# An All-American Boy

*Two different accounts were written about
a young boy who alone killed a 200-pound black bear with a .22 caliber rifle. In one
account printed August 6, 1931, in the **Rocky Mountain Husbandman**, the boy was
said to have discovered a big brown bear caught in a trap. Only the bear's hind foot
was caught and bruin uprooted the stake and climbed a tree. Meanwhile, another bear
came along, and "Johnny let the bear have the lead from the little repeating rifle as
fast as he could pump fresh cartridges in the chamber." The first bear, hampered by
the trap, could not climb farther, lost its balance and fell several feet short of the ground.
Nothing was mentioned of its fate.*

*A second account of Johnny's adventure was recounted the following year in the March
23, 1932 **Dillon Examiner** by Rex Healy. Healy's story differs from the first account
in that there is no mention of a second bear and Johnny was reported to have killed
the bear with only two shots. Healy's story, which is the one used below, paints the
picture of young Hardenbrook as "the All-American boy."[13]*

Alone, four miles from his home in the hills and armed with only a .22 calibre
rifle, Johnny Hardenbrook, 10-year-old Montana boy[,] faced a 200-pound bear
and conquered it!

While the average 10-year-old boy curls up before a glowing fireplace on a
cold winter's day and with pop-eyed enthusiasm reads fictionized exploits of
adventurous frontiersmen such as Daniel Boone, Buffalo Bill, Kit Carson and
Jim Bridger, young Hardenbrook, whose home is near Stanford, Montana, is on
the trail. He may be bucking sub-zero weather and deep snow drifts to track
predatory animals, be routing out coyote dens or engaging in encounters with
wild animals that would test the courage and skill of mature hunters and trappers.

And while many of his contemporaries are "roughing it" at summer camps,
Johnny probably is up in his native Rockies protecting and avenging his father's
stock against marauding animals that live by the law of kill. Already he has several
bears, numerous coyotes, badgers, bobcats and other destructive beasts to his
credit. And yet his equipment consists only of his small rifle, a .22 calibre pistol
and a few discarded traps he has salvaged and repaired.

The Montana boy is receiving and filling consignments for pelts from eastern
costumers and in his own section of the country is looked upon as a full-fledged
and talented hunter. In his classes at school he is just another youngster but on
the trail and in the mountain recesses, Johnny holds a full commission.

Twice he has succeeded in cleaning out coyote dens for a total of fourteen
pups, once after vanquishing the enraged mother. But his early preparations and
experiences are as interesting as some of his exploits.

John Bradford Hardenbrook was born February 28, 1921, on a cattle ranch
twelve miles from Stanford. He is the son of Mr. and Mrs. Bradford C.
Hardenbrook.

When but four years old he was allowed to play with a "BB" gun. Almost
from the beginning he showed aptitude in handling the air gun and two years

later he started shooting sparrows and gophers. He carried his air rifle with him constantly. It substituted for the usual toys and most of his games centered around it.

He had scarcely reached the age of seven years when the Stanford Juvenile Rod and Gun club instituted a contest for rodent extermination. Johnny began saving the tails of gophers and woodchucks he killed with his air rifle and when the final score was counted, he carried off the first prize—a .22 calibre rifle. The arms of the seven-year-old boy could just barely support the rifle and reach the trigger, but with the new repeating weapon he succeeded in winning cash prizes in two more contests. This provided money for shells with which to practice at targets and hunt small game.

But Johnny was not content with gophers and woodchucks. He wanted bigger game. While on one of his miniature hunting expeditions, he ran across a coyote den. Risking the chance that the old coyotes were in the den and disregarding the danger that they might return before he could come out, Johnny crawled into the dark interior of the small cave. Luck was with him. He found eight coyote pups whose eyes were not yet open. The entrance of the den was too small for him to lift the pups and carry them out so, placing his rifle by his side, where it would be handy if one or both of the parents returned, he lay down with his feet toward the entrance. One at a time, he placed the pups upon his heels and shoved them out of the cave before emerging himself.

In a matter-of-fact way he described the event in a modest way. "I put the pups in a sack," he said, "and brought them home, where I killed them. Some people might think this rather cruel, but if they could see the way coyotes kill my father's calves, I'm sure they would agree I did right to kill them."

This brought up another incident. "One day early this spring," he continued, "I came across a den and saw a big coyote in it, all prepared to fight if I came too close. With my '22' I shot into the den and killed her with one shot. There were six little pups, too, so I pulled them out of the den with a hooked wire and shot all but two of them. I took those home and tried to tame them but one got away. Hope I cross his trail some day. The other I chained in the back yard and before long he would eat out of my hand. One night a storm came up and the next morning I found him dead, caught in the fence. I guess Danny, as I had called him, was trying to break away from the storm."

Dr. W.H. Steele of Montpelier, Ohio, read a newspaper account of the boy trapper catching more than a dozen coyotes. He wrote a letter asking Johnny if he could get him a large coyote pelt. This marked the beginning of his "professional" career.

Salvaging from a junk pile a trap which his father had discarded as being too old and rusty for use on his trap lines, the lad prepared to fill the order of Dr. Steele. He scraped the rust from the trap, cleaned and oiled it and put it in working condition.

Johnny set the trap by a dead horse for bait and next day caught his largest coyote, which, incidently, is said to be one of the finest ever trapped in that section. The magnificent specimen measured 48 inches in length. The boy skinned the animal, dried the pelt and sent it to Dr. Steele, who sent him $20 in return, more than twice the usual price a coyote pelt would bring.

But his first bear kill was a real thriller. Yet he related the incident with less emotion than some boys might exhibit while telling of finding a birds' nest.

This quiet little son of the Rockies holds utter confidence in himself and complete trust in his rifle and aim. Few experienced hunters but who, when armed with only a .22 calibre rifle, would hesitate to engage a 200-pound bear.

In May, Johnny was inspecting a few traps he had set. When he came through the brush to where he had one hidden he suddenly became aware that a bear had been caught. The bear was too large for the small trap and was tearing the stake loose. In a few seconds he would be free and willing to vent his ferocity upon the boy.

"He made a lunge at me," Johnny said, "and I shot at him, but only hit him in the ear. He started scratching the other ear as the bullet didn't go straight through, but lodged in the other side and was burning him. It only made him madder. I shot the second time and hit him right between the eyes and killed him. I lost no time getting home to tell dad about it and we took the truck and went after the bear. We skinned it but the pelt wasn't very good at that time of the year.

"Another time last summer, I was hunting woodchucks about a quarter of a mile from the cabin and heard a badger digging in its hole. I had my rifle and .22 pistol with me. I started to dig and after some time got so near that the badger stuck his head out trying to fight and drive off the dogs and myself. Each time his head appeared I shot at him with the pistol. And can a badger fight?

"The battle lasted quite a long time as a badger has a slanting, thick skull and a tough hide. Finally I killed it. I ran home and got a wheelbarrow as he was a big fellow. I brought him home and skinned him. My aunt, who lives in the east, was visiting at the time so I gave her the pelt. She later had it made into a small rug."

Johnny also has several bobcat pelts to exhibit. Hawks, crows and other grain and poultry eating birds find the Hardenbrook ranch a poor place to practice their depredations as the keen-eyed boy wages a continual war against the feathered raiders.

He has his own pony, which he calls "Two Step," and which he has "gun broke" so that it will not be bothered by shooting and will stand still if left for a whlie [sic]. Two dogs are his constant companions around the ranch and on his hunting ventures.

With his small weapons and wide knowledge of the great outdoors and wild life, Johnny Hardenbrook faces the frigid Montana winters. Reading signs evident only to trained eyes, he pursues and ensnares his quarry in the woods and hills during summer. To meet and talk with this boy would undoubtedly be a pleasure, and probably instructive, to the sportsmen who depend upon their week or two-week annual hunting trips and their powerful rifles for their backwoodsmen adventures.

Still, the young Montana trapper has all the interests of modern youth. He is interested in mechanics, airplanes, radio, automobiles, football, basket ball, kites, marbles and most other things that occupy boys' minds. There is nothing in his actions, manners or speech that would set him apart in any group of boys. But his eyes might be a little clearer; his excellent little physique probably better developed than others' of his age; his face might reflect a ruddier, healthier glow, and he might display a little more confidence and self-reliance, gained through dependence upon his own resources.

He is typically an all-American boy.

# Unbearable Tall Tales

$\mathrm{B}$ ears of any species or size have been considered both awful and awesome simultaneously ever since man first encountered the animals. Attributes of their strength, ferocity, tenacity and intelligence have long been discussed. Naturally, when something is awful or awesome people's imaginations and exaggerations are often exercised beyond endurance. So it is with bear stories. In the early days and even today, a good bear story always finds a ready audience.

Frontier newspapers often featured human/bear encounters, and one newspaper in particular, the *Anaconda Standard*, had a propensity for publishing any type of bear story. It didn't matter whether the story was real or fabricated. In fact, contrived bear stories were often much better than the "true" bear tales. Often true tales were embellished anyway, so it was hard to know just what to believe. The important factor for bear stories was that the tale contained at least one bear. Some of the best western lies that ever appeared in print are found in the following chapter.

The first three bear stories, concocted by three Montana Supreme Court justices in 1898, were written for a prize bear story competition as a means to raise money at Christmas for two local charities. Contestants were requested to portray "apparent veracity" when writing their tales. The justice who wrote the best "truthful" bear story was fined $10; the second best author was fined $15; and the loser paid $25. Chief Justice-elect Theodore Brantly was chosen to exercise his supreme judgment in the matter, and he assessed the fines. The $50 was then divided between the Associated Charities in Butte and the Helena Orphanage so that the fatherless children in those two towns could have a happy holiday.

With its notoriety for printing bear stories, the *Anaconda Standard* published them in its Christmas edition, December 18, 1898. Upon reviewing the three tales, Brantly decided the contest was one of mendacity rather than veracity and discarded the proposed judging standard of "nearness to apparent veracity" to "relative departure from apparent veracity." A $10 fine was levied against the Honorable William Y. Pemberton for his tale titled "The Vindictiveness of the Bear." The Honorable William H. Hunt was fined $15 for his tale titled "The Ferocity of the Bear," and the Honorable William T. Pigott received a $25 fine for his tale titled "The Intelligence of the Bear."

# Vindictiveness of the Bear

*by The Honorable William Young Pemberton*

While I cheerfully contribute my remarkable experience with a bear to the columns of the Christmas Standard, I shrink from putting the story I have to tell in competition for a prize, because I know how prone men are to exaggeration whenever they are called upon to recite their adventures with bears. Yet I believe that my long years of residence in Montana justify me in feeling that no citizen of this state would for a moment suspect that, in telling my rather thrilling encounter, I would be tempted to depart from the truth merely for the sake of winning an award for highest excellence. I apprehend that, in this contest, the bear story that shows the marks of truth and veracity is the one that will, in the end, triumphantly carry off the first prize. But, however that may be, I shall write not chiefly with the award in view—but rather to relate an experience with a bear, which, I firmly believe, no man who tells a straightforward, honest bear story can match.

I was out one day, early in the time of my residence in Butte [Montana], walking along the brow of the steep hills that bound on the east of the valley which stretches in front of the city of Butte. I had started out in the companionship of a prospector long ago well known in Montana, and long since gone to his grave, and in a crude way I was learning from him how to do a little prospecting on my own account. We had climbed the hill near which the present Homestake tunnel of the Northern Pacific branch penetrates the range. My companion had gone several miles away in the direction of Beef Straight, while I, concluding to shorten my tramp, had ranged along until I came within sight of Butte at a point above the present poor farm in the valley. I had been climbing down the steep hill there and had just been taking a rest. I had not done much prospecting, in fact, I was neither a good loafer nor a good prospector. My total equipment was a little prospecting hammer, and that was the only weapon I had. I was not thinking of hunting, was not looking for trouble with man or beast, and indeed was not prepared for any trouble. It may be well supposed, therefore, that I was ill fitted for the events that ensued.

It was growing late in the afternoon, and I was thinking about going down home to the town, which I could see just beyond in its ragged outline. I was a bit tired and, as I have remarked, I was resting for a lazy half hour. All at once I heard back of me, or just in the sag of the mountain, a sound which at first thought I took to be made by a railroad train. This, of course, was impossible, for there was no railroad there. What then could be the cause of the tremendous puffing and the echoing blast which sounded like the challenge of the iron horse among the hills? I started to my feet and looked up the slope behind me, whence there came a crashing as though a stampede of cattle was coming down the hill through the brush and trees. It took but a glance to solve the riddle. It was a bear that was coming, a big bear. He was coming directly in my direction. It was the oddest looking bear that mortal ever saw. It was normal in appearance from the rear as far as its shoulders, and then it looked more like a sugar barrel than a bear. As a matter of simple fact, it was a combination of sugar barrel and bear. As I learned later, though I did not know it at the time, some miners working on ground near which the Kitty O'Brien five-stamp mill was afterward built, had put out this barrel purposely to catch this bear, which had been making trouble about the cabin. It is an old dodge,—I suppose everyone has heard of it. A number of long, sharp iron spikes are driven slantwise through the staves of the barrel or key, pointing backward. The bear sticks his head into the barrel to get at the sugar in the back end of it, and he can't get his head out again. Ordinarily, the rest is simple. The hunter comes up when he hears the bear begin to beg and ends the comedy with a bullet.

In this case it was not so simple. I do not know how long the old fellow had been thus entrapped. Be it long or short, the time was evidently long enough for Ephraim. You never heard anybody beg in all your life the way that bear did. He would sit down and whine and cry like a baby, putting up his hind feet to scratch at the barrel, in a way which made me laugh in spite of all I could do. Then he would get mad all over, and howl and scream and tear around, till the dirt flew as though there were a grand bull fight in progress on the mountain side. You never heard anything more terrible, and I could only pray that the spikes would hold. When the bear found that squalling did no good, and learned that he could not smash the barrel by pounding it on the rocks, he would lean the barrel down on the ground—he couldn't put his paws to his eyes—and he would sob as though his heart would break. To save my life, I could not help feeling sor[r]y for him.

At last the bear evidently heard me, for he turned up the barrel to one side, as though cocking up his ear. Then, slowly, and with a series of pitiful grunts and groans, he came on directly toward me, the barrel sticking straight out in front of him like a sore finger on a boy. It was plain as the nose on your face that he wanted me to take it off!

This was a rather odd situation, and one whose like I have not since experienced, nor do I think it by any means a common one. I was alone and defenceless. If I did not help the bear I took chances, and I took still greater chances if I did. In this case I tried subterfuge. I dissembled.

Reaching out at arm's length, I tapped along the surface of the barrel with my hammer, as though trying to knock it free. The bear caught the idea at once, and nestled the barrel, so to speak, against my person. This gave me a farther [sic] inspiration. Gradually receding, I continued tapping the barrel out toward its extremity, and the bear followed up the touch of the hammer, evidently wanting more of this effort to set it free. As I tapped, it followed, and soon I led it at a trot, coming after me down the mountain side. You may imagine the confidence the bear had placed in me. I should never have undertaken to abuse such confidence, and it came near costing me dear.

I was tired, but I feared to stop trotting, for it seemed best to let well enough alone. Acting upon the impulse of the moment I cast myself upon the bear's back, still reaching forward and tapping the barrel well on toward its outer extremity. In this I think I evinced a certain resourcefulness and ingenuity; at least, the proposition panned out well at first. The bear was apparently not conscious of my weight, or else thought it a part of the scheme of delivery, for it at once struck a sharper trot, and began to go at a pretty stiff pace, holding the barrel up at an angle in front of it. I wanted to get to Butte. I found that I could guide the bear by kicking lightly on the edge of the barrel upon either side as I wished it to change its course. It was a fat bear, and its hair was long and, barring the novelty of my situation, I could not call myself uncomfortable. The bear was treating me right, and evidently thought I was taking it off somewhere to get help. Now and then it uttered a sort of soft cooing sound, similar to the purring of a cat, though unlike any sound I have ever known a bear to make at any other time.

The trouble with me was that I was not satisfied with a good thing. I bethought me of my hammer, and the idea flashed across my mind that I would kill the bear with the hammer, and thus go on record as the most original bear slayer that ever was known in history. I might have known better, for even had the bear's head been exposed I could perhaps not have succeeded in my purpose. As it was, I did no more than make a mere dent in the mass of fur and fat against which I aimed my blow.

The effect of this blow was not what I could have wished. The bear gave a roar in the barrel. He evidently did not think that he was being treated right. In desperation I struck again, this time as far up on the neck as I could get. I must have struck a spike or at any rate I knocked something loose, for all at once the bear gave a wrench and a grab with his hind paw, and off came the barrel, with me still more than a mile from home. I had ridden more than a good mile down the mountain before I had made my mistake and I was then near what is now the Race Track.

It was a mistake. I sprang to my feet, and literally "lit running." I went across the level toward town at the best speed ever covered in that valley, though I got no mark for the record. I was about two jumps in front of the bear, but I could not gain. I could hear him panting and chuffing and bawling close behind me, and I knew if he ever got up to where he could reach a leg, the battle would be to the strong. I presume I would have been called the pace maker, though really this title belonged to the bear, for all I tried to do was to go as fast as he did.

I managed to keep up only by summoning all my energy. I was cheered by one thought. It occurred to me that perhaps the bear had no more occasion to run than I had, and that perhaps he too was tired. I even imagined that I gained on him at times, and when this seemed true I slackened my pace and fell back a couple of inches, in order to give myself a rest. I did not like to fall back too far.

When I reached the edge of town as it was then, at the crossing of Main street and Park there was not a soul in sight, and on the whole I am now glad of that fact. As I swung up Main street, I saw a clear path ahead of me, a sort of speed-way, as it were: but I could see no place where the race might be expected to reach a finish. I did not dare to try to attempt to get into a door, because the bear was too close. Not knowing what to do, I continued up Main street without any definite plan in view. I tried to yell for help, but my mouth was so dry I could not fetch a sound. I have never seen Butte more infrequented. It seemed to me that I had not a friend left on earth.

In this latter supposition I was wrong. It happened that just at that time, Judge [A.J.] Davis was shutting up his office at the First National bank, another man stood by him, and the judge apparently was about to go home—or, anyhow, to go away for a while. He stood for a moment on the steps, with his hands in his pockets, looking at us as we came along. "Well, I'll be _____!" said he.

By that time I was past him. I turned to the left abruptly from Main street, resolved to run again in front of the bank. I scrambled through what was then a gully back of the Davis bank, came out again on Main street near the corner of Broadway, started up Main, and having circled the block, I passed again in front of what is now the First National. When I passed there the first time I heard Judge Davis ask in his quiet way, "Is he after you?" I could only nod my head. I was too mad to speak anyhow. It seemed to me perfectly plain that the bear was after me. But I heard his voice in the distance remark "Oh, ho!" and the next time I came around, Judge Davis was not in sight. I thought I was forsaken, but a moment later I heard a shot ring out, and heard a scuffling in the dust behind me that told me I was safe. Judge Davis had stepped back into his office for his rifle, and his aim was fatal. I was barely able to thank him before I sank into a state of complete exhaustion.

When I started out on this recital I remarked that I did not care to be regarded as a competitor in the proposed bear story contest. I am inclined now to withdraw that remark and to admit that I am willing to let my story take its chances before the tribunal agreed upon, and I cannot help thinking, in view of the candid nature of this recital, that the story I have told will doubtless warmly commend itself for the highest mention. I am sure this would be the result but for one little disappointment, which has lately come across my path. I remarked in my story that when I passed in front of the bank another man was present with Judge Davis. That man was Judge [Hiram] Knowles, now of the federal bench. I know perfectly well that he was present; I cannot be mistaken and it occurred to me that a postscript added to my story, carrying Judge Knowles' certificate of its authenticity, would greatly strengthen my position in the competition. I have seen Judge Knowles and sought to recall the occurrence to his mind, but unfortunately he persists that he never heard of it, nor anything like it. Those who have the pleasure of a personal acquaintance with Judge Knowles are aware that he is very decided in respect to any opinions he holds. Knowing this myself, I have been compelled to abandon the hope of indorsement which I had anticipated at the hands of Judge Knowles.

I therefore submit my story on its merits, and I may be pardoned for adding that, if apparent veracity is to be the measure of relative excellence, I have no doubt whatever as to the rank which, in the competition, will be assigned to this tale.

# The Ferocity of the Bear

*by The Honorable William Henry Hunt*

I believe that the story I am about to tell will be recognized at once as of highest merit in the proposed prize contest. This I say not of personal conceit, but because my experience teaches that, in the pursuit of a bear, it is always best to start out with a great showing of confidence, no matter how discouraging things may prove to be later on.

The idea of a bear story competition is in its way unique and useful, and cannot fail to prove of popular benefit, inasmuch as it must bring to light, in the tale

I am about to tell, many interesting facts in natural history which otherwise might have remained unknown, or if not unknown, as least discredited. To my mind such a competition can have but one undesirable or, if I may, dangerous feature, and that lies in the disposition of certain individuals to give rein to the imagination in handling such material and in their failure to confine themselves to the simple and obvious truth. It is only through adherence to facts that we may attain scientific progress. Not even science is able to tell us why the subject of a bear story should predispose to fiction. Yet I presume that the habits of no other animal have been more covered with the gloss of lucid misapprehension. This preface I feel it incumbent upon me to make before adducing the facts, in themselves somewhat singular, which I am in position to add to the scientific data already recorded in regard to bears.

As further proof of the caution with which I wish to proceed in this matter, I beg to refer to a certain well-known and somewhat well-worn story which had often been related and which is sometimes referred to confidently as the "champion bear story." This is no less than the history of that gentleman who lived in Oregon and who was approached by a large and infuriated bear which had him cornered in such way that he was either obliged to jump over a precipice to certain destruction or face an infuriated animal, which meant equally certain death. In telling the story this man always insisted that he did not jump. "What then happened to you?" asked his hearers. "What in nature could happen to me," said the narrator, "except what did happen? The bear ate me up, right there." This story I give as showing the tendency to burlesque which is sometimes introduced into bear literature. The absurdity of the above denouement is of course apparent.

Yet there is a certain similarity between the above story and that which I am now about to tell—with this difference, that, while the former story contains no facts and adds nothing to popular education regarding the bear, the incident which I shall relate is not only curious, but truthful to a degree that entitles it to consideration. I mention the above story chiefly as a warning, lest the similarity between the two incidents, or rather the real incident in my case and the alleged incident in the other, might lead some thoughtless persons to charge against me either an imitativeness or a mendacity which I myself would be the first to deplore.

The facts are as follows: I was out hunting, one winter, during the period of my residence at Fort Benton [Montana], in the neighborhood of the mouth of the Musselshell river, which is known to be the natural habitat of a great many of the "white- faced" bears which formerly ranged far out over the plains, as recounted by General Marcy and other early travelers. These bears are the "gray bears" mentioned by Lewis and Clarke [sic], who always speak of them as possessed by unparalleled ferocity. In reality they are nothing but the grizzly, which is also the "silver tip"; but these range bears are thought to be more savage even than the average of their cousins of the Rockies, and very often they will attack a man without provocation. It is possibly true that the wild and solitary life they live in these forsaken Bad Lands predisposes them to this ultra ferociousness of disposition, and it is indeed quite enough to make one sad to think of spending a lifetime among such weird surroundings. It is an admitted fact that all creatures partake of the character of their environment—just as the trout takes on the color of the sand or shade of the stream which he inhabits.

I imagine that in this fact lies the explanation of the cranky and cross-grained temper of these bears.

As I have said, it was in the winter time that I was hunting. To be more exact, it was on the 23rd day of December, and it was half-past 2 o'clock in the afternoon, as I very well remember, for I had just looked at my watch, thinking it was nearly time for me to be turning back toward the ranch house where I was stopping. I was not really hunting bears at all, for every hunter knows that at this time of the year these animals have all gone into hibernation. In order to gain relief from the landscape these bears retire to winter quarters much earlier than is usually the case in the mountains, even at the high and colder upper ranges where the snow comes in October or November at latest. I had every right to suppose that every bear in that section of the country had been safely rolled up asleep for more than three months. I was therefore ill prepared and not a little startled, as I must admit, at what actually transpired.

I was walking along the edge of a little knife-like ridge which wound around between two deep ravines, or coulees, and I did not want to get down into either of these steep little gullies, for I knew it would be difficult to get out again. Moreover, I was aware how easy it is to get "turned around" in that wild country, and I did not wish to be too far from camp when evening came, as I am subject to frequent attacks of a rheumatic ailment which are much aggravated by night air, especially by the night air of a country where I am lost. Naturally, also, my position high upon this ridge gave me better command of the surrounding scene, and I felt pretty sure I would yet be able to get my deer, for I had seen some signs and had noted one buck at the edge of a cottonwood thicket some hundreds of yards ahead.

I was working my way along this hogback with my eye intently fixed upon the place where I had last seen the deer, and was not paying any attention to my immediate surroundings, when I was intensely startled by the apparition of a great gray monster which arose almost at my feet from out [of] the scanty shelter of a little transverse coulee which intersected the ridge along which I was traveling. This bear, for it was nothing else but a bald-face grizzly, and a very large one (I shall not say how large, for I had no means of measuring or weighing it, and I am no hand to guess at facts), rose before me at a distance of less than 20 yards, and gave a "Woof, woof," such as any experienced bear hunter knows very well is the expression of the grizzly who is surprised and not altogether pleased with the intrusion.

There was no apparent means of escape, and ludicrous as it may appear, there flashed over my mind the thought of the Oregon man who was once placed in a similar position and who was really eaten by the bear. "Can it be," thought I, "that I am to end my days in this miserable and inglorious fashion?" I must confess it seemed not unlikely, for a larger, a leaner or more generally cavernous-looking bear I never have seen in all my life.

I was carrying at the time a first-rate rifle. As the bear rose before me, balancing himself uneasily on the narrow ledge which gave footing to us both, I looked for one moment in his little piggish eyes. I thought how soiled and unlaundered would be my fate if he had his way and accomplished his evident purpose. At that moment, for some unaccountable cause, all trepidation left me, and I was as steady as I am as I write this chronicle. I jerked the rifle to my face and cut loose at the beast! He seemed to divine my purpose, for like a flash he threw up one paw. The bullet struck him just above the metacarpal bones of the forearm and tore the foot almost entirely free from the supporting bones and ligaments. I could see the great paw hang limp and useless. The force of the impact kicked the great beast off his balance, and he fell, roaring and growling, down the side of the hogback, at last rolling into the cover of the low undergrowth of the bottom, where I continued at intervals to hear his hoarse growls.

As soon as I recognized the power of my weapon and saw what damage I had done the enemy I was eager only to get at my prey. Yet I was wise enough not to advance at once, for I knew that each moment I waited gave so much more time for the animal to become stiff and disabled from his wound. I risked no catastrophe by any attempt to clamber directly down the side of the steep slope where my game had so recently preceded me. I presume it may have been half an hour or more before I got near to the spot where the wounded grizzly was lying. I cautiously crept up along the side of the hogback so that I might be above my game, always a desirable thing in approaching the grizzly, which can roll down hill faster than a brick can fall off a chimney. I got to the point which I wished to reach, and there, sir, I witnessed a sight such as I presume no man has ever seen before or ever will again!

I have said that this bear was gaunt and empty looking. I presume that for some reason the creature had failed to find a suitable winter hiding place, and hence had traveled for weeks, losing flesh and gaining hunger, instead of being rolled up comfortably with its nose in its fur. He may have been crossed in love. I do not know what had kept him out of winter quarters so late, and made him so ravenous as he undoubtedly was. Instinct for once served to offer no check to an insane desire.

The bullet, as I have mentioned, had cut away the forefoot of the bear so that it hung but by a thread. The blood had run down the injured member and frozen into a long red ribbon of congealed gore. I am able to describe only what I actually saw. To make brief as possible the horrid details, I will simply say that as it lay there the bear had eaten off its own front foot!

Shocked by this awful exhibition, I raised my rifle and again fired, with the intent to end the life of the beast. Accident again prevented complete success, for even as I fired the bear moved again, and once more I saw that I had only dismembered a foot, this time a hind foot. Again the bear reared and again it fled, going still deeper into the service berry bushes, where after a time it seemed to become silent. Crippled as it was, I made no doubt that it had died of its wounds, though I still retained a saving caution as I approached it. Peering through the bushes, I saw the same spectacle in process of repetition. The bear had actually eaten up its own hind foot in addition to its forepaw! Had I not seen this with my own eyes I myself should never had believed it.

I was by this time losing much of my nerve, and I admit I was shaky as I fired again. The same fatality attended this shot as had the preceding ones. Need I say that I shivered as I saw that I had once more failed of administering a mortal wound, but had only cut off a third foot, and the left hind foot! Nor was this all. As though to certify me in my suspicions, the bear now merely rolled over and began deliberately to chew his severed foot. He ate it, before my eyes and before his own eyes, we two being the only witnesses of this singular and impressive scene. I sank down trembling to the ground. I heard a rustling in the bushes and saw that the bear was seeking escape, injured as he was. Again

I fired, and this time, of course, I got his one remaining foot. In brief, he turned and ate it! Sick and weak from terror, I fired again and as I heard the bullet strike home I sighed with relief, for I knew there were no more feet for me to cut off, and saw that the end had come.

I crept up on my fallen quarry as fast as my now exhausted condition would permit, for I was much unstrung by what I had just witnessed. I stood at the very spot where I had seen the bear pause and whence I had heard the last indications of his struggles. I saw the trail plainly marked up to that point, but there it ended. The bear had gone no farther, for the bear was dead.

But the bear was not there! This statement I hardly expect to go unchallenged, but I make it, and, as I was the only witness to these facts, I alone am competent to testify, as is plain. The bear is not competent, because the bear is not here and he was not there. He was gone as utterly, if one may use the words of the novelist, and as literally as though he had been swallowed up. The conclusion was forced upon me that he had completed the work which I had seen begun.

There is no escaping the iron laws of logic. There was no other bear or other creature there except myself. I did not eat the bear. He must, therefore, have eaten himself, a thing which I saw begun in process of completion. This theory being that which reconciles the largest number of the known existing phenomena, must be accepted as the true and conclusive one, to which there can be no alternative and from which there can be no escape.

While I admit, as above stated, a certain similarity between this story and that of the Oregon man who was eaten by the bear, I wish to point out the essential difference between the two recountals, by which it will become obvious that the latter is absurd, whereas the former is natural and true. The Oregon man says that he himself was eaten by the bear, yet he appears himself to tell the tale! I do not claim that I was eaten by this bear or that I ate the bear. I only say that the bear ate himself, for there was nothing else that could have eaten him. At the spot where the bear disappeared I found a few claws which I sadly picked up and placed in my pocket, as the only collateral proof I might ever have to offer to the accuracy of the story which I was some day to tell—and which, I beg to add, I have never before this time felt at liberty to relate. When I came to Helena [Montana] to reside I deposited these for safekeeping in the First National bank; the reader will therefore understand that circumstances over over [sic] which I had no control deprive me permanently of the possession of the proofs of this bear story.

# The Intelligence of the Bear

*by The Honorable William T. Pigott*

There are people who have had more frequent dealings with bears than have fallen to my lot. I make bold to say, however, that the number of old-timers in Montana is not large of men whose adventures with these interesting creatures includes an experience so providential and, at the same time, so unique as the one which I confidently submit in the pending competition. I am not much given to hunting, yet I had an adventure in which any votary of the sport might justly take lifelong pride. At the time when it occurred I was a struggling young lawyer living in Virginia City [Montana]. Its scene is the Madison valley, in what is now known as the Yellowstone park. This was long before the region had been fully explored; indeed, my trip was made shortly after Governor [Samuel] Hauser and a few other adventurers had made their pioneer journeys. These first reports made by these early explorers were not believed though we know them now to have been far within the facts. In a similar way the facts in my story might have been doubted, until the growing knowledge concerning the physical phenomena of that wonderful region set them quite beyond the realm of doubt.

I was over in the lower park country, having gone in over the old Firehole trail, and was making a little journey into the section around the Fountain Geyser basin. I saw then for the first time the great hot springs of this playground of the giants, and I need hardly say that they excited in my bosom emotions of the extremest wonder. We visit this region now with carelessness and indifference, but it was not thus in the early days, when its possibilities were less thoroughly exploited.

My companion was an old-time friend who was an enthusiastic student of natural history. We went over the western range into the Firehole basin, in the early autumn, intending to make a rapid trip. We were not very well outfitted, having flour and bacon enough for a couple of weeks only, but we thought we could get all the game we needed to make up any deficiency, and so last it out for a couple of months. Of course, you know what a place that country is for sudden and heavy snow falls. Sometimes is [sic] snows three or four feet in a night, and keeps it up, so that when winter once begins it is impossible to travel.

We had not been in the geyser bas'n [sic] two weeks before there came the worst snow storm I have ever seen. It began about dusk on the evening of a day late in December. I remember we were talking about the good old Christmas times at home, which then seemed far enough away. It snowed fast and hard, and by morning we saw that we were prisoners in the valley. There was not a sign of game anywhere about us, and we were nearly out of provisions. All the elk had gone over to the Hayden valley and Pelican country, and we could not see so much as the trail of a snowshoe rabbit. Starvation seemed a very likely thing; but you know in those days men rarely worried about how they were going to get out of trouble until the trouble actually came.

That country was then, as it is today, one of the greatest bear countries in the entire West, and as this was in the early days, there were 10 bears where there is one now, and at any ordinary time we could have killed all the bear meat we wanted. It was now, however, too late for the bears, as they were all holed up in the mountains. We had no hope of getting a bear, though we could see where they had been scratching in the soft incrustation about the hot springs. My companion said that bears have rheumatism the same as human beings, and that they came there to get hot baths. I do not know about that; but it has really nothing to do with this story, which is confined to conditions and not to theories.

One morning we were out trying to find a little browse to keep our horses alive, when we saw in the distance the figure of some strange animal which loomed up big as a horse through the white, curling mists of morning in the geyser basin. The creature was acting in a curious way, now stooping, now rising, now bending over again, as though busy at some occupation to which it was giving its undivided attention. It had no notion of our presence. We crept up toward it a little way and soon found it to be about the largest grizzly bear that ever came down the Divide. That is to say, it seemed so to us; though I do not wish to make the claim that we saw the largest bear that ever was—it is such sweeping assertions that bring bear stories into disrepute. At least it was a bear, and a big one, and I shall submit that it was the smartest bear, as well, so to speak, as the most beneficial bear that ever was; and on this point I shall stand without fear of successful refutation.

When we discovered what this bear was doing, we could scarcely credit our senses. As you will very well remember, the Madison [River] is a stream abounding in mountain trout. At that time these fish could readily be taken in weight up to 10 pounds, though I bear in mind that this is no fish story that I am relating. It shows our own carelessness when I say that we had not thought of taking of these fish to eat, as we might easily have done, had we been properly prepared.

This big grizzly had evidently given the matter of commissariat better consideration than we had. We watched him at his work, which he pursued with grunts and whines of preoccupation, varied now and then with howls of exultation. In point of fact, the bear was fishing, and so great was his sporting instinct that he could not avoid giving vent to his pleasure when he found himself successful in landing an exceptionally large trout. His machinery was simple. The trout were unused to lures. The bear trailed a bright bit of gypsum in the water with one paw, and simply swiped out the fish with the other as they rushed up at the glittering bait. I had never seen this sort of angling before.

If it may be said that in thus supplying his wants the bear was not putting in use any extraordinary means, it will, I think, be admitted by all that at least the use to which he was putting this food, or rather the way in which he was treating it, was a most singular and unusual thing, and one displaying to the highest degree the marked natural intelligence of the bear, which is really one of the shrewdest of all wild animals. This bear was not only catching fish, but was also cooking them.

I make this statement with no intention of causing any surprise, for it is nothing new or startling. I presume that at least a thousand persons in the Yellowstone park have caught a trout on one side, in cold water, and have cooked it on the other side within reach of the swing of the rod in one of the many boiling springs which dot the country. Yet this feat had never, at that time, been performed by any human being; so that this bear can in no wise be accused of plagiarism or even imitativeness. He would catch a big trout as I have described, and then hold it head down in the boiling water of the adjacent spring for a moment or so, until it was thoroughly cooked. Then he would neatly pile it up with the other fish on his side, where he had raked up several little heaps, cob house fashion. After a while, when he seemed to have satisfied his notion about the thing, he grunted, stooped over, and, taking up his arms full of the cooked trout, he started waddling off through the snow up the shelf of a cliff which showed on the mountain side not far away. He had a trail plowed through the snow about as big as would be made by a Northern Pacific rotary.

I looked at my companion, he looked at me. We spoke not a word. We went back to our camp. We saw that the bear had left a few fish at the springs and thought he would return for these, in which supposition we were correct. In less than 20 minutes he came grunting and complaining down the trail again—he was very fat—and gathering up the rest of his catch he went back up the hill.

Our plan was very simple, and I make no doubt you have already heard of it, for the facts were generally known at the time: and I venture to advance them now merely because their age may give them an appearance of novelty at this late date. We simply took up our rifles and followed the big fellow to his home, which we found in a cave under an overhanging rock. It was so located as to give an excellent view of the whole geyser basin, this bear having evidently been a great lover of natural beauty in landscape. It seemed a pity to destroy so intelligent a creature, but we felt that our claims were first, so we shot him as he came out at the mouth of the cave. His robe was a fine one, not the largest in the world, as I have said, but big enough to keep us warm all that winter.

The oddest part of my story remains to be told. As we entered the cave we became conscious of a fishy smell, to which, however, our olfactories gradually became accustomed. We found the entire interior of the cave lined with neatly stacked rows and tiers of cooked trout, and I must say that I have never tasted trout done more perfectly to a turn. Of course, the bear had plenty of time, and had nothing on his mind to interfere with his cooking operations, which is rarely the case with most modern cooks.

We had plenty of salt with us, and, as we had all the bear meat and cooked trout we wanted, I must say that I never passed a more pleasant winter. We were rescued about March by a too zealous cousin of mine who, with a party of friends, came over before the snow was half settled. They lost four horses and two men trying to "rescue" us, only to find us really indignant at their interference. There was a breastwork of fish bones as tall as your head in front of the cave when we were discovered.

It is astounding to what extremes one's appetite will lead him in the pure, cold mountain air of the winter time, when he feels that there is no danger of indigestion and not the slightest risk of deficit in the food supply. We never kept any exact account, but afterward, in a rough way, we estimated that that bear must have caught, cooked and stowed away something like 4,326 trout, of an average weight of perhaps three and a half pounds. This fact shows alike the intelligence and the industry of the bear, for which animal I must confess I have since that time entertained the highest respect. While there was nothing immpossible [sic], or miraculous, or unduly sensational in this adventure, I believe it to be true that few people have had an experience with a bear like that which I have described.

# Riding Bear-Back

*A Californian, with a flair for fiction, created an entertaining bear story for the **Los Angeles Times**, in which the narrator preferred to ride a grizzly bear rather than stay in a certain tree a minute longer. The tale appeared in the May 13, 1900 **Anaconda Standard**.*

"Did you ever ride a bear?" asked Bill Ellis one night as we sat down at the campfire after hunting all day.

"No, I suppose not," he continued without waiting for me to reply. "Lot of folks haven't. In fact, I'm the only feller I ever heard of that ever did. All the ridin' is generally the other way. Bear seldom carry outside passengers. But Old Clubfoot packed me one day in great shape. That old sarpent used to range these hills and if there was anything he liked it was lead. He was a regular travelin' lead mine. He was so dangerous I never hankered after his pelt, but one day I nearly ran over him and he came for me, so that there was nothing to do but shoot. I fed him some lead right in the gizzard and all he done was to gulp as if it was good, and come right on with his mouth wide open for some more. I accommodated him right in the mouth, too, but one of his big white teeth flew into splinters that whizzed up into the air. I had a Sharp's rifle and just as I went to load it again the cartridge stuck in the chamber and I couldn't shut it. Disappointment seemed to make the old cuss only the madder and on he came, bent for a full breakfast.

"I suppose you'd have perspired, as they say in polite talk. I didn't have time to get a pore open, for luck was on my side and I was only a few yards from a live oak. I was young and pretty quick and swung myself in a jiffy onto a big limb. I felt a rip in my pants as I whirled over and, after gettin' well out of reach, I felt there and there was three or four slits six inches long where his claws had just missed my casin'. You may laugh all you please about folks that work with the seat of their pants, but if it hadn't been for the dry goods boxes down at the country store you wouldn't be entertainin' me with your ear to-night.

"I crawled along to the trunk of the tree and began to wonder how I was to get the rifle up. Old Clubfoot was there with his big paws clawin' down bark only two feet from my toes and tryin' to get up. His breath felt like the steam out of a locomotive and his eyes would almost have done for a headlight, he was so mad. I had seen mad bear before, when they had a foot caught in a trap, but I never saw such ragin' fury as this old scamp had when he found I was just beyond his reach and the trunk of that tree too straight and smooth for him to climb.

"Just as I began to think of a Sunday school hymn suitable for a saved sinner I felt a bite. Then there was another and another and something crawlin' up my sleeve and on my neck and up my ankles and more bites by the second, with the smell of ants gettin' mighty powerful. Then you bet I did perspire in no time. Did you ever try an ant bite? How many bites from one of the big red or black ants do you suppose it would take to kill a man? And how long do you suppose it would take? A horse stung by enough bees is dead before any pisen can possibly reach his vitals. A man dropped in bilin' water would be dead before any heat could ever reach his innards. It's the shock to the narves what does the business, and before the fifth bite was well in my narves was gettin' terrible shook up. Then I saw the tree was full of 'em and lines of hundreds of big red ants runnin' up the trunk. No use to mash 'em, for a hundred'll come to the funeral of every one you mash. It wasn't half a minutes [sic] before some still small voice inside whispered that I would have to get out of that tree, for it was certain the ants would kill me and with more sufferin' probably than I was likely to get at the hands of the bear.

"You'd a been mighty smart and slipped down the tree on the opposite side from the bear, wouldn't you? That shows what you know about bear. You can have 50 feet start and he'll climb your back stairs in just one and three-quarter seconds. I wasn't that variety of squash. It was over 200 yards to the next tree and that was a low one, where he might claw me down even if I was lucky enough to reach it. A grizzly standin' on his hind legs is mighty high and his durned claws add another foot onto his long arms, and when he stretches them out you've no idea how they reach. All he's got to do is get one hook into your meat and you're his'n. There was only one thing to do and that was to scare the stuffin' out of him. They're just like wild cattle on a plain. If you run from 'em they'll make a bulge on you sure, but if you run at 'em and wave your coat you stand a show of scarin' 'em off. There was only one thing to do, and that was to ride him, for swearin' at him didn't have no more effect on him than it does on you when you make a rank miss on a first-rate shot at a deer.

"There was no time to lay out any fine plans, for the ants bit worse and worse and came thicker and thicker. So I ran on a big limb and the bear followed me out there and looked up and showed his big white teeth and seemed to say— ain't you got some more lead to feed me? I'm tired of waitin' so long. I gave him my hat for a change, and as it fell to the ground he dropped his head and began to chaw on it. Before he had a chance to show any disappointment, because a bear's favorite teethin's ring—a man's skull—wasn't inside of it, I just dropped square a-straddle of his back.

"What are you lookin' so queer about? You don't believe it, eh? Well, now, I ain't a-tryin' to make out that I was particularly brave. It was only a stroke of genius. There wasn't any courage about it. It took more bravery to stay with the ants. There was a million of 'em and I just had to ride out of there. It was the only way to beat the grave. Of course, a man must be somethin' of a bareback rider and know how to keep his bearin's—no joke intended—but there's nothin' else to do, especially for the bear, for he had ridden so many hunters that I thought a change would be beneficial to his constitution. You might not have been as good a rider as I was and probably would have got off at the first pile of rocks we sailed through. But you'd have mounted him just the same as I did, because you'd 'a' had to.

"Did he snort? Not much. He had no time for that. Did you ever watch a fly sittin' on an arrow when you let go the string? That was about my fix, only I didn't drop off. Facts is, I didn't dare to, for he wasn't scared enough yet. He started fast enough, but when I got a good grip with each hand into his wool, dug my heels into his flanks and hollered 'Git out of here, you son of a gun!' he shot out like one of these rifle balls you hear tell of that gather speed so fast that when we went under the first tree I didn't have time to unload him and catch onto a limb and swing up again, as I had meant to. That would have been a dandy trick to play [on] him, for if he'd ever taken a notion to come back he'd never 'a' found the tree. A shootin' star might as well try to find the cloud it went through before it busted.

"In about half a second somethin' green whisked past. It wa'n't in my eye, for you never saw nothin' green in that when it come to a question of a bear. I'm green on theosophy and a few other fine p'ints of religion, but not on bear, thank you. It must a been another tree, but I wa'n't very particular about stopping to find out, so on I journeyed. Just as we cleared that, somethin' gray went a-swimmin' round on all sides with a thousand quails a whizzin', squealin', and dartin' around my head, and the durndest rattle you ever heard. It sounded as if the lightnin' had struck the pantry of the giants and bursted all the crockery and turned the flies loose. It might a been a rock pile we went through, but

I wasn't particular enough to get off and look. Just then I saw a couple of brown spots ahead, with somethin' behind that looked like the tail of a coyote, and then two streaks of brown went past us from the front, but they fell behind so fast I couldn't tell, but I rather guess they was coyotes.

"Just then there was another flash of green and then a regular cloud of it swimmin' round me, an' such a rippin' an' tearin' of clothes an' the awfullest smashin' an' crashin' of brush an' such a scratchin' of my eyes an' scrapin' off of my skin where the clothes had been, an' all at once I came to a dead stop so fast that it turned me upside down. As soon as I could get the blood out of my eyes enough to see, I found myself in one of those great, big mountain manzanitas, with my heels a lookin' toward the sky an' not a durned rag on me but a bit of court plaster I had on the back of one ear. I kept still for a second, expectin' a thunderbolt or somethin', but the coast was all clear an' the sun a smilin' as only our dear California sun can smile, with the birds all a singin' praises to their Maker and not an ant or durned thing in sight to bother anybody. Just then I heard some one holler, 'Get out of here, you son of a gun.' It made me jump up, but it sounded so natural like it set me to thinkin', and durned if it wasn't my own voice—just arrived.

"Oh, yes, he done pretty well for a lame bear, but, good Lordy, what sport I'd a had if I'd only had my spurs on."

# How To Spot a Phony

*J.A. Rueger wrote the following article for the December 16, 1900* **Anaconda Standard.** *His purpose for writing the story was to show readers how to recognize a fake bear story from a real one. Rueger's "true" tale certainly illustrates his point.*

There is something intensely fascinating in narratives of hair-breadth escapes from wild animals, and I have personally, on various occasions, listened to blood-curdling yarns of encounters with grizzly bears, mountain lions or some equally ferocious beasts. Most of the readers of the Standard may have themselves listened with bated breath as the narrator recounted his startling adventures, embellishing his narrative with an exactness of detail which carries conviction with it, and you listened with tense nerves as he gradually approached the climax where, just as the fierce animal is preparing for a final leap, a bullet from his trusty weapon, sent with unerring aim, brings the terrible adversary to earth, and so realistic was the recital that a cold thrill of horror shoots through you as you picture to yourself the narrow escape from a horrible death and you actually breathed a sigh of relief as the story concluded.

There are many such tales told, but they are not all true; in fact, the best of them are usually told by men who never saw any of the animals they describe outside of a menagerie, and the only firearm they are familiar with is the toy cap pistol, and usually their proficiency with this weapon has suffered through lapse of time. You can always tell the genuine hunter from these falsifiers if you know anything about the subject of hunting big game, but unfortunately only a comparatively small number are familiar with the sport. I will admit that it is exciting, especially when you run up against some "varmint" unexpectedly. The worst scare I ever had in my life came about just in that way.

I was with a band of sheep which I had bought only a short time before, having concluded like many another youngster that sheep raising was profitable if handled right and gave myself credit for knowing just how the thing ought to be done. I soon learned my mistake—but that is another story. At any rate I had taken the sheep into a ravine which opened into some of the foothills of the Rockies where there was running water and plenty of grass. I congratulated myself on my good fortune in stumbling into such desirable pasturage. I had two young fellows with me to help me out, but of course none of us had much to do just then, as feed was plenty and the sheep did not stray far; so we had ample time to do a little shooting now and then—usually small game, such as grouse and sagehens, which we often stirred up out of the underbrush. At any time we could get a shot at a rabbit, but nothing fiercer than the bands of coyotes which hung on our flanks ever showed up during our first week in the canyon, and although we now and then lost a sheep through these depredators, nothing else disturbed us.

One day in the early part of the second week the boys had gone up on the hillside with their light shotguns, leaving me in camp alone. I think I was writing letters or something of that sort, and doing the best I could with our limited writing facilities, when I heard the boys on the hillside blazing away as if they were out on a skirmish line. I stepped to the door of the camp-wagon wondering what they had run up against. I could not see from there, so I jumped down and walked ahead a little way in the direction of the shooting, for they were still firing with a persistence which thoroughly alarmed me.

I had gone perhaps a hundred yards when I saw them both standing on a boulder projecting from the hillside and firing down into the ravine at something below. They saw me just as I spied them, and at once they stopped shooting and both began to shout something at me which I could not understand, owing to the distance. It was evident that they had been firing to attract my attention, so I walked a little farther to try to hear what they were calling to me, but I had gone but a little way when they redoubled their shouts and began to gesticulate wildly, evidently warning me to go back. I did not understand at first and stood for a moment looking up at them while they continued their shouts and gestures with frantic energy.

I was just beginning to comprehend their meaning, when I heard a great crashing in the brush by my side and as I turned in alarm at the sudden sound, an enormous grizzly burst into the open with jaws dripping blood from a sheep he had slaughtered and was eating. I had interrupted him in his meal and he was coming to see me about it. I have heard it said that the bear is a slow, clumsy creature, but it didn't take me long to realize that this particular bear was pretty spry in spite of his enormous size, in truth, I felt that I hadn't a ghost of a show of escaping by flight. Worse than that I had come away entirely unarmed, for with my mind on my writing I had left camp without as much as a thought of a gun: all I had with me was a large hunting knife, which I always had strapped to me, much to the amusement of my companions, who always made it the butt of their jokes. It seemed like a pitiful weapon for such an encounter, but with flight impossible and driven to desperation by my peril I instinctively whipped it out and stood on my guard just as the grizzly came at me.

I don't know the usual method of this animal's attack, but this one lumbered fiercely toward me on all fours and I felt that my chances for defense were pretty slim, but just as he came within striking distance I involuntarily struck at him repeatedly with my knife. For an instant he stopped, then he rose on his hind legs, towering clear above my head, his powerful paws poised for tearing me with his immense claws, and with dripping jaws and blood-shot eyes he made a spectacle I shall not forget until my dying day. But in the attitude of the bear, with the quick perception of desperation, I saw my opportunity. Like a flash I ducked beneath the outstretched paws, and with a powerful slash of the keen blade I ripped the animal's abdomen from top to bottom. All his fierceness left him instantly—with a scream of anguish he pressed his paws against his wounded body, actually drawing the severed tissues together, and still retaining his upright position he tottered off into the brush, leaving a trail of blood behind him which indicated that he could not last long.

As he retreated and I realized that I had escaped, a faintness came over me and my head began to reel, but a shout from the hillside revived me, for it reminded me of the boys who must have been eye witnesses of the whole per-performance. In a moment they joined me, and never was a man greeted with more enthusiasm than I was at that moment. They showered congratulations upon me and plied me with so many questions that I could not answer the half, but I still remembered the bear, and having recovered sufficiently by this time, I at once stated the necessity of finding him.

While we were going to the camp-wagon for our rifles the boys told me why they had fired so incessantly. They had seen the bear plunge into the flock of sheep and in their excitement had begun blazing away for the double purpose of arousing my attention and of frightening the animal. They had never dreamed of my coming away unarmed and stumbling directly upon the ferocious animal, but when they saw me do that very thing they had tried in vain to warn me of my danger. However, I had passed through it absolutely unhurt and the next thing was to round up the bear and we were soon on the way properly armed for the occasion.

Naturally we proceeded cautiously, following the bloody tracks, which at first were perfectly distinct, but to my surprise gradually grew less and less so, until finally only an occasional drop testified to his passage. This circumstance made me decidedly suspicious and I warned the others to move with the greatest caution and we went forward like Indians, scarcely snapping a swig [sic] as we advanced. Suddenly we came to the edge of a clearing and it was well that we were moving so cautiously, for in the center of the space sat our bear and I stopped instantly, but if ever a man was stupefied with amazement I was that man, for sitting on his haunches that bear was actually engaged in repairing the damage done by my hunting knife!

He had some round discs about two inches in diameter which he perforated with his claws and by means of tough twigs from the brush he was actually sewing them to one side of the huge gash in his anatomy and on the opposite side at a point corresponding he would slit a short gash with his claws and was thus calmly buttoning himself up. I looked around at my companions. Both of them had their mouths wide open and their eyes stuck out so that you could have knocked them off with a stick. They glanced at me with mute wonder, but none of us said a word, neither did we offer to shoot, we were too dazed for that, but stood there watching the animal sewing on his buttons until he was all finished. I noticed when the job was done that his hide had wrinkled a little where the buttons drew, and that the tension caused by the overlap made him look somewhat gaunt, but otherwise he was as perfect a bear as I ever saw. Giving a kind of grunt of satisfaction as he finished he arose and not one of us interfered as he passed into the brush on the other side and disappeared. Then one of the boys broke the silence—"Well, I'll be blowed," he said, and that seemed about all he could say.

I stepped forward to the spot where the bear had been and found several of the discs used by the animal lying on the ground. I recognized them at once. We had camped in that identical clearing the first week and here I had first essayed making biscuits. They had never risen and having baked as hard as iron had by common consent been condemned and abandoned. Here they had lain, avoided even by the coyotes, until the bear happening upon them in his dire distress had seized upon them in his need and put them to the extraordinary use we had observed, and it is my belief that my remarkable escape sinks into insignificance in comparison with the extraordinary sight we witnessed as the direct result of it. Truly the sagacity shown by the animal passes comprehension and although I commenced this narrative more for the purpose of showing how a veracious hunting narrative differs from a willful prevarication I have entirely lost sight of my intention in my undying admiration of that bear.

# Cowboys and Bears

*Telling tall tales was a popular pastime for lonesome cowboys on the range, especially in Texas. Lieutenant J.M.T. Partelo submitted the following two Texan tales to the San Francisco Examiner.*

*These stories show what the sun and long hours can do to a cowboy's imagination. On September 14, 1890, they appeared in the Anaconda Standard.*

The finest rope-swinger in all the Southwest is Bud Carraway of Reeves county, Texas. It was my good fortune to be with a round-up party of cowboys last week who were out after stray steers, and among the number was Bud Carraway, the prince of lariat-throwers. One night while sitting around the camp fire smoking and telling stories, the subject of bears came up.

"Tell us the best true story you know, Bud," said one of the boys, "and don't be modest about it. Give us a good yarn."

"I'll do the best I can," answered Bud, "and what's more I'll not stretch it a bit, but give you straight facts." He filled the bowl of a big pipe, lit it from a live coal and settled back for the story.

"Last fall, you know, I was working for the Mill Iron Ranch company on the south fork of Red river. There was a great many nice fat yearlings on the range, and every day or two one would be missing, but as he had our brand on his hide we thought of course that he would be found at some one of the round-ups. The round-ups came, steers and cattle were gathered in, but only a very few yearlings were among them. After awhile the foreman set a watch by staking out a calf on the prairie over night, and next morning we discovered bear tracks, and big ones, too. Our boarder was in fact a big black bear, who required a yearling at least once in two days, and what was more, he preferred to do his own slaughtering. He was an old customer, for we had heard of him before in some of the adjoining counties. He had scorned all attempts to shoot or trap him, and actually fattened upon lead, winked at pitfalls, sneezed at traps and cunningly turned up his nose at poisoned meat.

"We did not known [sic] what to do. The fellow was cautious enough to keep out of sight, and every attempt or expedition against him failed until at last, by pure accident I managed to catch him myself when I least expected such a piece of luck. One afternoon in September I was out on the range horse hunting, when, as I was passing near a thick bunch of chaparal, I saw a monster black bear jump out of the bushes, knock a young heifer over with his powerful paw and draw the carcass back into the bushes again and out of sight. I could scarcely believe my eyes.

"Fortunately my mustang was a good one, and would not stir or move until I gave him the signal. I had no weapon; I was alone and miles from the home ranch, and only my pocket-knife and my trusty lariat with me. I rode around the bushes two or three times, feeling sure in case of danger that my mustang was fleet and quick enough to keep me out of trouble, but, to own the truth, I did not know what on earth to do. Unslinging my rope, I got it ready anyhow to use should an opportunity offer, determined to give him a toss if he dared to show his snout. Would you believe he actually did that very thing? Well, he did. He saw me, poked his head out to get a better smell, and then shoved his whole head out, I suppose to get a better view. This was my chance. Giving the noose a couple of turns to settle the loop, I let fly, and down it dropped snug over his head, but before I could tighten the line, blame my eyes if he didn't take his paw and lift it clean off. Then he dashed back into the brush and I was no better off than before. I waited some time and was about to go away when I heard a crashing and rustling some distance away. Looking to see what it was, blamed if the bear hadn't stole a march on me and was racing off ocross [sic] the prairie in the opposite direction."

"What a fool!" ejaculated one of his listeners.

"Well, I should say he was a fool. You fellows know that on the open prairie, with no tree or stump or hole to hide in, a big animal, be he a steer, a bear, or anything else, has no show, and that a rope is the best weapon on earth to have. I let Nance go, and before many minutes was within reaching distance of the black old sinner. Swinging the rope again, I let her fly, and caught him in the first cast right around the neck. He couldn't get it off this time, for it was range work with Nance and I, and she never let a slack or kink get into the line; so we had him fast.

"Now, you fellows know how to throw a steer, so you can imagine I had no trouble with the bear. I raced around him until the lariat trailed from the neck on the opposite side to the rump, and when I had it about the height of his knees I gave a short, quick jerk and pulled his feet from under him. Down he went like a cyclone, rolling over and over in the dust. You never saw a more surprised bear in all your life. Every time he rose up and started to run I did the same thing until at last he got very tired of the performance. The fun soon came to an end. He got up for a last run and started off like a steam engine. I let him go and waited until he was doing his level best, and then I gave him a good one which nearly broke his neck. He lay there stunned and quiet, and

I could see the breath had been knocked clean out of the old rascal's carcass. Cautioning Nance to hold taut, the same as for a steer you are going to tie, I approached carefully and with my jack-knife gave him a dig in the throat which settled his case for good. I went back to the ranch and got a team and hauled him in. When dressed he weighed 740 pounds. That's all."

"Well, that is a good 'un," said Old Hawkins, a gray and grizzled veteran who had spent a majority of his years on the Texas frontier. "Now, let me tell you a true yarn that happened up in the Panhandle a year ago last fall. We were riding near a bunch of timber, hunting for long horns and, after a long search, we found 'em jest coming out of a creek bottom, where the grass and water was good. I tell you them steers was mighty wild, and we had a tough time of it trying to persuade 'em to take the trail for the home ranch. At last we got 'em started, only four in all, and had gone about a couple of miles, when, upon passing through a bunch of mesquite and chaparel [sic], darn my buttons, if we didn't run upon a couple of black bears, who were sitting bolt upright on their haunches in the middle of the road. They were big fellows, and as none of us had agun [sic] or pistol only lariats we thought them steers was gone up sure. Well, now, would you believe they warn't, and that we got out of the difficulty without the loss of a hoof and not a scratch."

"How did you do it?" inquired one of the boys.

"We didn't do it all," answered Hawkins. "Them steers settled the question for us, and they just handled them three bears in fine style. While we were thinking what was best to be done, the foremost steer lowered his head, pawed the ground viciously for a few seconds, then, ballowing furiously, he went at them bears like a railroad train. With his long horns he caught the first bear under the ribs and sent him head over heels in the dust, with his side ripped open from the shoulder to the rump. They [sic] surprised bear thought an earthquake had struck him. He staggered to his feet, and all three of 'em started to run, but the other steers had caught the fever now and all of 'em came dashing down the trail hand over fist straight at them bears.

"They treated the bruins to several somersaults, and finally drove 'em into the timber. We could hear 'em bellowing, growling and snarling, but none of us cared to go in just then to see the circus. After a while the steers came out, and I tell you the first one was pretty badly used up. He was covered with blood, and to his horns clung bits of black fur, showing how he had gouged and smashed the black hides of the beef stealers. As they were pretty tired, we left 'em to graze and rest a while, and went in for ourselves to see what kind of a time they had been having. One bear lay dead on the ground and he was badly gored and trampled. The others warn't in sight, so we rightly guessed the steers had got the better of the fight and had chased 'em off. As the cattle had showed so much pluck and sand, we did not disturb 'em, but went back to the ranch by ourselves, leaving 'em alone to take their time and come home when they they pleased."

# Bear Kidnaps Baby

$M$r. Bear appears as a lonesome but friendly child abductor in this story. The tale, titled "A Bear Fondling a Baby," apparently came from the *Chico Record but was reprinted in the October 5, 1882 Bozeman Avant Courier.*

Henry Flynn, who resides up in the hills near Inskip, is in town [Bozeman, Montana] to-day, and had the following incident to relate in which a bear of the cinnamon species abducted his three-year-old daughter, not with any desire to harm the child, but through a strange kind of affection.

It appears that Mr. Flynn started one morning to take a horse to pasture, about two miles distant from the house, and as the little girl seemed anxious to go, he put her upon the horse's back and let her ride a short distance, perhaps forty rods from the house, where he put her down and told her to run home. He noticed that she continued standing where he left her, and on looking back after going a little farther saw her playing in the sand. He soon passed out of sight and was gone about an hour, expecting of course that the child would return to the house after playing a few moments. On returning home he made inquiry about her of its mother, who said she had not seen her and supposed he had taken her along with him. On going to the spot where he had left her, he saw a huge bear's tracks in the sand, and at once came to the conclusion that the child had been carried off by the bear.

The family immediately made search through the forest, which was grown up to almost a jungle, rendering their search very slow. All day these anxious parents searched for traces of their child; nor did they stop when darkness came on but remained in the woods, calling the lost one by her name. Morning came and their search was fruitless. A couple of gentlemen from below, who were traveling through the mountains buying stock, came to the house, and being informed of the circumstances, immediately set out to find her. The gentlemen wandered about, and as they were passing a swampy spot, where the undergrowth was thick, called the child, or else they were talking loud, when one of them heard her voice. He then called her by name, and told her to come out of the bushes. She replied that the bear would not let her. The men crept through the brush, and when near the spot where she and the bear were, they heard a splash in the water, which the child said was the bear.

On going to her, they found her standing upon a log extending about half way across a swamp. The bear had undertaken to cross the swamp on the log, and being pursued, left the child and got away as rapidly as possible. She had received some scratches about the face and arms, and her clothes were almost torn from her body; but the bear had not bitten her to hurt her, the marks of his teeth being only found on her back, where in taking hold of her clothes to carry her, he had taken the flesh also.

The little one says the bear would put her down occasionally to rest; and would put his nose up to her face, when she would slap him; and the bear would hang his head by her side, and purr and rub against her like a cat. They asked her if she was cold in the night, and she told them the old bear lay down beside her, and put his "arm" around her and kept her warm, though she did not like his long hair. She was taken home to her parents.

# Bears on The Range

*Colorado cowboys could spin yarns as well as any other professional liars. Honora DeBusk Smith tells three of their frontier fables for a chapter in a book on southwestern folklore. These tall tales were excerpted from* **Southwestern Lore,** *a publication of the Texas Folk-Lore Society, No. IX edited by J. Frank Dobie; copyright 1931.*[14]

Bear stories were always timely. Not only did they interest everyone, but they always reminded someone present of another. Hence I have a series of these. We'll start with a grizzly yarn told by "Sour-Dough" Charley, camp cook.[15]

"Scared? I'll say I have been scared. I'll tell you about the worst scare I ever had in all my frail existence. I was punching cattle over Magdalena way, and we were camped just off the range. Well, one afternoon I was coming down from the hills afoot, for I'd been out to get some fresh meat and had some rabbits. I was poking along when all at once I noticed underbrush moving not far away, and says I to myself, 'I'll just fire into that commotion over there, and see what happens. Maybe it's a coyote and again maybe it's only a rabbit.'

"So I whales away and fires into the moving brush, and, oh, my sakes alive, the size of a bear it was that riz slowly up from the bushes! He was that high I thought he'd never get clear stood up. He kept undoubling himself, like one of these here jointed telescopes, till he looked as high as that pine tree, and the mouth opened was as big as a cellar door. He was a grizzly, and a whooping grizzly at that.

"Well, I was scared, and I was scared bad. To begin with, I wasn't expecting a bear anyway, and then I'd never seen a grizzly before. My experiences had been confined to plain cinnamon bears, and bob cats, and such like small fry, and it gave me an awful feeling to see him keep rising and a-grinning like that. I shot and ran. I didn't take no careful aim either, I was in too big a hurry for that. I just fired promiscuous like and hit the road. And run! The way I ran was a caution. A dog with a firecracker tied to his tail is nowhere in comparison to the tracks I made.

"It was over a mile to camp. I got pretty well winded toward the end, but I didn't dare to stop, for I could hear that beast tearing through the underbrush after me, and he didn't seem to be coming slow, either.

"When finally I did reach camp, I just fell over on the ground, and I couldn't speak or move for a while, I was so run down.

"Of course, soon as I got breath enough to tell my story, some of the fellows started right back with me to look for the bear. When we'd gone about a mile and there were no signs of him, the boys began to rub it into me pretty hard. They said they'd often known folks that saw snakes and such like creations, but they never before heard of anybody that saw grizzly bears. And they wanted to know what kind of dope I'd taken to get such a boogering nightmare as all that.

"Well, when we got up the cañon, there the old fellow lay, not ten yards from the spot where I'd seen him. My first shot had wounded him and the second had finished him up. You see, he being so big, it was almost impossible to miss him if you fired in that general direction, even if your shot was shaky and promiscuous like. I figured it out that must have been how it happened, but the boys never could get over my hearing him tear along after me through the brush. That bear weighed 800 pounds, dressed. He was the only grizzly I ever had personal experience with, and I never want to meet another. They are too durn big."

Another of the cowboys took his pipe from his mouth, grinning expansively and sympathetically.

"Shucks, you make me think of that yarn Bill Jameson was telling about the time when he and Jim Wilson were going over to the Circle H round-up. They were going through the hills, bunching in cattle on the way over.

"Bill and Jim were always great pals, but they weren't a bit alike. Bill was one of these quick, spry, nervous fellows. Jim was long and lank and deliberate. Everybody called him 'Slow Jim.' He was that sleepy and easy looking that you couldn't imagine him ever moving out of that lazy, good-humored gait o' his'n. Right there was where strangers might make a mistake, though, for Jim could move, and mighty quick at that, when he got warmed up. He was a great fellow for horses and horse races, Jim was, always and eternally trying to get hold of the fastest bronc on the range, so as to put him up against the horses of all his long-suffering friends. He was riding a horse over to the round-up, which he declared was the swiftest on the range, and I guess he was about right. Blizzard his name was, not a very good looker, but he surely could run.

"So Bill and Jim, they started through a big cañon, or, rather, cañada. What is a cañada? When two cañons run together, making one big broad one, that's a cañada. Bill was to go through one side rounding in the cattle he found, while Jim did the same on the other side.

"Bill hadn't more than got good started when Jim came tearing over from his range.

" 'Come on, Bill,' he yelled. 'Here's the goldarndest old she bear over here you ever saw. She has three cubs. Let's us rope the bear and then we can get the cubs and take 'em to camp.'

" 'You go along, sonny, and rope her yourself if you want to', says Bill, 'but I reckon you'll have to excuse me. I'm not thirsting for excitement just now, nor yet for blood and gore. And a she bear is sure the unreasonablest critter on this foot-stool. You go ahead, and if you need me at the funeral, just give the yell and I'll be right along.'

" 'All right,' says Jim, 'I reckon I won't need any help, but I thought maybe you'd like to see the fun.'

"So Jim loped off, and Bill went on with his work. He didn't think any more about Jim and his bear, he got so interested in his cattle. But after a while he heard Jim let out a yell that made him face around and break for the other side of the cañada, fast as his cayuse could carry him, for he knew by the tone of voice that it wasn't any bear's funeral. 'Bill! he yells, 'Oh, Bill, come along, and for the land's sake come quick!'

"Pretty soon Bill sees Jim tearing down the mountain side, riding the most thrilling race he had ever yet participated in. It appeared that Jim had got the bear and then the bear had got him. He had roped her, but she was raging crazy, and made right for him. His horse took fright, and tore down the road, the old bear coming hard and fast behind. Every once in a while she would give the horse a dig before he could get out of the way. Jim's pulling on the rope only made things worse; so he was urging on the horse.

"Bill, he didn't know what to do. If he went to shoot, he didn't know whether to aim a little forward, so as to hit the bear, or a little back so as to keep from getting Jim or his horse. So he sings out, 'What'll I do, Jim? I dassen't shoot.'

"'Just pull the air out of the way, in front of me, so I can get through,' gasps out Jim. It was sure a good thing his horse was some speedy. As it was, he was about winded before Bill got a chance to lariat the bear and give her the back pull.

"Ever after that Bill wouldn't allow anybody to call his pard 'Slow Jim.' He said such a title was plumb unfitting for any man who rid the race he saw Jim riding that morning."

The next yarn has always been my favorite of·the series. The humorous, imaginative frills are deftly added to a probable experience, with that surprise twist at the end which is recommended by those who give university courses in short story writing. It must be remembered that these yarns were not intended to be written but to entertain a cowboy audience.

"Jake Elson was an old-timer and a great scrapper. He did love a row. Afoot or horseback, knives or pistols, clubs or fists, Jake was always right there. He would rather fight than eat.

"He was camping on the mesa over Bar X way, to look after some cattle. One morning he took a *paseo* [walk] down a side cañon, about sunrise. He shot at some coyotes along the way, just for orneriness, and so had about emptied his gun when he saw a big bear moseying along. The bear seemed to be starting up a cañon, and Jake was just coming out of another, a good piece away.

"Well, Jake stopped and looked at the bear, and the bear he paused and seemed to contemplate Jake. Gentlemen, but he was a whopper! Jake says he was one of the biggest he ever saw, broad and heavy, with a tremendous head, and a forehead on him like a forty-dollar roll-top desk.

"Of course, Jake had killed so many dozen bears in his day and time that the sight of this one didn't give him any particular thrills, even if he was almost the size of an ox. Jake began to consider whether it was worth while to kill him. He would like to, he thought, on general principles, just to be neighborly. It would seem sort of unmannerly and neglectful-like to pass a bear of those dimensions without even a salutation.

" 'But then', he argues to himself, 'the booger is so big it would take a double team of horses to pull him away, and moreover, it would be a day's job to skin him. And, as the Egyptian mummy said, I am pressed for time. I made a fire and put on the coffee-pot before I started out, and I'd better be getting right back for breakfast, for I've got to hustle off afterward. There's a day's work ahead of me with them Bar X people. I hate to, but I reckon I'd better let him amble along. What earthly use would I have for his old carcass, anyway?'

"As Jake came to this conclusion, the bear, who seemed to have been glancing him over kind o' contemptuous like, turned off kind o' scornful with a flirt of his paw, as much to say, 'You'd better let me alone.'

"That kind o' riled Jake a little. He began to wonder if his conclusion hadn't been a bit hasty, after all.

"'That big skin o' his'n would fill up beautiful all the middle floor of the living room in the cabin,' he says to himself. 'And that head, I never see[n] such a head, with that high rolling brow. If that head was mounted it would fill up that vacant space over in the corner like a beautiful vision in a dream. I guess I'll reconsider, for I might use his hide to pretty good advantage after all, and, moreover and besides, I didn't like that scornful way he turned off with that twist of his paw. It don't set well with me, and I don't propose to take no back talk from no bear, even if I am pushed for time. That bear is so fat he is plumb sassy.'

"So Jake lams loose and shoots at the old fellow. He thought he took fair aim, though rather a distant one. The bear turned around kind o' surprised and indignant like, and then headed straight for Jake. His powers o' locomotion didn't seem to be impaired none, and for such a big fellow he came on pretty fast, with a surprised, so-you-won't-let-me-alone-won't-you look on his massive countenance.

"Right then and there Jake found out he had used up all his shots. What's more, he hadn't no time to reload. In fact, time was at such a premium just then that he concluded he'd better look for a tree right off. By the time he had found the right sort of a tree, he hadn't time enough left to take his gun along. He scrambled up 'most any way, and thankful enough to get out of reach of the bear's claws.

"If he'd been just a black bear, he'd a-come up after Jake, I reckon, but, being as he was a grizzly, he sat down, with a patient, hurt look, as much to say, 'Well, I reckon I'll have to stay with you a while, if it does upset my day's program some.'

"Jake looked down at him and groaned. 'I might have known better than to insult a beast with a Gladstone brow like his'n', he says to himself. 'He doesn't carry all that forehead for nothing, either. I expect my coffee's boiled over by this time, and I'm some hungry all right. But I reckon there's no need of my feeling hurried or nervous, for it shorely looks like I'd not see the Bar X outfit this day.'

"He looks at the bear, who sits there in deep meditation and seeming lofty contemplation. 'I declare,' he said to himself, 'I believe that booger understands everything I say.'

"So he yells down to him, 'Say, old fellow, won't you hand me up that gun?'

"The bear looks at him, and then at the gun, and blest if he didn't waddle right over and pick the weapon up. He looks at it a moment, then turns it over and sees it is empty. And Jake swears that beast, when he seen the gun wasn't loaded, actually motioned him to throw down some cartridges.

"Now, of course, I maintain that the scare and all the exercise and excitement, coming on an empty stomach, had kind o' rattled Jake and he imagined this, but he is convinced it happened just that way. He began to get afraid of what the bear might do next.

"'If that gun had been loaded I'd sure have been a goner,' he says to himself. 'Wonder what ever made me such a fool as to meddle with an intellectual quadruped like that—me that don't need his hide anyway, no more than a chicken needs a tin bill!'

"But the bear didn't do nothing else, except to sit there and squint up his little red eyes at Jake. After a while Jake got that discouraged and hungry he thought some of throwing the bear some of the cartridges and encouraging him to put an end to the ridiculous performance. What made him maddest was to think that no tenderfoot could have cut a sorrier figure than he did, and he an old-timer as had killed dozens of bears! He kept getting madder as the sun got warmer, but the bear watched him pretty close, and seemed to mean business all right.

"It was nearly sundown when some punchers, going Cottonwood way, came within hailing distance. It sure did them worlds of good to see Jake sitting up in the tree looking so meek and woebegone. He didn't stir to come down till they were pretty close but began yelling, 'Right up that way's a bear you got to get, and for the land's sake hurry up or he'll be out o' reach!'

"They got the old fellow, and then they joshed Jake a good and plenty; put in most of their spare time at it for the next month, he said. Jake sure had a fine rug out of that bear, but never afterward would he have anything to do with grizzlies. Whenever he saw one with a forehead like a roll-top desk, he gave it a wide berth and advised his friends to do the same."

# Casey's Treasured Fiddle

*How a big, hungry cinnamon bear took to the fiddle and made music that caused a grown man to cry was the story told in the November 1, 1899 Anaconda Standard.*

George Munson, a prospector who has been working a claim near Lion mountain for a couple of summers, was in the city [Anaconda, Montana] yesterday buying his winter's stock of provisions. Mr. Munson is known among a large number of friends by the musical title of "Casey the Fiddler," not because he is an artist with the bow, but because he always keeps a violin in his cabin and guards it with the care that a fond mother bestows upon her first born. How he came into possession of the instrument is a story "Casey" is ever willing to relate, if he happens to be in a reminiscent mood. Yesterday he was in that kind of mood, and he told the story of the fiddle.

"Yes, I have the most valuable violin in the country," he said, when imposed upon to tell about how he came into possession of the old instrument. "The original owner of that fiddle was the crack musician of the part of the country we lived in 20 years ago. That was in Diamond gulch, and there was a good sized settlement there then. Bill Gray and I were partners in a mining claim, and we made some money those days, but that is not here or there so far as this story goes. Bill used to play for the dances and every evening after the day's work he would take the fiddle out of the case and saw away on some new piece so that he could have something fresh for the dancers the next time he was called upon to play for a dance.

"One Sunday afternoon in the middle of the summer I left Bill and went out for a cruise over the hills in search of almost any old thing in the shape of quartz float. Bill was sawing on the fiddle when I left, and it happened that he sawed all the time while I was away. I returned late in the afternoon, just as the sun was going down, and as I approached the cabin I saw a sight that took my breath away for a minute or two. I could see through the open door a big cinnamon bear sitting on a chair at the table, apparently in the act of taking a piece of bread from a plate. I advanced cautiously, intending to take old Bruin unawares, of course thinking that Bill had gone out and left the door open. As I neared the door I could see Bill sitting on the edge of the bed, where I had left him in the forenoon, his fiddle in his hand. He was sitting there like a man in a trance, as if riveted to the bed. I moved around toward the window, intending to take a shot at the bear from a point out of range of Bill. When I got to the window I saw that the bear was only enjoying a hearty meal from the leaving of the breakfast we had eaten that morning. Bill did not see me; neither did the bear, so I had the situation well in my own hands, and instead of making a noise to attract either Bill or the strange visitor, I just assumed a waiting attitude.

"The bear ate everything in sight and then with a grand swoop of his big left paw swept everything off the table and turned around on the stool and looked at my partner with one of those I-want- some-more expressions on his face. Bill did not move a muscle, but sat there with a firm grip on his fiddle. The bear reached out his paw and picked up Bill's pipe from the pillow on the bed, where the fiddler sat, and looked at it for a second or two, then fired it against the chimney rock, breaking it into atoms. Bill still sat motionless, and the bear reached out again and took the fiddle from Bill's hand and held it in his own for a minute or two, when he made a pass as if to smash it as he had the pipe.

"'Hold on, there', I said, at the same time poking my gun into the window in the direction of the intruder. 'Drop that fiddle or I'll drop you,' and the bear lazily turned his face towards me and looked at me as if to ask me where I had bought my chips in that game.

"Instead of making a demonstration, the bear took up the fiddle in his mouth and walked quietly out of the cabin and across the gulch towards the hills. I followed him and fired a shot, but missed. The bear did not quicken his pace; rather, he let me gain on him, and soon I was in certain range of him. I was about to take fatal aim, when the big fellow sat down upon his haunches and began to pick the strings with his claws, turning out what I thought was a pretty good article of music. I called for Bill, but he had not ventured out of the cabin. I supposed that he had been so badly frightened as to be unable to come out, so I just let it go at that and listened to more music by Bruin.

"I had now gained courage to venture closer to the musical animal, and soon, I found myself sitting as close to him as I am to you this minute. I could now distinctively hear the music, which was the sweetest I ever heard before. The bear was playing 'Home Sweet Home', and the tears were rolling down his cheeks as he played. I got the sentimental fever, and before another bar was played I was crying as hard as the bear was. I put my arms around the bear's neck and wept. The big cinnamon finished in the sweetest strain of that beautiful tune, and as the last note rippled away over the woodland the big bear fell back in a swoon from which he never recovered.

"Bill had actually died of fright. I was alone. The fiddle was mine, and why should I not cherish it? A fiddle that a bear has played upon you don't see every day."

# A Powerful
# (Boring) Speaker

*When confronted by a big bear, a Livingston, Montana, judge used masterful eloquence to subdue his adversary. This story from Livingston was written for the October 20, 1895* **Anaconda Standard.**

Judge J.A. Savage of this city [Livingston, Montana] met with a rather exciting experience the other day while duck hunting at Daily's [Dailey] lake in company with a party of Livingston people composed of Sam Wilson, J.A. McLaughlin, A. Brown, Joe Briggs, F.S. Webster, and C.C.H. Smith. The day in question several members of the party remained at the lake until the shadows of evening began to fall and then struck out for camp, some distance away. The judge became separated from his companions and in the gathering gloom lost his way and found himself in the mountain fastnesses, with nothing but a shotgun loaded with fine bird shot with which to protect himself should he encounter any of the wild beasts known to abound in the mountains around him. As he was wending his weary way around the base of a towering mountain the stillness of the trackless waste was broken in a sudden and startling manner by a big bear which the judge's dog had started from its retreat. Bruin had taken after the canine, and dog and bear came tearing down the side of the mountain, headed straight for the judge, displacing loose rocks which crashed on down thorugh [sic] the underbrush and made noise enough for an avalanche. His first impulse was to open fire upon the bear, but on second thought he concluded that this would be worse than folly. If his shotgun had been a rifle the judge would have felt no fear for his safety, but as it was he decided not to shoot until the bear was right upon him. There was not a single tree in sight; even if there had been the judge, with his 240 pounds of averdupois [avoirdupois], would have had a mighty hard time climbing it. It was too dark to run, besides the ground was so broken as to preclude the possibility of outfooting bruin. It was a ticklish position to be placed in but Judge Savage, always fertile in resources, was equal to this emergency.

In this connection it is pertinent to state that the judge is not only an eloquent barrister, but a polished gentlemen and a diplomatist as well. It has been his experience that human hearts are susceptible to appeals for mercy, but until he met the bear the other night the thought never occurred to him that the wild beasts of the forest could be brought under the patent spell of pleading eloquence.

As the bear approached, the judge fired in the air and, raising his voice to its fullest pitch, sent forth a blood-curdling yell. The ruse worked like a charm, for bruin came to a sudden stop, while the dog circled around and charged at the feet of its master. It was then that the judge, as if addressing a jury, began an impassioned appeal. It is not known to what lofty heights of eloquence the judge attained, as no one was present except the gentleman himself and his well-known modesty would prevent him from dwelling on his own address, even were he able to recall the language used. The judge volunteered the information, however, that at first the bear sat up on its haunches and then crouched down to the ground like a cringing cur. As he concluded his address bruin uttered a series of long, agonizing wails, half human in their appeal. The judge then cautiously backed away from the prostrate animal until its grizzled form was lost in the darkness. Mr. Savage, after wandering around for some little time, finally struck the trail and reached camp in an exhausted condition. He related his experience with the bear, but his companions were inclined to be skeptical, and in order to convince them of the truthfulness of the story he offered to take them to the spot in the morning and show them the tracks of the animal.

This was readily agreed to, and so when morning came and breakfast was over the entire party, with the judge in the lead, started out to view the spot where Mr. Savage held the audience with bruin [t]he previous evening. As the party approached the place designated by the judge, that gentleman uttered an exclamation of surprise and pointing to a dark object just beyond a clump of bushes, said: "There's the bear just ahead of us, right where I left it and in exactly the same position."

The judge's dog had already scented the animal and bounded towards it, awakening the echoes with its loud barking. But bruin neither moved a hair nor batted an eye. Several shots were fired in the air, but still the animal remained perfectly still. With leveled pieces the party approached close to the bear and found to Mr. Savage's great surprise that bruin was actually dead. The judge was then accused of having shot the animal, but this he strenuously denied. A critical examination followed, but not a particle of blood was found anywhere on the bear's body, neither was there a single wound, mark or bruise of any nature or description on the carcass.

The explanation is simple enough: The judge had actually talked the poor bear to death.

# Chewing Tobacco Can Be Hazardous to Bears

*A big grizzly followed a prospector to his cabin and made himself at home while the man spent an entire night in fear as a captive. Upon waking in the morning, the hungry bear ate some snuff for breakfast which had a deleterious effect upon his health. This tall tale appeared in the May 17, 1898* **Anaconda Standard.**

Oliver Hazard Perry Preston is in town [Anaconda, Montana], having just arrived from his mining claim in the mountains near the head of Ross' Fork of the Big Hole river. The snow, he says, is rapidly disappearing from his section of the country, and it now is no perilous task to make the trip from there to this city, although he was four days on the road. He walked every foot of the distance. He made the last trip in nearly three months ago, and of his experiences since he left Anaconda he spoke yesterday as follows:

"I didn't do any mining or prospecting on this last trip—I just dug a hole through the snow to my cabin and stayed in doors for six weeks. When the snow had melted down until it was about four feet deep I shouldered my old gun and started out after fresh meat. I traveled, I guess, about 10 miles from camp before I saw a living thing, and what I saw didn't please me a bit. It was a big grizzly bear. He saw me first, because when I caught sight of him he was sitting on his haunches looking at me with a bold, bear look of defiance. He wasn't more than 30 yards ahead of me, in a little open plat in the timber. If he had not moved a little, as if to settle himself more firmly for a stand against his supposed fierce adversary, I believe I would have walked squarely into his embrace. I wasn't thinking about bears or anything else in particular before I saw him move. Then I thought, and rethought and wondered how to get out of my unpleasant position without getting hurt. I wanted fresh meat, but you know, maybe, how it is to feel uncertain. Just then I lost confidence in my ability to shoot accurately. I'm no bear hunter; never was. I didn't want to leave such a tempting morsel without an effort to bag it, so I deliberately took aim and pulled the trigger. When I pulled that trigger I realized for once in my life how very tender is the thread of life to which a man so persistently clings. To miss meant certain death for me, I figured. Well, the hammer went down into place, but there was no report. I was trembling, for I thought I saw the bear coming towards me, but he wasn't; he was sitting there waiting for me to adjust the cartridge for effective work. I threw the lock and looked. No cartridge in the barrel, none in the magazine! Not a cartridge in my pocket. My weapon was useless, I was helpless, at the mercy of a big grizzly, and miles away from a human being. It was a terrible suspense, a painful fright.

"I involuntarily backed away and slowly, gradually turned my body about, still keeping my eyes riveted upon the bear. I walked, cautiously retraced my steps, hoping that my stealthy homeward movement would be unnoticed by the grizzly. I had gone probably 20 paces before the bear moved, and when he did move he started to follow me. I turned and ran with all my might towards camp. The bear kept about the same distance behind me until I got within a hundred yards of the cabin, when he closed in on me and we reached the door neck and neck. I sprang upon my bed and reached for my cartridge belt, but it wasn't there. It was hanging behind the door, and the bear was lying lazily just outside with his big paws carelessly thrown across the threshold. His eyes were focused on my frightened countenance, and I knew that if I attempted to get the cartridge belt he would slap my face and probably pile me up for good. So what did I do but just sit on my bunk and wait. The bear waited, too.

"A cold wind came up and was followed by a flurry of snow. Old bruin stood up, looked out onto the bleak open, shook himself, and politely walked into the cabin and stretched himself out right alongside of my bunk. He laid there, apparently as contented as a big Newfoundland in front of a fireplace on a Christmas eve. He emitted a hugh [sic] sigh and settled down for a comfortable night's rest, for it was now about 6 o'clock and the storm made it almost as dark as night. I was getting cold, but whenever I moved the bear moved, too, so I gave it up. I thought it would be as well to take my chances in the cabin with a quiet bear as to try to find comfort out in a snow storm.

"Horrible feelings of dreadful fear seized me as the daylight faded into darkness. Cold chills followed one another up my back in rapid succession. My teeth chattered, but I dared not move. I could plainly hear the breathing of the big bear, but could see nothing but the dark gray opening through the doorway. The wind howled and the snow scattered over the dirt floor of the cabin. An occasional gust would toss a handful of snow in my face, and I'd shudder again.

"A joyful throb of relief warmed my blood when I saw the faint outlines of the beast in the doorway. Surely he was going out and I could at least bar the door and load my gun. But he returned to his cot on the floor. He sniffed about and his warm breath touched my hand. I was now almost paralyzed with fear.

"After a while when I thought my impudent visitor was asleep I slipped over the foot of the bed, my gun in my hand, and started towards my cartridge belt behind the door. I reached it at last and was in the act of putting a charge into the gun when, biff, the rifle was snatched out of my hand with terrific force. The bear grunted and, I guess, returned to the bed, for I soon afterwards heard another of those sighs of satisfaction. I stood against the side of the cabin until daylight, while the bear comfortably snoozed the while away.

"Hunger was added to fright to make my situation worse. I feared the consequences of an attempt to escape by bolting through the door and out into the open. I still hoped that the bear would go outside. I could see, now it was broad daylight, that the beast was becoming uneasy. He began to walk around the room, and I saw in his eye clear indications of desperation. He quickened his pace to a dog trot, and in his merry-go-round he cast glances at me that chilled my blood and gave me the hiccoughs.

"All at once he stopped and stood stock still in the center of the room. He looked at me for a minute or two. I thought it was all off with me. I expected to be torn into shoestrings the next instant. But instead of striking me he walked over to a box of snuff I kept under the table and pushed it over. A plug of tobacco was in the heap on the floor. He bit off a chunk, chewed it up, swallowed it; took another chew, swallowed that and died.

"I have lived in the mountains for many years, but never before in my life did I put in such a night as I did with that bear. I dragged the dead animal out, after skinning it, and I was sick for two days afterwards. That's a straight story. I've got the skin and tobacco to prove it."

# Unusual
# Adventures

$T$elling bear stories was a popular pastime during the frontier days. Any story involving a bear was considered interesting, but some were better than others because they contained elements out of the ordinary. The tales in the following chapter range from amusing to cruel but all are unusual adventures. Some of the adventures include experiences roping or wrestling bears; others recount wild bull and bear fights and some relate amusing antics performed by those notorious Yellowstone National Park bears.

## Resurrection

*One fellow, while riding along in the mountains, sneaked up on a black bear and successfully roped it. Once the bear realized it was caught, bruin gave the horse and man quite a ride in trying to escape. The poor bear eventually smashed into a tree and was taken for dead. However, the dead bear came to life and the results of its resurrection were reported in the May 24, 1910 Anaconda Standard.*

The champion bear story of the year was brought into Butte [Montana] from Cameron, in the Madison valley, yesterday by Elgin Kellar.

"I have killed three fine specimens of the tribe of bruin," he told a Standard reporter yesterday, confidentially and under the promise that the story would not be printed until he left town. "Two of these were brown bears and one of them a silver tip, but it remained for my brother Bert to do something really exciting in the way of bear killing. The creek on which we live is called Bear creek. It is not the Bear creek of the comic supplements, but a real Bear creek and there are enough of the varmints in its valley and canyons to warrant the name.

"It was about a week ago that a real bear incident occurred. Bert went into the hills, riding a half-broken pony and without a rifle, for the nag he bestrode was not gun-broken by any means. When he was about 10 miles from home and after his temper had become seriously ruffled by sundry and various trips through thickets of timber, which scratched all of the fur off his chaps and all the hide off his face, he came out into a little clearing, where a yearling black bear was industriously trying to turn over all of the dead logs near the edge of the timber, in search of bugs, spiders, ants and other dainties.

"Bert saw how he could get even for his experience in the timber and, taking down his rope, got busy at once. He sneaked up on that bear and was within roping distance before bruin could think of anything else save to hunt for bugs. When he discovered an intruder was in the park he tried to forsake it, but the rope was the quicker and he brought up all standing when he ran to the end, for Bert had taken the precaution to tie the rope hard and fast to the saddle horn. There was never a horse that liked a bear under any conditions or circumstances, so the horse Bert was riding promptly stampeded, the bear trailing along behind through the timber, like Halley's comet. By and by a diversion came. The bear wrapped himself around the butt of a pine tree and locked a double hitch over the rope. The horse was compelled to stop by force of circumstances, for it was impossible for him to break the rope or get away. The man who was doing the riding act got off in a hurry.

"Bert sized matters up and concluded the bear was good and dead. There was not a quiver of life in him and it looked as if the animal's neck had been broken by the impact with the tree. Accordingly it was slung over the saddle and firmly tied, after the horse had been blindfolded, and the journey home was resumed. It was probably two miles before the bear came to its senses again. He had been tied pretty loosely and he was able to sit up in the saddle, give a growl and then put all four paws into the horse at the same time. The result was one of the prettiest bucking contests ever seen on the Madison valley, the real home of bucking horses. When it was all over the bear was surely good and dead. How he was killed is a mystery, but the general belief is that his neck was broken against the lower branches of a fir tree, which never showed a limb less than 20 feet above the ground. Anyway, my brother finally led a mighty mad horse into the barnyard about sundown, and it took two or three of us to tame the horse down sufficiently to untie the bear carcass.

"There were two good looking young Butte Dianas at the ranch. They had been bear hunting for a week and had never got sight of any member of the tribe of bruin. They more than made up for the discomfort on that bear hunt in the price they paid for the hide. The meat was no good, for it had all been bucked to a pulp by the various stunts that old horse cut up when the dead bear came to life and began testing his claws."

# Loses Britches In Battle

*Japanese workers idly watched a wrestling match between a mother black bear and their unarmed foreman near Missoula, Montana. This somewhat humorous, but no doubt dangerous, encounter was published as a dispatch from Missoula in the September 23, 1901* **Anaconda Standard** *titled "One True Bear Story."*

Bear stories are becoming so numerous that they have lately aroused but little interest. A new one came in to-day from up the canyon, in which Henry Oleson, section foreman at Clinton [Montana], is the hero and which is a little out of the ordinary in that Oleson killed his bear without the use of any weapon but a club and only after a desperate wrestling match with bruin.

Oleson, with his section gang, was clearing away cinders at the Clinton water tank Friday afternoon, when he was surprised by the sudden appearance of a trio of bears. One was a large one and the others were cubs, half grown. The bears nosed around curiously and Oleson resented their usurpation of the right of inspection that is the prerogative of only Roadmaster Mayne. This valiant Swede, therefore, proceeded to mix with the big bear. It must have been a contest that would have delighted the heart of a Cornish wrestler. When Oleson emerged from the mix-up he had lost his shirt, trousers and about all of his clothing except his shoes and stockings. He was somewhat scratched, but he had made connections with a small club in rolling around with the bear, and with that he hit bruin a rap over the nose that caused a suspension of hostilities. Before the bear recovered from the shock another blow, this time with an iron bridge bolt, settled the difficulty. Bruin was dead. The cubs made their escape during the wrestling match. The only wonder is that Oleson was not killed, as the Japs of his section gang lent him no assistance. He has as trophies of his valor a fine bear skin and a lot of fresh meat.

# Travels With A Bear

*While walking to a friend's house one evening, Mr. E. J. Morrison encountered a black bear. Being unarmed, the man became quite nervous, but the bear had no intention of harming the man. Bruin and Morrison just happened to be headed in the same direction, and the two of them trotted along together for about a half mile. Although the bear could have easily attacked Morrison, he didn't. Unfortunately for the bear, the man did not reciprocate this kindness when he had the advantage. This adventure was reported in* **The Great Falls Tribune,** *June 24, 1900.*

It was the latter part of October that I left the sawmill at the head of Roberts creek; Meagher county, Montana, on a trip to Oregon, taking with me "Rocky," a Californian, who wanted to get to his native haunts for the winter. "Rocky" had two saddle ponies, and, as I had a light two-seated wagon and harness, we decided to drive. I agreed to let "Rocky" drive on to Gogler's the first day, while I would walk to Hanson's, trusting to get a saddle horse to carry me forward from that point.

One can imagine my chagrin on finding no one at home, no horse in the stables or corral, and the place having every appearance of having been deserted for an indefinite period. As there was no food in the cabin, a supperless twelve-mile walk stared me in the face. It was then five o'clock and darkness was coming on. There was some danger attending such a walk, owing to the many cattle to be encountered on the way, which necessitated at times, keeping close to the river, where there were trees and brush for shelter and protection.

I was getting along very nicely, walking at about a four-mile gait, and keeping to the straight road. There was a moon, but I could see for a moderate distance ahead. All at once, I discovered an object ahead of me, near where the road led around the point of a hill, quite close to the river. As there were not any cattle near, I concluded it must be a cow or a steer which was sick or injured, as it had the appearance of being nearly a full-grown animal. As I was contemplating what to do, the animal arose, and I immediately saw that it was a bear, and a large one, at that.

It would be diverging somewhat from the truth to say that I was not somewhat disturbed at this discovery. For a moment I did not know what to do. As "Bruin" seemed to be prepared to contest the right of way, and as I was not then hunting bears, I concluded to give way to him and take my chances in the open country. Therefore, I left the road and struck across the hills in a northwesterly direction, aiming to come into the road again some two miles beyond. I was wearing a pair of new grain-leather boots, which were beginning to hurt my feet and ankles at every step. This condition was not improved by leaving the road and taking to the rough prairie. Therefore, my mind was made up to get into the road again as soon as I considered it safe. I did not take my bearings as carefully as I should have done, owing to there being more of a bend in the river than I had allowed for. Consequently I came into the highway sooner than I had anticipated. However, my fears were allayed, as I could see some distance ahead and, not seeing or hearing anything [of] that Mr. Bear, concluded that I was well rid of him.

As I walked on, hungry and lame, I commenced to reason with myself as to what I would do should I see the bear again which, of course, I was not expecting. Knowing that I could not outrun him and that, if he were in a quarrelsome mood, he would attack me anywhere, in which case I would be killed outright or severely wounded, and as the chances of being found would be much greater on or near the highway than on the open prairie, I concluded to stick to the road in any event.

About the time I arrived at this conclusion, I heard soft footfalls. Startled, I turned, and there was Bruin, so close that I could have put my hand on his back. He was trotting along, as unconcernedly as could be, and seemingly without fear, evidently realizing that he was master of the situation. Had he risen out of the ground, I wouldn't have been more astonished, and I could feel my hair actually raising my hat from my head. I commenced to run. Frightened? The word doesn't express my feelings, as the bear kept by my side, just as a large dog would do, for nearly half a mile, sometimes close, and sometimes at a short distance. All the bear stories I had ever heard in my life came to me in that short time. Among them I remember one: that in the event of being attacked by a bear, it is well to fall upon your face and lie perfectly still, as if you were dead: that the bear will not touch you so long as you remain perfectly motionless and he believes you inanimate. Another I remembered, which an old bear-hunter had told me, "Never attack a bear alone," said he, "unless every advantage is on your side, such as being out of his reach in the event of a shot not killing him, or mortally wounding him."

As in this case Bruin had the complete advantage of me—I having no weapons—I decided, in case of necessity, to adopt the former plan, and drop upon my face at the first move he should make toward me. I kept up a dog-trot, so as not to get out of breath, and, seemingly, without an effort, my friend, the bear kept pace with me. There he was, a grim reality, so close, at times, that I could have touched him. Once or twice he forced himself into the brush, whence he would again appear, as bold as ever. He evidently had business in the same direction—toward the mountains—in which I was traveling, and didn't proport [sic] to change his route. I had somewhat forgotten my extreme fear, when suddenly, as quickly as he had made me aware of his presence, he scooted into the brush, and then, splash! splash! I heard him as he plunged into the river to swim to the other side. To say that I felt a great relief doesn't express it. In fact, I can't find words to describe my feelings when I heard that bear in the water and knew he was crossing to the other side, and that I was safe.

The rest of the way I walked leisurely, and, at eight o'clock, could see the light at Gogler's in the distance. I arrived at the hospitable abode of Mrs. Barnes, who kept the tavern, at about nine o'clock. As they were expecting me, my supper was waiting, and, strange to say, almost the first dish brought upon the table was a steaming hot plate of bear meat. This, however, I avoided as the devil would holy water, as I had had all the bear I wanted earlier in the evening. The history of the meat they brought for my supper is interesting, and has a direct bearing upon this story. They told me it had been taken from the saddle of one of two great black bears that had recently been infesting the neighborhood. A few nights previous, these hungry brutes had broken into a sheep corral and committed considerable havoc among the sheep. One of the monsters was successfully trapped, but the other, a very crafty old bear, indeed, had eluded the vigilance of the hunters and proceeded upon his depredatory way, killing and gourmandizing until he was too full for utterance, and it is owing to the fact that he was stuffed almost to repletion that I unquestionably owe my escape. Bears never attack except in self-defense or on account of hunger. Upon reflection, I have concluded that, from start to finish, the bear was just about as nervous as I was. He had come upon me quite as accidently as I had upon him. Our paths converged to the main road, and we reached it about the same time. Bruin happened to be on the side next to the river, which the road skirted, and was evidently seeking for an opening in the dense brush along the precipitous bank. I dare say he was about as anxious to escape as I was to have him, and that, when he finally plunged down the embankment and into the river, the feeling of relief that he enjoyed was second only to my own. He had gotten his fill of lambs, had basked for a few hours in the autumnal sunshine, and was retiring with a well-lined interior to enjoy the sleep of the thrifty in his mountain lair. But, alas! that his dreams of rest should be so rudely shattered! The very next day he failed to stop a shower of bullets at the right time, with the result that, six months later, the beautiful, glossy skin of my late opponent in the trotting contest was in my possession.—E.J. Morrison, in *success.*

# Buffalo vs. Bear

*N*oted frontier hunter/dentist Doctor William Allen wrote about a battle between two bull buffalo and a grizzly he saw near Fort C. Smith. The winner of this gruesome fight was undetermined because Allen intervened and ended the battle by shooting the combatants. His eye-witness account of this bloodbath was taken from pp. 218-225 of Chapter XX titled "Buffalo v. Bear—A Strange Contest" in his book **Adventures With Indians and Game—Twenty Years in the Rockies,** published by A.W. Bowen & Company in Chicago; copyright 1903.

Once as I was returning from a trip to some mines, or supposed mines (which had been reported rich in gold, but upon examination had proved to be worthless), and was crossing a low range in the big mountains west of Rotten Grass, my almost exhausted pony suddenly recovered his animation and sniffed the air repeatedly. Being very much fatigued, I gave no heed to his demonstrations, but pushed on a few steps farther, where a clear, running spring invited me to dismount. Soon both horse and rider were eagerly drinking from the same fountain. I fastened the pony with a lariat, removed the saddle from his tired back and left him cropping the rich bunch grass with evident relish, while I began to prepare my own repast.

Soon I heard a snorting, and, hastening toward my pony, found the former strange behavior repeated with an increased energy and a great show of fear. I looked around, could see nothing, so I returned and finished my meal, took a bath in the water and was looking over my small pack, when my pony again ran toward me in great fright. I then took my rifle and walked rapidly in the direction whence his look said he apprehended danger, and about four hundred yards away I saw a dozen buffaloes, quietly grazing near some quaking asps [aspen].

I crept up as close as I could without disturbing them, and had selected a fat calf for my victim, when a full-grown bull came tearing out of the bushes and ran toward the herd. I did not know how to account for this strange freak; and I saw him looking in the direction from which he came, shaking his ponderous head in an angry manner. Only a short time was given me to wonder what would happen next, when a full-sized grizzly bounded out after the bull and rushed toward the herd.

The cows began to form a circle, while the calves were rushing wildly around. The latter were quickly surrounded by the cows, thus keeping the little fellows on the inside, as is the custom of the buffaloes when danger threatens. The bull took up his position in the rear, with a manner which indicated his determination to protect the females and their young, with his life if necessary. It was soon evident that some of the herd would become a meal for his bearship, unless they acted immediately in their own defense.

The bull saw just how matters stood, and, when the bear was almost at his heels, turned swiftly and met bruin as a mountain ram meets his antagonist. They came together with a thud, which fairly stunned them both, and they rebounded from the concussion like balls, and paused for an instant to recover from the shock. The bear then made a fresh start for the herd, but was again confronted by the bull.

The bear seemed to understand fully the motives which actuated his opponent, so he raised upon his haunches, and prepared to do battle with the bull, before he made another attempt to secure a fresh young calf. At that moment the bull lowered his head, shot forward with his tail standing straight in the air, and struck the bear full in the stomach. The bear in turn caught him around the neck and proceeded to tear the flesh from his shoulders, while the bull gave the grizzly some terrible wounds with his horns, and he finally made a desperate charge which compelled the bear to relinquish his hold, when the buffalo ran over his body and attempted to join the herd.

Wild with rage, the bear quickly regained his footing, pursued and overtook the bull, who then turned like a flash and gave him another charge. This time bruin sprang upon the buffalo's back, and fastened his claws and teeth in the great fellow's flesh, a surprise for which the bull was not prepared. But he was equal to the situation and showed no small skill as an imitator of the bronco bucker. The buffalo plunged first one way, then the other, while the bear held on with a death-like grip, until it also was surprised by the bull's turning a complete somersault. Before the bear could recover the bull was upon it with his feet, and buried his horns deep in its shoulder. The bear then dealt the bison a blow with its paw, which sounded far off and made the bull shake his head with pain.

All this time the herd stood awaiting orders from their leader, and, whenever there was a lull in the battle, he glanced anxiously toward them. The bear was now deeply wounded in the shoulder. The bull was fearfully mangled about the neck. The blood flowed freely from both, while great bunches of hair were scattered in every direction. The bear now made a leap for the bull's back, but was caught between the fore-legs on the horns of the latter and received a terrible wound. It was then thrown upon its back and the bull plunged over it, goring it the while with his sharp horns.

The bear seized the opportunity to catch its enemy in the flank, tearing off a great mouthful of hide, but the bull turned and jumped upon it with both fore-feet and gave the animal another wound. The bear then caught his antagonist by the back of the neck and they rolled over together. They were now in the wildest state of excitement, both suffering severe pain, each looking like a great mass of animated sand and blood. They started apart and stood within twenty feet of each other, panting like race-horses. The bear's mouth was full of hair and blood, while the bull's horns were red with gore for more than half their length, showing how deeply they had penetrated the body of the bear.

They stood apart but a few moments. The bull kept glancing toward his little family, while the bear approached one step at a time and raised itself on its hind legs, preparing to renew the conflict. I could hardly keep myself from sending a ball through the bear's worthless body, for I found myself in sympathy with the bull from the first, but I was curious to see how the affair would terminate. The battle had carried them closer and closer to the herd, and a two-year-old bull, seeing how matters stood with his defender, and burning with desire to test his own strength, came upon the scene, pawed the ground, bowed his back, and rushed upon the bear with all his force, but was repulsed with a blow on the side of his head that turned him halfway round.

His old friend was close at hand, however, and taking advantage of the situation gave the bear another goring. The young bull kept shaking his head the while. The blow he had received had evidently stunned him, but he walked up within a few yards of the bear, turned himself sidewise, took a few steps, then flew again at his antagonist, plunged his horns into its bowels, making a gaping wound that allowed part of the entrails to fall out. Maddened with pain, the infuriated bear caught him by the hump with its claws, and tore the flesh from the back of the youngster's neck with his teeth, leaving the bones bare. The little bull roared as though imploring mercy, while the old one came again to his rescue and struck bruin a heavy blow in the back.

I now began to feel sorry for the grizzly, as he could no longer raise himself upon his haunches, and so I gave the old bull a shot through the heart, just as he was making another charge upon his fallen foe. The bear paid no attention to the shot, but seemed determined to have satisfaction out of his remaining enemy, though the young bull seemed willing to give up the struggle and depart in peace, taking warning perhaps from the fate of his friend.

Picking himself up as best he could, bruin made another attack, dealing the young buffalo a blow on the top of its head which staggered it. The bear now lay upon his back a mass of gore, evidently dying, and the bull had received a blow from which he could not recover. I then walked up close to them, and out of sympathy shot the bear through the brain. The bull was still standing, throwing his head up and down, the blood pouring from his nose and ears, so I released him from an existence which had certainly become unendurable, and saw him stagger and fall over the body of the bear.

This was one of the bloodiest battles between animals I have ever witnessed, and was maintained on both sides with equal courage and determination. The combatants had fought with all the strength and ferocity of their savage natures. "He who fights and runs away may live to fight another day." Animals seldom possess this element of cowardice when contending for their rights, or when satisfying the demands of appetite. I stood looking upon the remains until my heart grew sick within me, then mounted my faithful pony, and was soon flying down the valley.

At nightfall I drew rein near the spot where Fort Smith used to stand, refreshed myself with a few mouthfuls of supper, and turned in on my saddle blankets for the night, under the sheltering boughs of a large cottonwood. The roar of the waters, the rustling of leaves, the cries of coyotes and the howling of wolves, robbed me of sleep and made me feel that the infernal regions could not be very far off. I fired two or three shots in a vain attempt to frighten the brutes into silence, then built a fire and lay down to rest but not to sleep. I reached Fort Custer by noon the next day, having had no adventure worth relating, save the battle I had witnessed.

# The Fur Flies

*This story bears an uncanny resemblance to one written by journalist J. Ross Browne titled "A Dangerous Journey," which appeared May 1862 in the* **Harper's New Monthly Magazine**. *However, the details here have been altered slightly and the author has embellished his tale by mentioning eagles and wolves that are ever ready to prey upon the victims of the battle. The story below was published in the October 17, 1899* **Bitter Root Times**.

"Some years ago, as agent of a big firm of cattle speculators," said a prominent traveler to the writer, "I spent a good deal of time in the great northwest. One day, while fishing, I saw a small herd of wild cattle standing off to my right. Among them was a young bull, a splendid specimen of his kind, who came towards me. I can't say exactly how it was done, but it wasn't many seconds before I found myself in a cottonwood tree, out of reach of the bull, who was immediately under the tree, pawing dirt and acting as if very mad. The bull pawed and grumbled a few minutes and then turned and walked toward the thicket, on the creek side of which there was a water hole. I saw him push his way into the thicket, and the next instant I could see that he had got into trouble of some kind, and that trouble proved to be a grizzly bear. A fierce struggle followed in the thicket. Scarcely two minutes elapsed before the bull broke through the bushes. His head was covered with blood and great flakes of flesh hung from his fore shoulders. But instead of showing any signs of defeat, he seemed literally to glow with defiant rage. Instinct had simply prompted him in his retreat to seek an open space. But scarcely had I time to note all this, when the bear, a huge, repulsive looking brute, broke through the bushes into the opening. When the bear made his appearance out of the thicket the bull did not wait for his charge, but, lowering his great head to the ground, rushed madly upon the bear. The latter seemed to appreciate the abilities of the bull, and summoned all the wariness of his nature to his aid. He waited until the bull was almost upon him, and then sprang aside with marvelous quickness, seized his assailant's horns in his powerful grasp and pressed the bull's horns down against the ground by his great strength and the weight of his enormous body, biting the bull's nose and tearing the flesh from his cheek and shoulders with his long, sharp claws. Presently both animals paused in their desperate struggle, but the bear did not relax the hold he had obtained on the bull. The cessation in the struggle had probably been of ten minutes duration when suddenly the bull made one desperate lunge, broke the embrace of the grizzly, hurled the bear from off his head and backed away some ten paces. The bear lifted his huge head and stood ready for the next assault. The herd of cattle had by this time gathered in from the plain and surrounded the combatants, mooing and bellowing and pawing up the ground, and maintaining a terrified neutrality. The bull did not remain at rest a moment after backing away for a new charge, but, rendered furious by his wounds, he gathered all his energies and, with a resounding bellow, rushed with impetuous force and ferocity upon the bear. The latter attempted to use the tactics that had served him so well at the first onslaught, but the second charge of the bull was irresistible, in spite of the bear's terrific blows with his paws, and the grizzly went down in the dust before his crazed antagonist, and vainly tried to defend himself. The bull thrust his horns under the bear, caught him in the belly with one of the sharp weapons, and with one furious sweep of his head, ripped a great gash in the grizzly's under side. The grizzly rose to his feet, and with a howl closed with his foe, and for a long time the two fought.

"While the fight was going on two eagles appeared from some mysterious eerie and sailed and circled above the scene of the conflict, leisurely and gradually dropping nearer to the earth. Almost simultaneously with the appearance of the eagles I saw the heads of half a dozen hungry wolves emerge from the bushes where the fight had begun. I knew that the battle must soon end.

"The desperate struggle continued. The ground was torn up and covered with blood for many feet around. Both animals were grievously wounded. It was plain that neither could hold out much longer. Maimed and gory, they fought with the certainty of death, the bear rolling over and over in the dust, vainly trying to avoid the fatal horns of his adversary [sic], and the bull ripping, thrusting and tearing the grizzly with irresistible ferocity. At last, as if he determined to end the conflict, the bull drew back, lowered his head and made a third terrific charge; but, blinded by the streams of blood that poured down his face, he missed his mark, stumbled and rolled headlong on the ground. In spite of frightful injuries and great exhaustion, the bear turned quickly and sprang upon his prostrate foe. He seemed to have been suddenly invigorated by this turn of the battle in his favor. With merciless sweeps of his huge claws he tore the flesh in great masses from the bull's upturned side.

"The bull and the bear rolled over and over. Nothing was now to be seen but a heaving, gory mass, dimly perceptible through the dust. As to weight, the two fierce and determined brutes must have been about equally matched. The unfortunate result of the bull's last charge on the grizzly indicated that the latter's qualities would in a few minutes more settle the fight against the bull and I was in momentary expectation of seeing such a termination, when, to my astonishment, I saw the bear relax his efforts, roll over from the body of his prostrate foe and drag himself feebly away from the spot. The grizzly had no sooner abandoned his attack on the bull than the latter was on his feet, bearing himself as erect and as fierce as ever.

"Giving his head a shake, he lowered it for the fourth time, and again charged. As the bull hurled himself against the grizzly the latter braced himself for a last desperate struggle. He struck out wildly with his paws and the bull fell back with the force of the grizzly's blows. The bear sank to the ground, writhing in agony. The indomitable courage of the bull here prevailed. Blinded and crippled as he was, he dashed wildly at his foe again. With a last frantic effort the bear sought to make his escape, scrambling and staggering through the dust. But it was useless. His great strength was gone. The bull plunged his horns again and again into the huge form of the dying brute as he lay stretched helpless in the dust. The bear's muscles quivered and contracted. He drew his immense paws up once or twice in convulsive clutches, raised his huge head, gave one agonizing groan and fell back dead. The victorious bull raised his head, gave voice to a deep bellow and, shaking his head triumphantly, turned and walked away.

"His progress was slow and painful and he stopped and turned at short intervals and listened as if to know whether his foe would renew the battle. He walked nearly a hundred yards with the herd gathering and bellowing about him. Presently his head dropped from its proud position. He spread his legs apart as if to brace himself against the weakness that was telling upon him. Suddenly he fell as if he had been shot, a mangled, bleeding mass, and was soon dead. When I climbed out of the tree to leave the scene of the terrific combat the herd of cattle had disappeared on the plain and the eagles and the wolves were screeching, snarling and fighting over the mangled carcasses of the bull and the bear."

# A Day's Diversion

*Roping bears seemed to be one of those activities young cowboys felt compelled to do at least once. Usually one experience with a roped grizzly prevented it from becoming habit-forming. Back in the late 1870s, a couple of cowboys moving horses through eastern Montana spotted a grizzly and with their youthful spirit of adventure lassoed the bruin. Their tale was recounted in the June 18, 1930 **Dillon Examiner**.[16]*

Plaz Price of Hinsdale, Elmer Cain of Tampico, the Garrison boys of Saco, Harry Rutter, now of Deer Lodge, and Lem Branson of Nashua are among the few still living of that border legion of youthful cowboys who came up the long trail from Texas in the late seventies and early eighties after the Sioux had been corralled on reservations. They arrived on the Montana ranges while the campaign for the extinction of the buffalo was at its zenith.

The N-N was among the first of these Texas outfits to settle in Montana in what is now Valley, Phillips and Roosevelt counties. The international boundary was hazily defined in those days and the range boss for the N-N spotted the home ranch first at a point at the head of Rock creek on the Canadian side. When the first hard winter came and drifted cattle southeast to Milk river and to the Missouri, it was concluded to re-establish the home ranch near the site of the present town of Oswego [Montana]. A bull camp was established on Rock creek near Hinsdale.

On one occasion it became necessary to move 500 head of saddle horses from the Milk river country through to Casper, Wyo., to be loaded for shipment to Denver. It fell to Plaz Price and Carl Williams to move them across the Missouri, down the Big Dry en route to Miles City and south.

Well up the Big Dry, an ancient trail, a small drain miscalled Timber creek comes into the Dry from the east and out of a small wash broke a giant silver tip grizzly, loping off down the course of the Dry. Plaz and Williams decided to rope the grizzly.

Several "throws" failed and the bear finally found refuge in a deep wash at the bottom of a cut coulee under a cut-bank, disregarding clods and other miss[i]les and attempts to dislodge him.

The hunters decided to tie Plaz' fur overcoat to a "ketch rope" and drop it off the cut-bank to dangle before the bear in an effort to bring him into the open. The coat was dropped over the ledge and brought to a sharp stop just at the grizzly's head. Instantly the bear let out a roar and embraced the coat, clawing it to shreds. He then ran out into the open. Taking after him, the cowpunchers overtook him and finally roped him [sic] head and hind foot. They had left their firearms with the bed wagon and were unable to kill the bear.

The tug of war continued, the bear first making for one of his tormentors and then for the other, able to travel only as far as the slack of the ropes would permit, all the while losing strength with the strangling pressure of the loop about his throat. The cowpunchers were afraid their fast failing and terrified cow ponies would stumble and fall or be overtaken by the mad rushes of the bear. Finally old silver tip gave up the struggle but so great was the respect he had inspired by his gallant resistance that his opponents set back on their ropes for the largest part of an hour before daring to dismount to administer the coup de grace.

The N-N was owned by the Niedringhouse family of East St. Louis, famous manufacturers of enameled ware and tinware and proprietors of Granite City, Ill., where their large factories still produce trainloads of manufactured goods daily. The silver tip hide is still displayed in the lobby of the Niedringhouse hotel in Granite City.

Carl Williams died last winter at Wolf Point [Montana]. His partner, Plaz Price, still lives on Beaver creek, west of Hinsdale, at the water hole and timber patch where he settled in the nineties.

# Rassling Old Rizzo

*W*alter I. Shay wrote an amusing article about how a braggert was tricked into wrestling a little black bear. However, the man quickly changed his mind when he realized the "little" bear was not so little. Mr. Shay also told what happened later to the bear and its companions which kept them from returning to Montana. His story appeared September 5, 1928, in the **Dillon Examiner.**[17]

Butte's sporting fraternity has witnessed every form of sport from a bull fight to a cock main and besides the championship baseball given the fans by John McCloskey, who went from Butte to the St. Louis Browns, horse racing which established two world's records and every type of prize fighter from the pork and beaner to champions, Butte at one time boasted of the best Cornish style wrestlers in the country.

Tim Harrington, who lived there for years, was the champion of this style of grappling and a big 200-pound son of Cornwall, named Thomas, claimed he could throw any man in the world except Harrington at Cornish style.

Thomas had several bouts and while he was no Carkeek or Harrington, he was fairly clever with the "Jacket" and possessed enormous strength. He was overboastful and a clique of Cornish miners employed at the same mine where Thomas worked, framed on him, more to stop his boasting than for any other reason.

In those days every summer a couple of Italians would tramp from town to town in Montana with a pair of performing bears. They would give an exhibition on the streets and would pass the hat. One of the bears was a small brown bear weighing not to exceed 200 pounds. The other animal was a mammoth black bear, named Rizzo.

Rizzo, who weighed as much as an average cayuse, would waltz, go through a crude manual of arms with a broomstick and would finish the exhibition by wrestling with one of the Italians.

"Give a nick, give a dime, it is a'worth da half dollar to see Rizzo rassle like a da mans," one Italian would shout as he passed through the crowd with his hat outstretched.

A secret deal was made with the owners of the bears and Thomas was brought down from Centerville [Montana] to see the little bear.

"Hi 'ave made a bet that no bloody bear h'as small as 'e could throw a Cousin Jack," said the leader of the jobbers, as he showed Thomas the little bruin. Meanwhile Rizzo had been taken out of sight and to the rear of Jack Hawke's livery stable, where the Montana Auto garage is now located.

"Put a jacket hon the bloody beast and Hi'll rassle 'e ," said Thomas. "Course the bloody bear must wear a muzzle, for Hi'll ave no bloody bear chewin' my neck."

The match was arranged to take place the next Saturday night at the Silver Bow saloon, which was located a few doors south of Clark's bank.

At 8 o'clock it was next to impossible to get inside the saloon. All the tables were jammed to capacity, a double row of men stood at the bar and scores stood up near the stage, which was in the rear of the building.

As Thomas shoved his way through the jam to reach the platform, members of the gang who framed the job made a number of "wash" or framed bets with Thomas the favorite over the bear, at odds of three to one. As the Centerville wrestler stepped upon the platform he was greeted with cheers.

At one edge of the mat was a chair and Thomas, after bowing to the many cheering men, sat down and started to unlace his shoes.

"Bring forth the bloody bear," shouted a man with a scoop of beer in one hand and a hot pasty in the other. "Hif a bloody Dago can throw a bear so can a Cousin Jack."

Suddenly the noise and commotion in the crowded saloon was stilled. One of the Italians was leading the bear to the platform from the alley, which runs behind Green's.

Thomas had one shoe off and was unlacing the other when the platform quivered. He looked up and instead of the little bear he had had [sic] seen a few days before, the owner was leading Rizzo upon the mat. In keeping with the agreement, Rizzo was muzzled and a huge canvas, large enough to make a tent, was tied around his front quarters.

"Up, Rizzo, up lik'a da mans," shouted the Italian and the huge bear stood on its hind legs. To Thomas the beast looked 10 feet high.

Without a word Thomas laced up his shoe and hurriedly pulled on the other shoe.

"What's the matter?" yelled one of the men in on the job.

"Damme if Hi'll rassle a bloody beast that takes hon a thousand pounds weight in three days," replied Thomas as he jumped through the rear exit. He never again boasted of his wrestling ability.

A week later Rizzo, the little bear and the two Italians were in Marysville [Montana] giving a street exhibition.

"Put in da nick, da dime, Rizzo, he rassles lik'a da mans," yelled the Italian passing the hat, while his companion had Rizzo waltzing with the grace of some of the modern black bottom artists.

Tom Bailey, well known wag who later died in Alaska, gave a boy a quarter and sent him to a nearby store for a package of firecrackers, and a fish hook.

Bailey tied one end of the Fourth of July package to the fish hook and as the Italian leading Rizzo passed close by, Bailey lit the other end of the crackers and jabbed the fish hook into Rizzo, an inch from the base of his tail. A combined terrific squeal and roar, which shook Marysville followed as the big bear jumped forward.

Then the firecrackers started. Rizzo may have been a fair wrestler but his specialty was running. Notwithstanding the ring through his nose to which was attached a chain, Rizzo started in the direction of Helena, the Italian hanging on to the chain, his feet touching only at the high spots in the downhill grade.

An hour later the other Italian led the small bear down the road and that was the last time the Italians and the two bears were ever seen in Montana.

# An Impish "Ghost-Bear"

*Milton P. Skinner studied bears for many years while working in Yellowstone National Park and wrote several books about the park and its notorious bears. In his book* Bears In The Yellowstone, *Skinner related an amusing story about a mischievious black bear cub who found entertainment in disturbing different camps and scared the dickens out of a superstitious black man. The following account was excerpted from pp. 2-4 of that book, published in Chicago by A.C. McClurg and Company in 1932; copyright 1925 in Great Britain.*

. . . Especially full and rich in promise are the bears, both black and grizzly; for bears in the Yellowstone are the most easily observed of all its larger animals. And furthermore, they are interesting because each bear is a study by himself. Just because we have seen one bear doesn't mean that we know them all. For each bear has certain individual ways and traits of his own, a fact unsuspected by most people. It was first brought home to me by two black bear cubs belonging to the same litter. Born together, having the same mother, and always traveling, eating, sleeping, and living together, they had seen exactly the same life and had exactly the same training and experience. Yet one was cheerful and obedient while the other was sullen and morose. When their mother sent them up trees, the one was prompt and always up first, while his more sullen brother required a second command and an occasional cuff on the ear. When the mother called them down again, the cheerful one always responded first and so promptly that he was down soonest even though he may have started from the top of the tree.

One showery day as I was riding along the Yellowstone River near the Grand Canyon of the Yellowstone, I passed a solitary camp almost hidden in a pretty glade amongst the trees. It was an attractive place but at the time there was no one about that I could see. Still the flap of the tent was half open, and although it was not raining just then, it might begin soon. As I debated whether I ought to go and close it, a small black bear came waddling ludicrously out on hind legs, and clasped tightly in his arms was a beautiful [fifty-pound] sack of flour, at least he seemed to think it so, and he carried it proudly to the side of the tent and set it down. Immediately, he was inside the tent again and brought out another sack which he set beside the first one. Then he squatted down on his haunches to gloat over his prizes. Not for long, however. Somehow he seemed to feel he wasn't getting all the fun out of the occasion that he ought to have. So he reached over one paw and grasped the first sack by its top and held it dangling just above the ground, while he drew his claws down through it, and I could fairly hear him chuckle with glee as the flour cascaded out from the slit bag in four wonderful white streams. When the bag was empty, he threw it aside and reached for the second sack which he treated just as he had the first one. For a time the falling flour fascinated him. Then he began stirring the piles about tentatively with one paw, until by chance some of it fell into a small puddle of rain water. This started a new train of thought in bruin's brain, and soon he had a fine white bed of wet flour. Then he rolled in it and plastered himself well with the white, gluey mixture. And just about the time he was good and white, the campers came back and put him to flight. After such an escapade I quite naturally thought that would be the last I should see of that bear. But he was bent on achieving more publicity. My own tent was about a mile away and close beside another in the edge of the public auto camp. About midnight I was awakened by the most blood-curdling yells from my neighbors' tent. The cries were so unearthly and so filled with terror that I rushed out, prepared to battle for my life. My neighbors were southerners and had brought their own negro cook with them. The old fellow was a good cook but somewhat given to gambling. Strangely enough his employer had scolded him that very day and threatened to sick a bear on him if he played again. The old negro was superstitious and one can imagine his feelings when he looked up from an enticing crap game to see a huge white form—"a ghost-bear," he called it— coming into the tent with every indication that he meant "to get that nigger."

Now there are not many of us that have ever had a "ghost-bear" after us, but most visitors to the Yellowstone usually see some bears. Everyone has heard of the free-and-easy, friendly bears that are to be seen on every hand. At the present time there are about a hundred and fifty black bears and forty grizzlies in the Yellowstone National Park. Probably there were never very many more than that, for this number is abundant for the territory considered, as bears need lots of "elbow room." The greatest number I have ever seen at one time, was on August 2, 1916, at the Canyon feeding station where I had twenty-nine in sight. In spite of his confidence in man about the regular feeding grounds and established camps, all the bears, especially the grizzlies, act quite differently when away from those places.

# The Chaperone

*Those park bears could be pesky all right. One particular black bear caused much trouble the summer of 1930 in Yellowstone National Park. After routinely annoying the chef at the Mammoth Hotel by knocking over all the garbage cans, the bear would then go to the girls' dormitory to disrupt the nightly romancing of the young park employees. The unpopular bear made news headlines in the September 4, 1930* **Rocky Mountain Husbandman.**

True love, someone once said, never runs smoothly, and if left to employes at Mammoth in Yellowstone National park, they would be unanimous in their opinion the person who said those words probably had them in mind, for if it isn't bears, it's something else that always is butting in.

Any way, there's a big black bear that makes a nightly trek to the Mammoth hotel kitchen door. This bear and the chef are on the outs and no foolin'. Bruin climbs a stairway leading to the kitchen, sniffs around a minute or so, knocks a row of garbage cans for a goal and begins his evening repast. But this doesn't register at all with the chef, who straightaway puts the run on bruin with a pan of water. Bears are not easily discouraged, though, and this particular mammal waits until the chef is indoors, then returns to his banquet, but not for long, because always, out pops the chef. As a consequence the chef gets angrier and the bear gets madder until finally bruin starts off on a lope and the strange part of it is, always toward the girls' dormitory, directly back of the hotel.

Now, bears and girls and boys never did jibe, especially when the girls and boys happen to be "rotten-logging," which, in plain English, is spooning. And let it be said that the porch of the girls' dormitory is a popular place for such a pastime. To continue, though, this particular bear always heads for the dormitory porch and in less time than it takes to tell, he succeeds in driving the love-sick youths indoors. This is repeated night after night and all say there ought to be a law against it, because 'tis said many a lad had been deterred from "popping the question."

# Bagging Bears—Voices of Experience

This chapter presents some frontier hunters' advice and personal experiences concerning bears, most notably the grizzly. Some of these accounts include advice from noted bear hunters Theodore Roosevelt, Colonel William D. Pickett and William Wright. Most of these writers gave sound advice and interesting information about bears, which they gleaned from personal study and observation. Unfortunately, not all would-be bear hunters heeded the experienced bear hunters' warnings: keep a clear head when confronting bruin, possess a dependable weapon, and know how to shoot accurately.

Most of the hunters in this chapter agreed that bears were more likely to flee than fight. Furthermore, they maintained that wounded, startled or mother bears could be dangerous adversaries. If tackling a mother or wounded bear, extreme caution was necessary and often two men were recommended. Many of these men not only actively hunted bears, but they also carefully studied bears, learning their traits and habits.

Today, most of the mentioned hunting areas are now absent of grizzlies.

## Hunting Grizzlies— A Realistic Appraisal

*Theodore Roosevelt, America's most famous frontier hunter, observed and shot almost every type of big and small game in this country and abroad. Although he loved to hunt as much as any frontiersman, he had a strong sense of conservation that kept him from the mass slaughter that was common during his time. Both black and grizzly bears fell to his sharp scrutiny and to his rifle, and he wrote about his experiences in numerous books. While he believed the grizzly could be dangerous, he thought tales of the bear's ferocity were exaggerated and that men with high-powered rifles and accurate aims could get the better of bruin. In the following account, Roosevelt described what qualities make a good bear hunter. He did not expect men to foolishly risk their lives in pursuit of a wounded bear, but he believed a good hunter should be able to skillfully track the animal and kill it. Roosevelt's attitude toward bears and conservation was not shared by most frontiersmen.*

*The following excerpt was taken from **The Wilderness Hunter—An Account of the Big Game of the United States and Its Chase With Horse, Hound and Rifle** by Theodore Roosevelt, Vol. II. Dakota Edition; published by G. P. Putnam's Sons—The Knicker-bocker Press: New York, 1907. Copyright by Putnam in 1893; pp. 93-95.*[18]

. . .On the whole, the danger of hunting these great bears [grizzlies] has been much exaggerated. At the beginning of the present century [1800s], when white hunters first encountered the grisly [sic], he was doubtless an exceedingly savage beast, prone to attack without provocation, and a redoubtable foe to persons armed with the clumsy, small-bore, muzzle-loading rifles of the day. But at present bitter experience has taught him caution. He has been hunted for sport, and hunted for his pelt, and hunted for the bounty, and hunted as a dangerous enemy to stock, until, save in the very wildest districts, he has learned to be more wary than a deer, and to avoid man's presence almost as carefully as the most timid kind of game. Except in rare cases, he will not attack of his own accord, and, as a rule, even when wounded, his object is escape rather than battle.

Still, when fairly brought to bay, or when moved by a sudden fit of ungovernable anger, the grisly [sic] is beyond peradventure a very dangerous antagonist. The first shot, if taken at a bear a good distance off and previously unwounded and unharried, is not usually fraught with much danger, the startled animal being at the outset bent merely on flight. It is always hazardous, however, to track a wounded and worried grisly [sic] into thick cover, and the man who habitually follows and kills this chief of American game in dense timber, never abandoning the bloody trail whithersoever it leads, must show no small degree of skill and hardihood, and must not too closely count the risk to life or limb. Bears differ widely in temper, and occasionally one may be found who will not show fight, no matter how much he is bullied; but, as a rule, a hunter must be cautious in meddling with a wounded animal which has retreated into a dense thicket, and has been once or twice roused; and such a beast, when it does turn, will usually charge again and again, and fight to the last with unconquerable ferocity. The short distance at which the bear can be seen through the underbrush, the fury of his charge, and his tenacity for life make it necessary for the hunter on such occasions to have steady nerves and a fairly quick and accurate aim. It is always well to have two men in following a wounded bear under such conditions. This is not necessary, however, and a good hunter, rather than lose his quarry, will, under ordinary circumstances, follow and attack it, no matter how tangled the fastness in which it has sought refuge; but he must act warily and with the utmost caution and resolution, if he wishes to escape a terrible and probably fatal mauling. An experienced hunter is rarely rash, and never heedless; he will not, when alone, follow a wounded bear into a thicket if, by the exercise of patience, skill, and knowledge of the game's habits, he can avoid the necessity; but it is idle to talk of the feat as something which ought in no case to be attempted. While danger ought never to be needlessly incurred, it is yet true that the keenest zest in sport comes from its presence, and from the consequent exercise of the qualities necessary to overcome it. The most thrilling moments of an American hunter's life are those in which, with every sense on the alert, and with nerves strung to the highest point, he is following alone into the heart of its forest fastness the fresh and bloody footprints of an angered grisly [sic]; and no other triumph of American hunting can compare with the victory to be thus gained.

# Roosevelt's
# Prized Trophy

*In 1889, Roosevelt was hunting alone in the Big Hole country when he encountered a large grizzly. Roosevelt aimed and wounded the big bear. However, when he shot again, the enraged bear charged him and several more shots were necessary to kill the bear. Teddy was very proud of this particular specimen because of the circumstances under which it was taken. His account was excerpted from pp. 87-93 of The Wilderness Hunter.*[19]

I spent much of the fall of 1889 hunting on the head-waters of the Salmon and Snake in Idaho, and along the Montana boundary line from the Big Hole Basin and the head of the Wisdom River to the neighborhood of Red Rock Pass and to the north and west of Henry's Lake. During the last fortnight my companion was the old mountain man, already mentioned, named Griffeth or Griffin—I cannot tell which, as he was always called either "Hank" or "Griff." He was a crabbedly honest old fellow, and a very skilful hunter; but he was worn out with age and rheumatism, and his temper had failed even faster than his bodily strength. He showed me a greater variety of game than I had ever seen before in so short a time; nor did I ever before or after make so successful a hunt. But he was an exceedingly disagreeable companion on account of his surly, moody ways. I generally had to get up first, to kindle the fire and make ready breakfast, and he was very quarrelsome. Finally, during my absence from camp one day, while not very far from Red Rock pass, he found my whisky-flask, which I kept purely for emergencies, and drank all the contents. When I came back he was quite drunk. This was unbearable, and after some high words I left him, and struck off homeward through the woods on my own account. We had with us four pack and saddle horses; and of these I took a very intelligent and gentle little bronco mare, which possessed the invaluable trait of always staying near camp, even when not hobbled. I was not hampered with much of an outfit, having only my buffalo sleeping-bag, a fur coat, and my washing kit, with a couple of spare pairs of socks and some handkerchiefs. A frying-pan, some salt, flour, baking-powder, a small chunk of salt pork, and a hatchet, made up a light pack, which, with the bedding, I fastened across the stock saddle by means of a rope and spare packing cinch. My cartridges and knife were in my belt; my compass and matches, as always, in my pocket. I walked, while the little mare followed almost like a dog, often without my having to hold the lariat which served as halter.

The country was for the most part fairly open, as I kept near the foothills where glades and little prairies broke the pine forest. The trees were of small size. There was no regular trail, but the course was easy to keep, and I had no trouble of any kind save on the second day. That afternoon I was following a stream which at last "canyoned up," that is, sank to the bottom of a canyon-like ravine impassable for a horse. I started up a side valley, intending to cross from its head coulies [sic] to those of another valley which would lead in below the canyon.

However, I got enmeshed in the tangle of winding valleys at the foot of the steep mountains, and as dusk was coming on I halted and camped in a little open spot by the side of a small, noisy brook, with crystal water. The place was carpeted with soft, wet, green moss, dotted red with the kinnikin[n]ic berries, and at its edge, under the trees, where the ground was dry, I threw down the buffalo-bed on the mat of sweet-smelling pine-needles. Making camp took but a moment. I opened the pack, tossed the bedding on a smooth spot, knee-haltered the little mare, dragged up a few dry logs, and then strolled off, rifle on shoulder, through the frosty gloaming, to see if I could pick up a grouse for supper.

For half a mile I walked quickly and silently over the pine-needles, across a succession of slight ridges separated by narrow, shallow valleys. The forest here was composed of lodge-pole pines, which on the ridges grew close together, with tall slender trunks, while in the valley the growth was more open. Though the sun was behind the mountains there yet plenty of light by which to shoot, but it was fading rapidly.

At last, as I was thinking of turning towards camp, I stole up to the crest of one of the ridges, and looked over into the valley some sixty yards off. Immediately I caught the loom of some large, dark object; and another glance showed me a big grisly [sic] walking slowly off with his head down. He was quartering to me, and I fired into his flank, the bullet, as I afterwards found, ranging forward and piercing one lung. At the shot he uttered a loud, moaning grunt and plunged forward at a heavy gallop, while I raced obliquely down the hill to cut him off. After going a hundred feet he reached a laurel thicket, some thirty yards broad, and two or three times as long, which he did not leave. I ran up to the edge and there halted, not liking to venture into the mass of twisted, close-growing stems and glossy foliage. Moreover, as I halted, I heard him utter a peculiar, savage kind of whine from the heart of the brush. Accordingly, I began to skirt the edge, standing on tiptoe and gazing earnestly to see if I could not catch a glimpse of his hide. When I was at the narrowest part of the thicket, he suddenly left it directly opposite, and then wheeled and stood broadside to me on the hillside, a little above. He turned his head stiffly towards me; scarlet strings of froth hung from his lips; his eyes burned like embers in the gloom.

I held true, aiming behind the shoulder, and my bullet shattered the point or lower end of his heart, taking out a big nick. Instantly the great bear turned with a harsh roar of fury and challenge, blowing the bloody foam from his mouth so that I saw the gleam of his white fangs; and then he charged straight at me, crashing and bounding through the laurel bushes, so that it was hard to aim. I waited until he came to a fallen tree, raking him as he topped it with a ball, which entered his chest and went through the cavity of his body, but he neither swerved nor flinched, and at the moment I did not know that I had struck him. He came steadily on, and in another second was almost upon me. I fired for his forehead, but my bullet went low, entering his open mouth, smashing his lower jaw and going into the neck. I leaped to one side almost as I pulled trigger; and through the hanging smoke the first thing I saw was his paw as he made a vicious side blow at me. The rush of his charge carried him past. As he struck he lurched forward, leaving a pool of bright blood where his muzzle hit the ground; but he recovered himself and made two or three jumps onwards, while I hurriedly jammed a couple of cartridges into the magazine, my rifle holding only four, all of which I had fired. Then he tried to pull up, but as he did so his muscles seemed suddenly to give way, his head drooped, and he rolled over and over like a shot rabbit. Each of my first three bullets had inflicted a mortal wound.

It was already twilight, and I merely opened the carcass, and then trotted back to camp. Next morning I returned and with much labor took off the skin. The fur was very fine, the animal being in excellent trim, and unusually bright-colored. Unfortunately, in packing it out I lost the skull, and had to supply its place with one of plaster. The beauty of the trophy, and the memory of the circumstances under which I procured it, make me value it perhaps more highly than any other in my house.

# Making It Hot For Bruin

*Colonel William D. Pickett, (1827-1913), veteran of the Mexican and Civil Wars, settled in the West after the Civil War. For many years, the avid hunter served as a vice president of the Boone and Crockett Club, representing Wyoming. He recorded many of his western hunting adventures in diaries, which are now preserved in the Montana Historical Society Library archives.[26] George Bird Grinnell edited Pickett's diaries and incorporated them into* **Hunting At High Altitudes—The Book of The Boone and Crockett Club,** *published by Harper Brothers in New York; copyright 1913. Pickett's diaries made up the first chapter of the book titled "Memories of a Bear Hunter." Grinnell noted in this book that Pickett "has had an experience hunting the grizzly bear greater probably than that of any man who ever lived." Below is one of the Colonel's bear hunting experiences in Montana in 1878, in which he arranged a trip into the Judith Mountains with an Englishman, Charles Messiter. For this particular hunt, Pickett hired a guide, teamster, cook and a two-horse wagon with team. Pickett successfully killed a grizzly and like most hunters of his day claimed the bear was "the largest of his kind." The bear was estimated to weigh 600 pounds.*

*This account was taken directly from his unedited diaries as found in the small collection #1436 of the Montana Historical Society Library archives, folder 3/7, pp. 3-7.[20]*

On the tenth of September [1878] we make a good drive to camp on Armell's creek near the foot of the Judith mountains. I determine to camp here until [Charles] Messiter comes up, intending to send Hayden [the teamster] and team back for him if necessary.

Today I killed two bull buffalo for bear baits. Fishel [the guide] killed two, in different localities. We also killed several antelope and deer for camp meat and are now prepared to live better.

In hunting for elk on the eleventh of Spetember [sic] I ascend the end of Judith mountain[21] and have a magnificent view across the Missouri valley (which stream is about forty miles distant,) with the Bear Paw mountains and Little Rocky mountains about seventy miles to the north and Moc[c]asin mountains to the west. Return to camp and have a fine sleep with my blanket laid on a fat bed of willow brush.

On September thirteenth C. Messiter, my hunting companion, arrives, coming out with Major Reed's [A.L. Reed—Indian agent at Fort Browning, Montana, from 1868-71] team with all baggage.

Stretch our two tents and make things comfortable, just in time for a rain and snow storm that commences about three o'clock p.m. and continues all night,

Major Reed stopping with us.

September 14

About three inches of snow on the ground, the snow continuing until about 10 o'clock a.m. Fishel reported that upon examination that one of the buffalo killed by me, from a high point thro[ugh] field glasses in the forenoon, indicated that some animal had disturbed the carcass, so we determined to investigate.

Upon ascending a bench of the mountain, about one mile from the bait, we discovered a large bear making off from the bait, in the opposite direction, he evidently having discovered us. We at once spurred up our horses, taking a direction to get ahead of him. But he was too fast for us.

In attempting to follow the trail, for the snow was fast melting I became separated from Fishel and Messiter and they struck his trail first and followed it until it entered a dense willow thicket on a small creek. On examining the opposite side to ascertain whether he had passed on, a huge bear rushed out and charged fierc[e]ly at them. Their horses did not at first take in the real situation and the bear was close to their heels before they got up the proper move. Fishel had started to camp to bring out a grey hound that Messiter had brought with him, when I met him. He then told me of the incidents just related and I hastened on to the scene of action and found Messiter perched on a high rocky point overlooking the thicket, his horse being tied some distance in the rear. The thicket was very dense and in area about one hundred yards up and down the small creek and fifty yards across.

The small creek six or eight feet wide and two feet deep with cut banks meandered thro[ugh] the thicket as shown on the accompanying sketch.

We held a council of war across the thicket and determined to stir the bear out, so that we could shoot thro[ugh] the brush with solid balls and by wounding him, he might become mad enough to rush out. I approached within twenty steps of the thicket on my side but failed to hear any movements. As Messiter had some idea of where he lay, it was determined that we would fire into that locality from each side and cause him to move around. About this time Fishel came with the grey hound but no persuasion could get him into the thicket near the bear. Then Messiter and myself commenced a bombarding of the supposed locality of the bear. I shot a 450 grain solid bullet with 90 grains of powder that penetrated the willow brush admirably. Messiter's rifle, was a double-barrel "Lang" rifle, that used a 160 grain express bullet with 120 grains of powder. This bullet was too light to penetrate far. We finally made his hiding place so warm that he rushed to the upper end of the thicket and charged out fierc[e]ly to Messiter's side. We each got in a shot and each wounded him. He retired to the thicket though badly wounded and was again still.

Messiter then left his perch, mounted his horse and came up on the opposite side of the thicket.

I forgot to say that the creek bottom outside the thicket was covered with rose-bushes and buck brush about as high as [a] horse's belly and it made it difficult for a horse to turn around quickly.

He was evidently wounded for his breathing was audible. We approached the edge of the thicket as close as we dared, about thirty feet and guided by his breathing kept his vicinity pretty warm by our bullets.

The old rascal watched his opportunity, crept to the edge of the thicket on my side and charged fierc[e]ly at me. I gave him a shot but overshot him, for he came on and was close to my horse's heels before he could be turned around in the thick buck-brush and gotten under way. I stood not on the order of my going, but went as fast as spurs could persuade the horse. I lost my hat in the scrimmage and before the horse was gotten in hand, for he had gotten up a scare, and another shot delivered, the bear had returned to his lair. Guided by his breathing we kept up the bombardment and managed to move him around.

In course of half an hour, he crept along the bed of the little creek to the edge of the thicket, near the point where I was stationed, and watching his opportunity charged out on me the second time. I gave him a deadly shot in the chest with a solid bullet as he approached which dropped him in his tracks and with such fashion that I yelled out "I have got him." But not so; for before I could load and give him a second shot (about fifteen feet off) he was up again and in a rage rushing for me. My horse barely got out of the reach of his claws before getting headway, (though as a matter of precausion [sic] he was headed outward on account of the buck-brush.)

We had now spent more than two hours around this bear and a blinding snow storm had "set in" which made it more difficult to hear or see as he moved about in the thicket. He was evidently badly wounded in the lungs as was evidenced by his breathing so loud as to be audible. We kept up the bombardment for some time but neither got in a good shot as we had to aim by guess. He was evidently fast dying; the storm, a wet snow, continued fierc[e]ly and a council of war was held, as to whether we should, on foot boldly approach him or wait till morning, as we felt sure he would be found dead. We finally concluded that discretion was the better part of valor and the latter alternative was the best.

Had we ventured in on foot and the bear possessed more vitality than anticipated, we should have stood no chance against such an infuriated monster in brush so dense as to prevent the effectual use of our rifles. During this time Fishel and Mason, a friend of Messiter's were perched up on the rocks overlooking the thicket and were quiet but safe spectators of the scene.

We reluctantly withdrew from these exciting incidents, without getting the full fruits hoped for, reaching camp, about two miles away, about half past five o'clock, wet from the driving snow storm and disappointed that the bear robe had to be left on the carcass.

After a hot supper which instantly revived our spirits stormy as it was, we gathered around a huge camp-fire and spent a hilarious time in discussing the various incidents of the evening fight and in expressions of astonishment at the size, fierceness and great vitality of that brute. The only bear of subsequent experience, his equal in ferocity (anticipating a few years), was that one killed in 1880 near the north fork of Stinking Water.[22]

After a night rendered the more comfortable in contrast to the storm raging without and a warm breakfast, we mounted our horses determined to ascertain the fate of that bear.

On passing the buffalo carcass, it was found that a bear and two cubs had visited it as was apparent by the signs in the snow, but we determined to give them attention later.

On approaching the thicket everything was quiet. Messiter and myself gave our horses to Fishel to hold and we pushed our way cautiously in the direction of the locality he had been left the previous evening. Being all ready the brush was carefully pushed aside and there the brute lay stark and stiff, in a hastily improvised bed.

After congratulations all around he was turned over and carefully examined. He was the largest of his kind, the grizzly bear, of a brownish color gradually turning grizzly or silver tip and in two months would have been called a silver tip bear. Standing on his feet he would have been about three and a half feet high and seven or seven and a half feet long from the end of his nose to the end of his tail. Standing on his hind feet, straight, he would have measured eight feet with his head level. He was in good order but not fat and would have weighed as he lay about six hundred pounds. His robe was not as well furred as it would have been later in the winter, but it was a large one. I secured the bone of his tally-whacker as a trophy.

On returning towards camp after skinning the bear Messiter and Fishel took up the trail of the bear and cubs, whilst I packed the bearskin to camp. The[y] followed the bear trail until the snow gave out from melting and soon returned.

# Big Gun/Cool Head

*In his book* Through The Yellowstone Park on Horseback, *George W. Wingate advised sportsmen about hunting grizzlies. He told them to be sure of themselves and their weapons before trying to tackle the tenacious grizzly. Wingate also described the various types of bears that inhabited the Rocky Mountains during the frontier days. The following two passages were excerpted from pp. 42-43; 217-220 of his book, published by O. Judd Company in New York; copyright 1886.*

The sportsman who goes to the Great West needs the most powerful rifle he can get, as the game is large and hard to kill. If he is going for bear he must be sure of himself as well as his rifle; and above all be certain how the latter carries at close quarters. Few appreciate how much the ordinary rifle overshoots at short distances, and how apt one is, for that reason, to miss. Some people talk about walking up to a grizzly and putting a bullet between his eyes at ten paces. If you have the nerve and skill to do it, it is all right, but failure is death. I knew of one man, who was armed with a rifle like mine [45-75 Winchester repeating rifle] (but using the ordinary bullet), who fired at a grizzly when 100 yards off. The bear rushed for him and he fired seven shots, while bruin was covering the distance, but although every one hit in a vital place, the bear was not stopped until the very last, a fortunate shot in the head dropped him when not ten feet from the hunter. Only the latter's wonderful nerve saved his life. Another bear, with two Express bullets through his heart made a rush up a hill at his assailant, and the sportsman's life was only preserved by a lucky shot which broke the animal's foreshoulder and swerved him from his path; he lived for some moments afterwards, time enough to have torn the hunter to pieces. Some of the coolest and best riflemen I know have refused to fire at a grizzly when alone, and in such close proximity that they had a chance for but a single shot. For my own part, although very anxious to kill a bear, and having a reasonable degree of confidence in my own nerves and skill, as well as in the power of my rifle, I was not at all desirous of having a single combat with one under the circumstances in which Mr. [Theodore] Roosevelt kills his bears. As an army friend of mine said, "I value a grizzly's hide, but not enough to bet my life against it." With fifty or sixty yards clear space so as to be able to get in several shots, it would, however, be another thing. But even then, no one should try it unless he knows he can shoot fast and straight, when under the excitement incident to a grizzly's coming for him like a tornado. . . .

The bears of the Rocky Mountains are the Grizzly, Silver-tip, Cinnamon, Smut-face, Black, and Silk bear. The Hog-back, or real California Grizzly, is one of the largest, most ferocious and dangerous animals on the Continent. The Silver-tip is a little smaller. Its coat of hair is longer and is tipped at the ends with a glistening silvery white. The Cinnamon is of a reddish brown color and is also smaller than the true grizzlies. The Smut-face is still smaller than the Cinnamon and has a spotted face. There is very little difference in disposition between all these varieties; the grizzlies and the Smut-face bear are said to be the most meddlesome and pugnacious of the bear family. The grizzly lives in the mountains, but comes down about September, where he is frequently found in the little parks and ravines, feeding on plums, berries and wild fruit, of which he is very fond. He is also a great admirer of ants, and it is common to find old logs which have been torn to pieces by him in searching for them. He is much less dangerous than is generally supposed, and he will always run away if left alone, if he thinks he can do so. If he is wounded, however, or thinks he is "cornered," he attacks his assailants with the utmost ferocity and desperation, and utterly irrespective of their numbers and weapons. The spectacle of an enraged grizzly tearing down upon you with the speed of a horse, roaring at the top of his voice, is appalling. His strength is so immense, his tenacity of life so great, and his disposition, when aroused, to kill his assailant so inflexible, that the average frontiersman is very much disposed to leave him alone. As he says, "he hasn't lost any grizzly," and does not care to hunt for one; and regards with scorn those "tenderfeet" who do. I have already written something upon this subject at page 42, [See Above] and I would repeat that no one should attack this bear except when armed with the most powerful rifle, and with some one to support him. He should also be provided with some good dogs who will divert the bear's attention by snapping at his haunches when he makes a rush. When a hunter can steal up to a bear and get a steady shot, a bullet in the forehead or butt of the ear with almost any rifle will produce instant death. But a shot at the head is very uncertain. If the front sight is drawn too coarse, or the animal raises his nose or moves his head when you are in the act of firing, a miss is almost inevitable. If the bullet only makes a flesh wound, the hunter is apt for the first time to appreciate the full force of the expression "as mad as a bear with a sore head." In that case he will want a rifle which will shoot quickly and strike a smashing blow—and will want it badly. While I was in the Rocky Mountains, there was a party there who were hunting for grizzlies, but they were provided with traps of such a size that a large lever was required to open the jaws. These were chained to a heavy log and put in a place where a grizzly would be likely to come. If a grizzly kills any animal, he eats what he wants of it and covers the rest with decayed logs, rubbish or stones, either remaining near the body or returning to it nightly. If the trap is placed in the neighborhood of such a carcass it is very apt to catch him, or the hunter may, if he prefers, conceal himself in the vicinity and shoot him if he comes up. If dogs are used, small dogs who will run around and snap at the animal's haunches are better than those who will attempt to fight. The latter are short lived. I was told of an English gentleman who had two imported bear hounds as large as a man, which he let loose on a grizzly. The first dog jumped at the throat of the bear, who gave him a single hug with his fore-paws, which mashed every bone in his body, and as the second dog jumped past him, the bear dropped the body of the first and struck the second a blow with his fore-paw which broke his back, disposing of both dogs in less than a minute, and if the owner of the dogs had not been fortunate to have several good shots with him, his own chances for life would have been no better than those of his dogs.

# Another Hunter's Advice

*Dr. William Allen, prominent frontier dentist and hunter, also advised novice bear hunters. Allen's advice reflected his own inexperience when he shot his first grizzly. The story of his first grizzly kill and other hunting adventures are found in his book* Adventures With Indians and Game— Twenty Years In the Rockies. *Below is an excerpt taken from pp. 82-84 of that book published by A.W. Bowen and Company in Chicago; copyright 1903.*

. . .These bears [grizzlies] make a savage fight when wounded. They ransack the country, eating all kinds of berries, bugs and worms. They are wonderfully clever in finding game that has been killed and left by hunters; I have known them to scent a dead elk several miles off. A wounded animal stands no chance of recovery near one of these bears, for it is hunted down and devoured.

That bears are slow on foot and very awkward is an idea prevalent among people who have never seen nor hunted them. They imagine that a good spry fellow can dodge them very successfully. Let me give a word of advice to those who are thinking of visiting the Rockies to play with the grizzly for the first time. The mouse does not play with the cat, but vice versa; a man in the power of a bear has little or no chance of escape; the bear is as quick as a cat in proportion to his size; what more can be said of the man and the mouse? To hunt bears one needs a 45-60 Winchester, or something as good, if it can be found, and a sharp bowieknife. Armed thus, a man may tackle the grizzly with safety, providing he knows how and when to use his weapon.

After the hunter has sighted his game, he approaches it as closely as possible, keeping on the leeward side. He takes his stand near a tree, or where he will have some means of escape should his first shot fail to do its work. When all is ready, if he is unobserved, he draws a bead on some small object to see how it is with his nerves; if all is right, he takes a good breath, gets his rifle in position and gives a shrill whistle. When the grizzly deigns to raise himself gracefully upon his haunches to take a look at the hunter, a bead is drawn just between the eye and ear; or, if he be facing the hunter squarely, a ball is given him in the center of the throat. If the shot is well directed, one is apt to say, "Well! I don't think it is much of a job to kill a bear." If the animal is only wounded, it is the part of wisdom to climb the tree before it is too late. Many have lost their lives by underrating the strength of a wounded bear. Heavy undergrowths of brush and bushes do not slacken the speed of a thousand-pound grizzly, though it may sadly inconvenience the hunter. I have seen them mash down bushes three inches in diameter while making a charge.

# One Down,
# Another 100 to Go

*Probably the foremost expert on grizzly bears during his day was William H. Wright, who alone killed over one hundred of them. In his book **The Grizzly Bear**, Wright not only offered advice to bear hunters, but also related his findings he learned from studying the animals for many years. The following excerpt was taken from pp. 55-62 of Chapter VI titled "My First Grizzly." This book was originally published by Charles Scribner's Sons in New York; copyright 1909. However, the excerpt was taken from the 1977 reprint by the University of Nebraska Press in Lincoln and London, reproduced from the 1913 edition published by Charles Scribner's Sons in New York.*[23]

Hunting grizzlies requires more quiet, more skill, and more patience than any other kind of hunting, and at the best there will be more disappointments than killings. It took me several years to learn this. I started out with deep-rooted but mistaken notions, and these had to be knocked out of my head by failures, and new ones hammered in by experience, before I understood the grizzly well enough to even occasionally get the best of him.

The best way to hunt them is to study their habits, familiarize yourself with their range, and lie in wait for them near their feeding grounds. Trailing them is more than uncertain. It is, to be sure, a supreme test of woodcraft and endurance, but it must be a good hunter indeed that can take up the trail of an old grizzly and hope to get a shot at him.

I am often asked what is the best gun for grizzlies? My answer is that the best gun is the one the hunter is most used to and hence has the most confidence in; any of the high-power guns are all right and will, if the bullet be well placed, end matters at the first shot. My own first hunting rifle was an old .44 Winchester that I brought from the East. It had already done good service for deer and black bear, but the extractor had become worn, so that it would not always draw the shell unless I put my thumb on it and bore down. This worked satisfactorily as long as I thought to do it, but there were times when I forgot and then there was trouble. The cartridge then had to be cut to pieces before it could be taken out, and it required a pocket-knife and some labor to accomplish the result. For a year or more I had been thinking of getting another gun, but this one was so accurate that I clung to it, and at last it got me into difficulties.

I made a number of trips after grizzlies and I had got sight of several, but they had always seen or heard me first, and when I would see them they were just disappearing over some ridge or into some jungle. So one spring, having made up my mind to go after them and not return until I had one, I started out in May with a few pack-horses and went to the Bitter Root Mountains, which form the dividing line between Montana and Idaho. A friend went along with me to look after the horses, help do the packing and, as he said, skin the bears.

For nearly three months we cruised about this rugged wilderness and enjoyed life to the utmost. We killed plenty of black bears, but up to September had not bagged a grizzly. We found an abundance of their tracks and saw three bears, but they were so wild that we could not get near enough to them for a shot, and twice, when it seemed as if one could not possibly escape, it quietly slipped out of sight at a point I had not calculated upon.

We had, during this time, killed several deer for meat, but though we had seen some elk and one or two moose, we had not shot them since we could not care for so much meat and had no way of carrying the heads. At last, however, having, perforce, given up getting a grizzly, we turned our faces homeward, and I determined to kill an elk and pack out the head and what meat we could.

We therefore left the divide we had been following and struck off to the right to reach a stream of considerable size flowing into the main north fork of the Clearwater River. We had been told by an old miner that there was a large lick on this stream about twenty miles from the trail, and he directed us as to where to leave the ridge, and where, after we struck the stream, we would find the lick.

We followed his directions and arrived at the creek about noon the second day. The stream was very swift and cold, since we were near its source, and it flowed from the snow-banks only a few miles away. We set up our tent, turned the horses out to graze, had a quick lunch, and I, taking my rifle, went to search for the lick, leaving my friend to attend to the camp. The weather was warm, and expecting to return before dark, I did not take my coat. I found the lick where the miner had stated and saw plenty of fresh tracks of elk and deer. There was no timber nearer the spot than across the creek, except some two hundred yards down the stream, but close to the lick, on its lower side, there were some small bushes three or four feet high. Into these, then, I crawled, and finding an old log that had been left there by high water years before, I cut some of the bushes and made a rough bed on the lower side of it.

This was my first experience in watching such a place, and I did not know that, at that time of year, the game did not come every day. Judging from the trails, I took it that they did. They had, without a doubt, been there that morning, and so I curled down and prepared to wait. At first it was not uncomfortable. The sun shone in upon me and I found myself dozing several times. Later, when the sun sank behind the mountains, I began to feel the need of a coat, but still I did not care to give up, and determined to stick it out until I got an elk or it became too dark to see.

Every few minutes I raised my head above the bushes, but nothing seemed to be stirring. Finally it became so cold that my teeth began to chatter and I looked at my watch and made up my mind to stay just five minutes more. When these were gone I raised up, took another look, and seeing nothing in sight, concluded to remain another five. This I did several times. Finally I was nearly frozen and I determined that the next five minutes should be the last and that I would not wait longer for all the elk in the country. When the time was up I took a good look about, but not a living thing could be seen. Then I looked up-stream and, just around the point of the hill and out in the bottom about a hundred yards away, I saw what seemed to me to be the old grizzly I had seen in the cage when I was a boy. He had the same carriage, had the same big forearms and the gait I would know again anywhere as long as I lived. Best of all the brute was headed straight for my log. I ducked back to my bed and waited almost breathless for him to get nearer. I had laid no plans. I simply wanted him to get near enough that there might be no possibility of his escaping. It now seemed certain that my dream was to come true.

I waited for what seemed an unconscionable time, and hearing nothing, began to fear that this bear, like the others, had given me the slip. Finally I raised up to look about and there he was about seventy-five yards away. He had evidently been standing still and had resumed his walk just as I looked up. I did not drop down again, but just stooped so that he would not see me, and waited for him to reach a spot from which he could not get away once I had opened up on him.

When some forty yards off he turned a little to the left so as to avoid some bushes, and this being just what I wanted, I straightened up, aimed carefully just on the point of the shoulder close to the neck, and pulled the trigger.

It never entered my thoughts but that the bear would drop in his tracks. One can, therefore, imagine my surprise when he gave a roar like a mad bull and came my way on the jump. I threw the lever of the rifle forward to pump up another cartridge, but that roar, and the grizzly's tactics, had so surprised me that I forgot to thumb my old Winchester and the shell was left jammed in the breach [sic]. Here was a situation not down on the programme, and it began to look as though I was going to have all the grizzly I wanted. I took one look, dropped the gun, and lit out for the creek, and as I reached it I jumped down the bank, which was about three feet high.

Underneath this bank the dirt had been washed out by the river, leaving a considerable hollow below the roots of the bushes, and when I saw this space I ducked into it, figuring that the bear, if he jumped after me, might jump clear over me and give me a chance to climb back up the bank and make for the timber down the stream. The water was ice cold and I had been nearly frozen before taking to it, but I had no regrets. I waited for what seemed to me a half-hour, but I could hear nothing beyond the rush of the water as it surged around the boulders, and at last it got so cold that I felt that I would as soon be clawed by a bear as frozen to death. So I tried to make my way up-stream, thinking to reach a point above the bend and there get out and go to camp; but the water was so rapid and seemed to me to make so much noise as it struck against my neck, that I was afraid the bear would hear me if he was listening, as I supposed he was. He was behaving so differently from the bears I was accustomed to that I was at a loss how to size him up.

When I found I could not go up the stream, I decided to go down, and by hanging on to the roots, slid noiselessly along for about fifty yards. Then, as I still heard nothing of the bear, I concluded that he had either left the spot or was keeping quiet and watching for me to reappear, and, determined to at least have a look, I got up on my knees, scraped the water out of my shirt, and peered cautiously over the bank. But I was still too low to see over the bushes, so I crawled ashore and raised up enough to look about me. Still I could see no bear. I now began to fear that he had escaped me, instead of I him, and I made up my mind to creep to my gun, cut the cartridge out, and hunt for him.

It makes me laugh to this day when I think of the picture I must have made, first crawling a few feet, then lying still and listening. It was the most conscientious stalking I ever did. When I reached the log and looked for my gun I could, at first, see nothing of it. But, raising my head a bit, I spied it lying where I had thrown it in my haste to get away, and I at once cut the shell out, carefully thumbed it while I pumped in another cartridge, and then, my own man again, I stood up and looked about me.

And the first thing I saw was that terrible bear, as dead as a stone, and not more than twenty feet from where it had stood when I shot it. Moreover, it had turned a complete somersault and was headed the other way. The bullet had entered between the shoulder and the neck, had hit no bones except a rib, and had passed over the heart, severing the large blood-vessels.

Since then I have found that nearly all grizzlies, if shot when they are not aware of the presence of the hunter, will, for some reason, run in the direction from which the wound is received. This, I believe myself, is why so many claim that grizzlies always charge them. The next time my attention was drawn to this I shot across a ravine at a grizzly that had just come out of the bushes. I obtained a side shot at about a hundred and fifty yards, and I made it sitting down, aiming close up to the shoulder. At the crack of the gun the bear turned and charged straight at me, and I could see the brush in the gully sway, and could hear him tearing through it. I ran back a few yards from the edge of the brush so as to get a clear shot at him when he came out of the ravine, and when he emerged I made a movement to shoot. Like a flash he saw me, evidently for the first time, and turned so quickly that, as I was not expecting such a move, I did not have time to fire. He only made a few jumps after seeing me and changing his course, before he fell dead.

Since then I have seen many bears do the same thing, and I am convinced that, although they generally, in these circumstances, run toward one, it is not by any means always with the intention of charging.

# Trailing The Clubfoot Bear

*John Griffin, noted frontier bear hunter in Oregon, wrote about one of his many bear hunting expeditions, in which he pursued a notorious livestock-killing grizzly dubbed the Club Foot Bear. Griffin's dogs, Trailer and Ranger, were as famous as their owner because of their superb tracking and fighting abilities. While hunting the Club Foot Bear, Griffin and another hunter killed four black bears, three bucks, two bull elk and one wolf. Their adventure appeared on pp. 3-7 of the January 1919* **Forest and Stream** *magazine, titled "On The Trail of The Club Foot Bear."*

As this is the first story I have written for *Forest and Stream,* I will just say for the benefit of the readers that these stories are written from actual experiences in hunting big game for over twenty years in the Cascade and Siskiyou Range, when elk, deer, bear, and big timber wolves were roaming the forest practically undisturbed except by myself and dogs. During half of this time I had with me Trailer, who was supposed to be, and no doubt was, one of the best bear and cougar dogs on earth. He often treed two cougar in one day, and three and four bear in a day, a feat that is seldom done by any dog, and this he often did alone, without a helper. These facts are well known by any amount of people in Southern Oregon. As it is claimed that a cougar will kill on an average of fifty deer a year, it will be easy to see that Trailer saved the lives of a great number of deer to say the least.

I never allowed Trailer to run deer, only when wounded; and you can believe me when I tell you that whenever I drew blood, and sent Trailer after a deer,

I was sure to get it. And when Trailer struck a bear or cougar track that was fresh it was nearly a sure shot that it would be climbing a tree in a short time.

In those days I used to go on hunting trips of several days' duration, taking along pack horses, and often had to dry or jerk the meat, as it would be too heavy to pack in fresh. Often I went alone, but at times I was accompanied by some friend who wished to take an outing. On the hunt that I intend telling you about in this story I had with me a man by the name of Templeton, who had never hunted big game before, but who afterwards became quite a hunter and was with me on a number of occasions when we had to handle our Winchesters pretty lively. He was a very excitable man, as you will find out when you read this story. I will call him Temp for short as that is what I always called him in those days.

I had heard of an immense grizzly that was ranging in the region around Mt. Pitt. Occasionally it would take a stampede and get over in the Buck Lake country and kill a few sheep and sometimes a cow, or a big steer, and then hike back to his old stamping-ground north of Four Mile Lake, and would not show up in that locality for quite a while again. The sheep belonged to a man named Reddick, who tried all kinds of plans to trap him, but the old scamp was too foxy to be trapped. He probably had been in a trap before, as he had a crippled foot and made a peculiar track which gave him the name of the Club Foot Bear.

I received a letter from Reddick offering me one hundred dollars if I would come and kill the bear. At the time he wrote Old Club Foot had swooped down and killed a big four year old steer and he wanted me to come at once. So Temp and I started out one morning with our outfit of horses and dogs, Trailer and Ranger, and before noon the next day we landed at Reddick's camp on Buck Lake prairie where the steer had been killed.

That afternoon he went with us and showed us where the steer lay. The bear had not been there for a day or two; however, we could follow his tracks and found he had gone north toward Black Butte. The trail led us through a big burn for three or four miles where it was easy to follow, but after a while we struck the timber and brush. Then it was all off, and we went back to camp.

After holding a consultation with Reddick, we came to the conclusion that he had gone back to his old range. So the next morning we packed up and struck out for Four Mile Lake, at the foot of old Mt. Pitt, and the hunt was on for the trail of the Club Foot Bear. Our route lay through a level timber country for several miles, as we avoided the high hills and swung in by Lake of the Woods, and that night made our camp on Grouse Creek, where the grass was high as a horse's back and huckleberries grew by the bushel. The next day we laid over and took a scout out around the side of old Mt. Pitt, east of camp, but failed to find any sign of the Club Foot Bear.

I told Temp that probably he was taking it easy and it would be three or four days before he would get back to his old range probably. As there were lots of huckleberries on the hill east of camp, we concluded to give the bear a round-up for a few days, and then go on one and make another camp near where the old Club Foot ranged. So next morning we were off bright and early. I took Trailer with me, and took a route nearly northeast from camp, and Temp went nearly east, which would put him on the lower side of the hill from me, as we thought that would be the best thing to do in case Trailer should start a bear. The country was covered with open pine timber, with scattering brush all through it, and was an ideal place for deer. I had not gone more than two miles from camp when out jumped two big bucks within forty steps of me and bounded off through the timber. The Winchester came to my shoulder in double quick time, and catching a bead behind the shoulder of the one that was in the lead, I pumped away and had the satisfaction of seeing him spring high in the air, run a few yards and fall. This disconcerted the other one, and after running a short distance he stopped to look back. This was easy, as it was only about seventy-five yards. I caught the bead and fired, and down he went with a bullet a little high behind the shoulder. One was a sixpronged buck and the other nine on one and ten on the other. I dressed them, hung them up as best I could and started on and had gone no more than half a mile when Trailer struck a bear track that was fresh, and away he went, yelping at every jump. I followed slowly along, thinking perhaps he would overtake and tree it near where Temp was, as it went in that direction.

I could hear him going, going, for quite a while, and finally he passed over a ridge and out of hearing. I stood still and listened a while, and then started on down in that direction. All of a sudden I heard him again, this time coming back towards me. I got up on a log and waited. I could hear him coming nearer, nearer, all the time, and in a minute I saw the bear coming just as straight as a line right to me. When he got up to within one hundred yards, Trailer had got near enough so that he was in sight of him. Now he quit barking and came on like the wind to overtake him. It was a pretty sight to see them come. The big black fellow lumbering along straight to his doom, as he was close enough now so that I could fill him full of bullets before it would be possible for him to get away especially with a dog behind him that had never failed to get his game, and was gaining on him at every jump. On he came and as he got closer I held my gun on him ready to pull the trigger if he ever made a turn. But he did not know that I was there and just as he got up and was pausing within ten steps of me Trailer overtook him, and, making a lunge, caught him by the ham and give [sic] him a yank. Around he went, and struck viciously at Trailer, but the dog let go and got out of the way. The bear turned to go, and Trailer came full tilt to get him again. Just then I fired and he sunk right down in his tracks. Trailer was coming so fast that he lit on top of the bear's back, and grabbing hold, commenced to shake at him, but old B[r]uin was done for and the scrap was over.

But another was coming which I little dreamed of when I was dressing this bear, which did not take long. I picked up my gun and started down the slope thinking that perhaps I would run across Temp down in that direction. In this I was not mistaken, for I had not gone more than a mile when, bang, went a gun off to my right. I threw up the horn which I always carried and gave it a toot, and I heard Temp hollering for me to come. I sent Trailer and followed up as fast as I could, and when I got there I found Trailer and Temp at the foot of a big fir; upon looking up the tree I saw two cub bears, one about half way up, and the other away near the top. He told me that he had shot at the old one and missed, and she had run off leaving the cubs. I asked him what kind of bear it was, and he said she was a big brown one. He was awfully excited and was in for shooting them out without any ceremony; but I cautioned him not to be in a hurry, for I knew that in his present excitement he couldn't hit a barn door. So he waited a while but finally got so eager to shoot that I told him to go ahead.

But I warned him—"Let me tell you something, Temp. If you make a bad shot on them cubs and cause one of them to squall we will have a fight on our hands just as sure. For the old one will come just as sure as she hears."

He said he didn't care; he wanted to kill them. He had never killed a bear in his life.

"All right," I said. "Go to it."

He pulled up to shoot, and I saw he was shaking like a leaf, so I said, "Hold on, Temp. Wait until you get over that." But he paid no attention and bang, went his gun, and the cub commenced to squall. I called to him to look out, and ran over to a tree about thirty steps away, and stopped with my gun ready. We did not have long to wait, for she came sure enough, and like a cyclone. Trailer met her just as she dashed into the opening, straight for Temp. She passed the dog, but he was too quick for her, and sprang at her, seized her by the ham, swinging her clear around, and let go to get out of her way. Just then I shot, striking her in the shoulder, breaking it. By this time Temp had got turned around and got his gun into action, putting a bullet through her body. Trailer kept working on her hams, and we kept pouring the bullets into her until she rolled over. Temp now had only four cartridges left, and commenced to shoot at the cubs, but missed every time. I was going to shoot them out then, but he begged me to let him have my gun, as he had never killed a bear. So I gave him my gun, and after shooting eight times he brought them down at last and was happy.

We now had four bear and two bucks on our hands, so we had a job of packing in the next morning. During this time Temp killed a five point buck and it took all that day to get them in and skin them and two days more to get the meat jerked so we could handle it. Then we sacked it and hung it in trees where it would be safe until we came back, for we were on the trail of the Club Foot Bear, and were bound to give him a round before we quit.

We broke camp the next morning and landed at Four Mile Lake at noon. There we met with two hunters who told us they had just come through from the head of Red Blanket and had seen elk signs near Summit Springs as they came along, but being short on provisions, they did not stop to hunt them up. This set Temp wild as he had never seen an elk, and as this was in the vicinity of where the Club Foot Bear ranged, it was just what we were looking for. So after dinner we set out, and after traveling a few hours we came to a nice place where the grass was high as the backs of our horses, and nice running water; an ideal place to camp, under a large spreading maple tree. We spent the balance of the day fixing up the camp, as we did not know how long we would be there; for we were in a country where big game abounded, and where seldom a white man had ever trod. So we intended to make the most of it while we were there.

I told Temp we would start out in the morning and go in different directions to size up the country and get an idea of how the ground lay; for it might be of great benefit to us in case we had to follow a bear that would not climb. So next morning I struck out through the timber in a northwest direction and Temp bore off about north or northeast.

I hiked along through a level timbered country for perhaps two miles, when suddenly I came to a small prairie of perhaps four or five acres, and on the opposite side the hills showed up and the timber was scattering, with thick patches of buck horn brush. I had seen a number of deer tracks as I came along, but had seen no game that was worth shooting at, so I made up my mind that

I would go across the prairie and take up the mountain on the other side. So I started out and as soon as I got in the open ground I began to see elk tracks. Before I got to the other side of the opening I saw great holes pawed out where they had been lying and big trails leading out into the timber. I followed one of these trails for about two hundred yards, when all at once I saw where a big band of elk had come in to the trail and gone on up the hill. It was no trouble to follow them, so I hurried on after them, feeling sure they were making for some high ground on account of flies, which were very bad in the open prairie. I could tell by the tracks that they were taking it easy, as now and then they would nearly all be out of the trail feeding on browse; but it would not be long until they were back in the trail, and going again. Finally the trail led me out of the timber on to a ridge that was covered with low buckhorn brush. I followed up this ridge for probably a mile, then they turned down around the side of the hill and crossed a deep gulch and on over the next ridge. As I approached the top I was very cautious, and stood and looked a long time, but there was not an elk anywhere to be seen.

I now went on across this gulch and climbed up to the top of the next ridge. Here they had scattered around some and worked along up the ridge for a short distance and turned down again. In front of me the brush was high so I could not see across on the opposite side, so I kept on up for sixty or seventy-five yards to where the short buck brush was, and, upon looking over, there on the opposite side just above the edge [of] the thick brush stood an immense bull elk, not over one hundred yards from where I stood, and not another elk in sight.

Say, believe me, that was a sight that made my heart leap for joy, for in those days I was a dead shot and did not have a thought that he could get away. He held his head straight up with his big horns back astride of his shoulders, and they were big ones too. If you will believe me, there were seven on one and eight on the other. I thought to myself, as I thought a great many times when my dogs were fighting a bear, how many there were who would give a thousand dollars to stand where I stood and have the chance that I did to kill that elk—it would have been worth the money.

It was a big mark, but I drew my bead carefully behind the shoulder and pulled. At the crack of the gun he lunged forward. The Winchester cracked again and another bullet went crashing through him; but it was not really necessary. The first had done its work, passing square through the butt of the heart, and he reeled and fell, never to rise again. But down below the brush was thrashing and crashing, and the whole band was tearing down the canyon toward the timber at a tremendous rate.

I ran down a few yards and got sight of one of the hind ones, and bringing the gun to my shoulder I caught a bead and fired. The elk was out of sight in little or no time, but when I went down I found blood. I followed up and after a while it left the bunch and took off to itself, and I concluded to go back and take care of the one I had. It was a big job to take his entrails out and get him in shape, but I got through with [him] in due time and started to camp. It was a long hike and the sun was down before I got half way. I was hurrying to get to camp when I suddenly heard the long lonesome howl of a big gray wolf. I listened a minute and not hearing an answering howl I hurried on again. In a few minutes I heard him again and far back. I was sure now that he was following me, as my shoes had gotten bloody from the elk. I began to study what to do, for I knew if he followed along like that others might fall in, and it would place me in a dangerous position, as the only chance would be to climb. I was thinking fast as I hiked along when I happened to look out to one side and saw a large tree that had fallen, and the point lay the way I was going. I hurried and went a little past the top, then ran back and walked back to the butt of the tree, which lay high off from the grounded [sic] and waited.

I looked to see that the cartridges were in the barrel and, dropping the muzzle of the gun, I stood ready with my thumb on the lock and my finger on the trigger. I did not have to wait long for he soon came in sight, a long, lanky fellow, trotting slowly along, and every few yards would stop and stick his nose in the air and give a long mournful howl, then he would listen, but no answer came. I was listening too. Then on he would come. I could have shot him, but did not want to take any chances on missing him, for he had to pass in thirty steps if he stuck to my tracks. Closer and closer he came, and when within fifty yards I could hardly resist the temptation to shoot, but smothered it and waited. Now he was in forty yards and stopped. He did not howl this time, but stood a few seconds and listened, then came on. Just as he got opposite me he stopped and sitting back on his haunches gave one of the most dismal, hair-raising howls I believe I ever heard. While his nose was in the air I brought the gun up and drew a fine bead on his head; and just as he started up, while the sound was still reverberating through the woods, I pressed the trigger. The bullet caught him just at the butt of the ear and over he went with feet straight in the air for a few seconds, then commenced to kick around lively for a while and straightened out dead.

I went over and took a look at him, and lit out for camp, arriving a little bit after dark, tired and hungry. Temp had been there quite a while and had supper ready, but was very much excited. He had run across the track of the Club Foot Bear and was so eager to tell me all about it that [he] did not think to ask me if I had killed anything. So while we ate he told me how he had been traveling through the woods and came to a prairie covered with high grass, and near the middle he ran onto a spring or hole of water, and there had been a bear there only a short time before, as the water was still muddy. When he went on out he left a trail of water and mud for a short distance, and then Temp could see his track plain, and it was sure enough the track of old Club Foot. Right there and then Temp turned back as he had no desire to come in contact with a grizzly, for he had heard they were ferocious beasts and would fight at the drop of a hat. I told him this was a fact as I had tried them, but that is another story.

He was right in for starting out the next morning. But I told him we couldn't do that as I had another job on hand. He wanted to know what it was, and was astonished when I told him about killing the elk and wolf and wounding another elk. I told him we would take the horses and dogs and go to where the big buck [bull] was, and leave the horses and take the track of the wounded elk and follow it up. This suited Temp fine, for he stood as good a chance to get a shot in as I did.

In the morning we saddled up, taking five head of horses and arrived about nine o'clock where the big elk lay. We tied our horses up and took up the trail of the elk. When the dogs smelled the blood they were eager to go, but I wasn't ready yet. I had Temp put a string on Ranger and keep him back, then I let Trailer slow track the elk for a long way across gulches and over ridges and finally we came to where he had been lying down, but was up and gone. We followed to the top of a ridge and upon looking down discovered that the gulch was very brushy, so I decided to let the dogs go; but before I did so I sent Temp back down the ridge with orders to shoot like the dickens if it came his way. I waited so as to give him plenty of time to get there, then I slipped the rope off Ranger's neck and told them to go. And away they went down into the head of the gulch, and I heard the brush begin to crash, and away went the elk down the mountain side, and both dogs right after it, yelping at every jump.

Temp heard them coming and was on the alert. He did not have long to wait as the elk soon came by on the opposite side of the gulch, and old Temp began to string bullets after it, and as luck would have it hit it once so that the dogs soon overtook it and then the fight commenced.

I ran down the hill as fast as I could and overtaking Temp we hurried on down and soon came in sight. And such a sight! To see two of the finest trained bear dogs, almost, on earth, fighting a wounded elk. It was simply wonderful the way those dogs would get around and seize it by the ham, and get out of the way of its hoofs. I will not try to describe it, but will say that after we had stood and watched them quite a while I told Temp to watch his chance and put a bullet behind its shoulder and end it, which he did, and the fight was over.

I sent Temp back after the horses while I skinned it and got it ready to pack. It was only a two year old and we packed it on two horses. When we got to the other one it took us quite a while to get it ready, but we finally got loaded and racked [sic] out for camp. We did not bother about the wolf and arrived at camp just about dark, hungry as wolves, and happy as clams.

Temp wanted to start right out the next morning after old Club Foot, but I said, "No, we are going to cut this meat up and salt it tomorrow and let the dogs rest up, and the next day we will go." I told Temp if he thought we were going to have a picnic when the dogs got after old Club Foot he was badly mistaken, as I was sure he would put up a great fight and we would have to get a good ready on. Well, we stayed in camp all next day. Got the meat all cut up and salted, and the next morning filled the Winchesters with cartridges, our pack sacks with grub and were off.

It took about an hour to get to the prairie where Temp had seen the sign and upon going out to the wallow we found he had been back. Trailer and Ranger took up the scent and were off pell mell after him, and the chase was on; out across the prairie and up the hill on the other side and over the hill and out of hearing. We hiked out for high ground, and when we got up on top we could hear them away down below us, and we could tell by the sound of their voices that they had overtaken him, and the fight was raging fast and furious. I told Temp to go straight down the ridge until he got entirely below them and wait. Temp lit out on a run, and after waiting a while I struck out and in probably twenty minutes I was close enough to shoot, but could not see them on account of brush. I kept moving up closer and closer when all at once I heard old Club Foot go crashing through the brush down the hill toward the creek. I ran now as fast as I could in hopes of getting to see them as they went up the hill on the opposite side, and sure enough up he came after stopping at the water a few minutes, with both dogs going after him savagely. First one would catch him by the ham, but as he swung round to deliver a blow the dog would let go and get out of the way, and the other dog would do the same. Now was the time for me to get in my work, and the Winchester began to crack. Once, twice, three times, down he went, and the dogs piled in on him. But he was up in no time and scattered them right and left. Just then I heard Temp's gun begin to crack and down the hill came bear, dogs and all, straight toward me. I began to pour the lead into him, as it was evident now that he was going to try to get me. I called to Temp to give it to him, and as he was above him he could do good execution. But down in the creek he came, and as he climbed the bank I commenced to put bullets into his breast, and he rolled back and began to chew the bushes, and soon rolled over dead.

Temp was literally wild with delight and hugged first one dog and then the other, declaring over and over that they were the best on earth. All we could do now was to take the hide and head of the bear, which we proceeded to do, leaving the feet on the hide to show that it was really the Club Foot Bear.

This wound up our hunt, and I will say to the reader if you wish to see some of the teeth out of the mouth of old Club Foot, and also the horns of the elk, come to my house near Kerby in Southern Oregon, and I will show them to you.

# Hunting Grizzlies With Bows

*Famous archers Dr. Saxton Pope and Arthur Young contracted to kill grizzlies in Yellowstone National Park for museum specimens for the California Academy of Sciences. Since grizzlies were already extinct in California, the men had to pursue silvertips in Wyoming. However, for sporting challenge, Pope and Young decided to hunt the bears with bows and arrows instead of firearms. They didn't go after those begging bears hanging around the campgrounds and garbage cans; they headed for the high country in the spring where the bears were wary. Both men were proficient with their handmade weapons and successfully secured the required specimens. Dr. Pope wrote of their Yellowstone experience for the October 1920* **Forest and Stream***. His article titled "Hunting Grizzly With The Bow" appeared on pp. 533-536; 565-568.*

The California Academy of Sciences has in its museum in Golden Gate Park some of the finest habitat animal groups in the world. But the California grizzly bear is not among them. He is extinct. It was decided, therefore, to secure specimens of the Wyoming grizzly, the "silver tip," a species whose range extended westward to the Sierra Nevada mountains, and which in size and general characteristics closely resembles the California great bears.

Permit was obtained from Washington [D.C.] to take specimens for museum purposes in Yellowstone National Park. We offered our services as professional bear slayers with the object of delivering those specimens to the Academy, incidentally to kill these beasts with the bow and arrow, and strange to say, our offer was accepted.

As a sporting proposition, a great many people will say shooting bear in Yellowstone Park is rather a tame pastime. These people think that bear are all over the park, playing around the hotel garbage pile and pillaging camps. This is true to some extent, but it is also a fact that there are 8,000 square miles in the Park. The highest portion of the Rocky Mountains is also there, and the time the pelts of the bears are in best condition is before the park opens to tourists, when the bears are in the mountains.

Don't imagine, however, that because a bear comes up and eats out of your hand near a camp he may not take your arm off if he gets a chance. In fact, William Wright, whose book [The Grizzly Bear] on the grizzly is the best authority we have, states that these same bear that frequent the hotel dumps, when beyond the confines of civilization, are just as wary and just as dangerous as any bear in Alaska, or any other wild area.

During the past few years no less than four people have been badly mauled or killed by Grizzlies in Yellowstone Park. One man was seized while asleep and dragged out of his tent, being bitten through the arm and in the chest. At another time, a bear entered the tent of Ned Frost, the famous Yellowstone guide, and attacked a sleeping man. Frost, hearing his cry, sat up in bed and hurled his pillow at the bear, which immediately turned upon him, seized him by the thighs and dragged him from the tent. The bear carried Frost fifty yards or more, shaking him so violently from side to side, that he was thrown entirely out of his sleeping bag. While the bear still worried the bag, Frost escaped in a thicket of jack pines. Although his thighs were badly bitten and the flesh torn, he managed to climb a tree, while friends came to his rescue, driving off an enormous grizzly.

Jack Walsh,[24] a teamster, sleeping under his freight wagon at Cold Springs, was attacked by a large grizzly. His arm was practically bitten off at the shoulder and his abdomen was ripped open. Walsh died of blood poison a few days later.

The question may be asked, "Well, if you have to shoot a grizzly bear, why worry him with a bow and arrow; why not take a gun and shoot him like a man?" Most people can only picture to themselves the little willow bow they used to shoot when children, and they imagine that if any animal were accidentally hit with an arrow his death might possibly result from nervous prostration and insomnia, but hardly from any damage done by the arrow.

In a way, killing a grizzly with a bow is an experiment in anthropology, to learn exactly what can be done with this primitive old weapon. Secondly, it is a much more sportsmanlike thing to use a bow to kill any animal than a gun.

Every big game hunter will tell you that there is no danger and very little excitement in killing a bear at a hundred or two hundred yards with a modern high power rifle.

For some years back, Arthur Young and I have hunted with the bow and arrow. We have killed ground squirrels, quail, duck, rabbits, skunks, wild cats, mountain lions, deer and black bear, with this noble old weapon. We have found it more humane to shoot an animal with an arrow than with a gun; he never gets away when wounded severely. It is a fairer contest of strength and cunning when one pits his own nerve and vigor against that of his quarry. The bow as a game weapon makes for fair sport, careful hunting and stands on its past record for honorable service.

Our bows we make ourselves of Oregon yew. They are 5 feet 8 inches long and pull about 75 pounds. Our arrows are birch dowels, 3/8 of an inch in diameter, a cloth yard long, or 28 inches, feathered with the pinions of the turkey and tipped with tempered steel broad heads. The extreme range of such a bow is about three hundred yards, but our hunting range is from twenty to one hundred yards. It takes a great deal of practice to attain any proficiency in shooting the bow, but it is worth while. You must earn your right to hunt.

Having obtained the services of Ned Frost, of Cody, Wyoming, as our guide, a man who knows the grizzly thoroughly and has killed over three hundred himself, we landed in Yellowstone late in May while the snow was still deep on the ground. The Canadian jay and the woodchuck seemed to be the only animal life left in the Park, the winter having been the worst in thirty years. Contrary to all past experiences, there were no bear around the camps. Our hunt started near the Canyon; the Sour Creek region, Sulpher Mountain, Alum Creek, all good bear grounds in the past, were explored. There were but few tracks in evidence, mostly those of black bear.

At the end of three or four days, we located with a glass five grizzlies at the head of Alum Creek, a sow, three large two-year-olds and an old male. But they were too far off and it was too late in the day to attempt getting them.

Arthur Young and I were armed only with our trusty bows, a dozen arrows apiece, and hunting knives. In camp, of course, we had a second bow and a box of twelve dozen broad heads, the finest collection of archery tackle since the battle of Crecy. Ned Frost carried his modern destroyer, a 35 automatic rifle. This was to be used only in case of emergencies. We knew that the bow could not stop the mad rush of a bear. This embarrassing position of being charged by a grizzly had entered fully into our considerations. We knew we could kill him because he is only flesh and blood anyway, and the arrow can slay any beast that lives. But what he does between the time he is hit and the time he dies of hemorrhage opens up a wide field for conjecture and deliberation.

Perhaps you doubt whether an arrow can pierce the thick hide of a bear, and it does seem strange that a missile whose velocity is only one hundred and fifty feet a second, and whose weight is only an ounce and a quarter, can possibly do what a bullet often fails in doing. We have found that with a blunt arrow we can shoot through an inch of pine board, and with steel arrow heads three inches long by one and a quarter wide, sharpened like daggers, we can shoot feathers and all clean through any animal in America.

Broadly speaking, a bullet kills by shock, an arrow by hemorrhage. The bullet shatters bone, tears out large areas of tissue, destroys the brain and nerve centers and breaks down the animal's power of motion. Hemorrhage is a secondary phenomenon and a bullet often passes over large blood vessels without enough injury to cause bleeding.

An arrow cannot crash into the heavy brain pan of a large animal. It cannot fracture large bones, although it has no difficulty in severing ribs. Any place it enters it cuts like a knife. It opens up every artery and vein that lies in its way; the hemorrhage is tremendous. A bullet mangles the tissue, leaving a badly damaged but clotted area. The arrow wound is clean and its incision liberates few tissue juices to cause a clot; technically speaking, it liberates little *thrombo kynase,* or clotting ferment.

The ability of the modern hunter to break down his quarry has led him to abandon other methods of defence, when attacked. The aborigine used stealth, the ambush, the protected position, the spear, and fire, to frustrate the beasts' counter attack. We considered all this, but decided that for the sake of safety we would sacrifice our sporting honor and resort to the gun when the tables were turned.

Frost was told, however, that such an exigency must be considered a failure in our eyes. We hoped to get one or two bears clean and compromise on the rest.

The next time we saw our grizzlies on Alum Creek we made out at a distance of three miles a large female with three half grown cubs, large two-year-olds. They were digging roots on a half uncovered side hill. The morning was early, the wind was right, and we decided to attack immediately. Frost led off at a fast pace; we stuck close to his heels, bow and quiver at our sides.

Down the river banks, through the swales, up the ravines, deep into the timber, a long way round we circled. At last we emerged on a sheltered point a quarter of a mile down wind from our bear. There they were, feeding slowly up the valley, working toward the snow line for a forenoon rest.

We rested. Young and I put the finishing touches on the edge of our arrow heads with a file. I took off my socks and dried them in the sun. The bear went leisurely up on a snow bank and lay down near the crest of the hill. We could approach them with the wind in our favor, and shoot over the ridge not more than fifty yards away from them. Ned gave the order to advance—Indian file— and we crept upon our first grizzly.

Well, what does one think of when he goes out to shoot his first big bear? For months he plans and dreams and fits himself for the test, and now it is at hand. Can you hit him? What will he do? He may charge, then what next? Do you feel excited, or have you that intellectual detachment so essential for success? As for me, I felt happy and confident.

Perhaps Young was thinking of camp hot cakes. I do not know. Soon we reached the top of the hill. Right over the top were four fine bears. Ned took out his green silk pocket handkerchief and floated it, to test the direction of the wind. Yes, everything was O.K. We drew three good arrows apiece from our quivers, and nocked one on the string. All ready, crouch low and advance without a sound. Now we stop, stick the two extra arrows in the ground, take off our hats and rise up. There they are, four intermingled hearth rugs on the snow, not twenty-five yards distant from us.

I pick out the far one because he looks good to me, and glancing out of the corner of my eye signal to Young to shoot. We draw our powerful bows to the full arc and let two deadly arrows fly. My bear rears up, an arrow planted deep in his shoulder. There is a roar like dinner-time in a menagerie. Quickly I nock another arrow. The beasts are milling around together, biting, pawing, mad with pain and surprise.

I single out my boy pinioned with an arrow. He has thrown himself on his mother in his rage. I shoot and miss him clean,—too much action. I nock again. One large bear stands out in the circling, roaring bunch. She is biting, cuffing, rearing on her hind legs, the blood runs from her mouth and nostrils in frothy streams. Young's arrow is deep in her chest. I drive a shaft into her, below her foreleg.

The confusion and bellowing increase, and as I draw a fourth arrow from my quiver, I glance up in time to see the old female's hair rise on her back; she steadies herself in her wild hurtling and glares straight at us for the first time. "Now," I say to myself, "she will charge." And she does. Quick as thought she bounds towards us. Then a gun goes off at my elbow. The bear is literally knocked head over heels backward and falls over and over, in backward somersaults down the steep snow bank. There she gathers herself and attempts to charge again, but her right fore leg fails her. Like a flash two arrows fly at her and disappear through her heaving sides. She wilts, and as we draw to shoot again, she sprawls upon the ground, a convulsed, quivering mass of fur and muscle. She is dead.

The two-year-olds had dispersed at the boom of the gun. We saw one making off at a gallop three hundred yards away. The snow bank before us was vacant.

We went down to view the remains. Young had three arrows in the old bear,— one deep in her neck, the point of emerging back of the shoulder. He shot that as she charged. His first shot struck anterior to the shoulder and entered her chest, cutting her left lung from top to bottom. His third arrow pierced her thorax through and through and lay on the ground with only the feathers in the wound.

My first arrow cut her below the diaphragm, penetrating through the stomach and liver, severing her gall ducts and portal vein; my second arrow had passed completely through her abdomen and lay on the ground beside her. It had cut her intestines in a dozen places and opened large branches of the mesenteric artery.

The bullet from Frost's rifle had entered at the right shoulder, fractured the right humerus, blown a hole an inch in diameter through the chest wall, opened up a jagged hole in the trachea and dissipated its energy in the lung. No wound of exit was found, the soft nose copper-jacketed bullet having apparently gone to pieces after striking the bone.

Anatomically speaking, it did the necessary thing, knocked the bear down and crippled her, but it was not an immediately mortal wound. We had her killed, but she didn't know it. She certainly would have been right on us in another two seconds. The outcome of this hypothetical encounter I leave to those with vivid imaginations. We hearby express our gratitude to Ned Frost.

Now we had to rush off and get the camera and the rest of the boys. We had my brother, G.D. Pope and Judge Hulbert of Detroit along with us to see the sport and to give dignity to the party. Inadvertently they had gone in other fields in quest of bear.

Ned tramped off across bogs, streams and hills, and within an hour we all got together to view the wreckage. The skinning and autopsy having been completed, we looked around for our other bear. There was his trail, with here and there a blood spot, and there was our little friend huddled up on the hill side, my arrow nestled to his breast.

One broken arrow, with its head deep in the thorax, pulmonary artery wounds, and a dead bear. He had traveled about two hundred yards. Half grown as he was he would have made an ugly antagonist for any man.

His mother was a fine, mature lady of the old school, showing by her teeth and other lineaments her age and respectability. In autumn she would have weighed four or five hundred pounds. We weighed her in instalments and found her to register three hundred and five pounds. The juvenile *ursus* weighed one hundred and thirty-five. So we measured them, gathered their bones for the museum, shouldered their hides and turned homeward.

That night Ned Frost said: "Boys, when you proposed shooting grizzly with the bow I thought it a fine sporting proposition, but I had my doubts about the success. Now I know that you can shoot through and kill the biggest grizzly in Wyoming."

Our instructions on leaving California had been to secure a large male,—*Ursus Horribilis-Imperator,*— a good representative female and two or three cubs. The female we had shot filled the requirements, but the two-year-old was at the high school age, and was hardly cute enough to be admired.

So we set out to get some of this year's vintage in small bear. Ordinarily, there is no difficulty in coming in contact with bear in Yellowstone; in fact, it is more common to try to keep them from eating at the same table with the family, but not a single bear, black, brown, or silver-tipped, called upon us.

We traveled all over the beautiful Park, from Mammoth to the Lake. We hunted over every well known bear district, Tower Falls, Mt. Washburn, Dunraven Pass, (under 25 feet of snow), Antelope Creek, Specimen Ridge, Buffalo Pens, Steamboat Point, Cub Creek, Pelican Meadows, and kept the rangers busy looking out for bear. From eight to fifteen hours a day we hunted. We raked the side hills and valleys with our glasses. But bear were as scarce as hens' teeth. We saw some few tracks, but nothing compared with those seen in other years.

We began to have a sneaking idea that the bear had all been killed off. We knew they had been a pest to campers, wrecking automobiles and chasing visitors up trees. We suspected the Park authorities of quiet extermination.

Then the elk began to pour back into the Park; singly, in couples, in droves, they returned lean and scraggy. A few began to drop their calves. Then we began to see bear signs. The grizzly follow the elk, and after they come out of hibernation and get their fill of green grass, they naturally take to elk calves. Occasionally, they include the mother on the menu.

We also began following the elk. We watched at bait. We sat up nights and days at a time, seeing only a few unfavorable specimens, and these were as wild and wary as deer. We found the mosquitoes more deadly than bear. We tracked big worthy old boys round in circles, and had various frustrated encounters with she bears and cubs.

They say that the Indians avoided Yellowstone, thinking it a land of evil spirits. In our wanderings, however, we picked up on Steamboat Point a beautiful red chert arrow head, undoubtedly shot by an Indian at an elk years before Columbus burst in upon these good people. In Hayden Valley we found an obsidian spear head,—another sign that the Indian knew good hunting grounds.

But no Indian was ever half so anxious to meet grizzly as we were. Our party began to disintegrate. My brother and the judge had to return to Detroit. A week or so later Ned Frost and the cook had to go back to Cody. Before they left us, however, they packed Young and me with our bows and arrows, bed rolls, a tarp and a couple of boxes of grub upon the head of Cascade Creek.

We had received word from the rangers that there was an old bear traveling between Tower Falls and the Canyon, killing elk around Dunraven Pass. Frost, Young and I scouted over this area and found his tracks—eleven inches long. We saw that he used certain fixed runways in going up and down canyons.

Then Frost gave us some parting advice, left us his 35 automatic, and went home.

We soon found plenty of bear signs, and the bear found us. We began to lay plans to ambush the enemy. In the meantime, they captured our supply trains, getting everything that was not enclosed in tin.

The moon was nearly full. We built a blind on the up-hill side of a steep bear trail, some forty yards off. With fallen trees and a rocky eminence between us and the trail, we utilized a natural point of vantage. Here we proposed to stand our ground.

So we watched early and late. The first night bear passed us, dim shadows shuffling by. We distinguished an old female and three yellow cubs, but did not deem her suitable for our purpose. And then the big fellow came along.

Our first view of him was from a distant trail at dusk. He strode down the mountain side like an impetuous monarch,—magnificent! As large as a horse and having that grand, supple strength given to no other predatory animal. He was dark brown, with just a suggestion of rust and silver on his coat.

The next night we heard him pass. He was chasing a large black bear and treed him back in the timber a couple of hundred yards. Such growls and roars one seldom hears. As he ran, the big fellow made a noise like an elephant, his claws clattered on the rocks, and the ground shook beneath us. We shifted the automatic into a more handy position, and filed a fresh meat cutting edge on our arrows. It is humiliating to admit we had the automatic along, but experiments are sometimes costly.

Next night we decided to get one of the little cubs if we could. The old sow came along. I was detailed to pot the infant. Choosing the one that nearly resembled our previous specimen, I let fly a broad head and struck the little fellow in the ribs. Without a sound the whole flock of bears disappeared. Then we heard a plaintive bawl; we saw the little fellow fall against an obstructing log and lie still. His mother came back several times, gazed at him sadly, then softly disappeared.

Daybreak came. We picked up our little two-year-old,—one hundred and twenty-pounds,—deprived him of his coat, long bones and skull, and performed the autopsy. The arrow had cut a rib, gone through his left lung, shaved a piece off the left ventricle of the heart, severed the coronary artery and imbedded itself in the sternum. His chest was full of blood. We packed him home and had delicious bear steaks for supper.

Next day it rained all day, and evening came clear and fresh with the fragrance of the ground and woods. The moon was full and beautiful, so we went to the blind early.

One morning, before this, we had crossed the trail of a fine female and three cubs. She winded us; the cubs squeaked and the solicitous mother whirled about, rose up on her tiptoes, and advanced in our direction. We held still as death while she looked, sniffed and growled, and then reluctantly went off, turning back from time to time. She was wonderful,—so imperious and strong, eager to fight for her own. We heaved a sigh of relief as she would have been a most dangerous animal to encounter.

This night she came; dim shadows, soft velvet foot-falls, and there she was, family and all. I whispered to Young, "Get the cubs." We waited till they were 40 yards off, then drove the arrows at them. There was a squeal, a jumble of dark figures, a roar from the mother, and they all came tumbling toward us.

Just then the big fellow appeared on the scene. We had five bears in sight. Turning her head from side to side, trying to find her point of danger, half suspecting the big bear, our dame came toward us. I whispered to Young, "Shoot the big fellow." At the same time I drew to the head and drove an arrow at the oncoming female. A dull soft thud; I saw her rear; she yelled with rage; the yell turned to a groan; she staggered sidewise twenty yards and fell on her side; rose again breathing hard, and slowly sank down. She was dead in less than twenty seconds.

The cubs had run up hill past us. One came back and sat up at his mother's head a moment, then disappeared in the dark forever.

All this time the big male was up stage, ramping back and forth with mixed emotions. Young shot three arrows at him; I let fly two; then off he packed. We missed him! We missed him! And only fifty or sixty yards. It is true he was in deep shadow, but we should have landed! He was as big as a house!

We were deep in despondency. We waited an hour or two but the bear procession had passed, so we got out of our blind and started skinning the female. She was a beautiful bear, weighing about 500 pounds, and no fat. Her coat was like that of her lord and master, dark brown, a little curly and rusted, here and there the silver shining through.

My arrow had cut a rib or two, penetrated her lung and entered the right ventricle of the heart. The hole in the thick heart wall would admit two fingers. Her thorax was occupied by one huge blood clot.

We finished skinning at daybreak, then went off in search of the cubs. We found one under a log a hundred yards distant. An arrow was lodged in his head and he had breathed his last. Look as we would, we could not find the other. Young's arrow was missing, so we assumed that only a skin wound had been inflicted and the little fellow would recover.

Just for curiosity and to pick up our arrows, we went over the ground where the monster passed. One arrow was gone. This gave us hope, so we journeyed on. There was blood! We trailed him. There were spatters of blood, as if sprayed on the dewy grass. Here was a pool of blood, and more pools, clots! Then began the tracking. He had wandered in and out of the little clumps of jack pines. We followed, cautiously, peering under the limbs, watching piles of fallen timber, as he had wandered round in circles.

Then we picked up the anterior half of Young's arrow, deep stained with wet blood. More pools of blood! Then we picked up the feathered end of the arrow. It had been drawn out by his teeth. Now the bleeding stopped, with only an occasional spatter.

The trail then entered the open forest, where we could track him only as he crossed fallen logs, and left his bloody smear. Here he had dug shallow holes in the earth and lain down. Four of these were close together. He must have been badly hurt!

Then his trail disappeared. We went over every inch of the hard ground. We circled; we went back; we went in big circles; we cross-cut every trail that left the country. We searched up and down the creek, but he was gone! For five hours we hunted in vain.

We sat down, ate a little food, took a nap, and woke up to discuss the problem. He must be near. It is impossible for a bear to live that has lost so much blood. We viewed the last wallow he made. There it was in the soft loam beneath a big fir. No tracks left the area. He must have gone down in the ground, or straight up in the air. We looked once more along the rim rock. There was a patch of blood! Below was a trodden trail. We clambered down, and there he lay, great hulk that he was, on a rock straddled across a tree! He was as dead as Caesar, cold and stiff! His rugged coat was matted with blood. Well back in his chest the arrow wound showed clear. I measured him;—twenty-six inches of bear had been pierced through and through. One arrow killed him. He was tremendous. His great wide head, his worn and glistening teeth, his massive arms, his vast, ponderous feet and long curved claws,—all were there. He was a wonderful beast. It seemed incredible. I thumped Young on the scapula. "My boy! I congratulate you!"

We started to skin our quarry. It was a stupendous job, as he weighed one thousand pounds and was on a steep canyon side, with no bottom. But by means of ropes and braces, by flashlight, acetylene lamp, candle and fire light, by using up all our knives and by assiduous industry for nine straight hours we finished him, after a fashion.

In the middle of the night we stopped long enough to broil some grizzly cub steaks and open up a can of beans. We literally hacked the hide off that brute, and to decapitate him, dissect out his feet, shave off and clean his leg bones was a Herculean task.

At last another day came. We gathered our trophies together and staggered somehow to a trail; packed our camp stuff, hired a machine to get us out of Yellowstone, and sallied forth dripping with salt brine and bear grease, dead for sleep. We were weary almost to intoxication, but the possessors of the two finest bears in Wyoming.

We left our hides with a ranger to flesh and re-salt, and so the day ended.

Now, as I write this on the train speeding back to California, it all seems very tame and sweet, but as the cigarette ads. say: "It satisfies."

As for the gun, we forgot all about it, until the time we shipped it back to Frost. Not a shot fired!

The California Academy of Sciences will have a handsome representative group of *Ursus horribilis imperator[.]*    We have the extremely gratifying feeling that we have killed five of the finest grizzly bear in Wyoming,—killed them fair and clean with the bow and arrow.

# A Different Approach To Bear Hunting

$M$any unusual methods were employed to rid the West of bears during the frontier days. Since bears were undesirable animals, they were killed by any means available. Shooting bears was considered the most practical and safe way, but sometimes firearms were not handy. Besides, if a bear could be killed without a gun, the bear slayer was not only considered a brave hero but an ingenious one as well. Tales of bear slayings in this chapter all involve pursuing or attacking bruin in some strange fashion. Roping, bombing, kicking, spearing, chopping, knifing, you name it, people did it to bruin. One man who harbored a grudge against grizzlies crawled into a bear's den to administer a dose of chloroform; he then dragged the drugged bear out of its lair to photograph it before shooting it.

## Hatchet Makes A Dandy Bear Killer

*An old timer told of an exciting encounter with a grizzly in which a brave old man killed a charging bear with a hatchet, while a group of terrified young men watched in utter amazement. The narrator of the story was one of the scared young men, and after he witnessed this hand-to-hand battle concluded that a hatchet was the only sure bear killer. His account appeared December 2, 1902, in the* **Anaconda Standard**.

"The proper weapon to hunt bear with is a hatchet." The speaker, an ex-army officer, was one of a little group of men who, in a cozy corner of a down-town hotel, were discussing President [Theodore] Roosevelt's bear-hunting excursion. "I mean by that," he continued, "the hatchet is the main reliance of the real, 'sure nuff' bear hunter—the man who tackles Bruin single-handed and alone, and who never declines such combat.

"When I was out on the plains in the '70s there were lots of these typical professional hunters left. Buffaloes then abounded in enormous herds from Montana to Northern Kansas. Elk [,] deer, antelope, foxes, wolves and coyotes were as plentiful as prairie chicken. All these came as grist to the professional hunter's mill. The first consideration was, of course, the pelt; the carcass was only secondary. In this the American hunter differed from the Indian, because the latter was as careful to save every pound of flesh of his quarry as the great packing houses of to-day are in their slaughter of cattle. An experienced plainsman could always tell an American hunter's work from that of an Indian in looking over the remains of a buffalo found newly slaughtered out on the prairie.

"But to return to our muttons, or rather our bears, as the Frenchman says. The grizzly bear is a dear lover of fresh meat. In this he differs from the black bear, after which the president went hunting, or the cinnamon or brown bear of the northwest. The latter two species will not eat flesh so long as they can obtain anything else. But Mr. Grizzly is carnivorous by choice. He will slouch along after a professional buffalo or deer hunter and glut himself on the remains which the nimrod leaves. Unlike his relatives, the black and cinnamon bears, Mr. Grizzly will stand up and fight on almost any occasion. He is not a "quitter" in any sense.

"It requires strategy to get a fight out of a black or cinnamon bear, but all your hunter needs to do is to locate grizzly if he is looking for trouble. What will happen afterward all depends on how much pluck the hunter has and how much he knows about the business of hunting grizzlies.

"Of course, it is one thing to chase a little black bear down with a pack of hounds and then shoot him from some convenient cover when he has been about fagged out. But I would like to see a pack of hounds tackle a grizzly. What would be left of the hounds after the preliminary encounter would not be sufficient to establish a kennel of the most modest pretensions. And as for gunshot wounds, brother grizzly regards the average rifle shot with about the same indifference as a target on a rifle range. Even if a hunter should be lucky enough to get a heart shot through him with an ordinary sized rifle bullet, the chances are that grizzly would go right on doing business for the next half or three-quarters of an hour. And what a grizzly bear can do at close quarters in 30 minutes would fill newspaper columns if related in detail. Indeed, a rifle is almost a useless weapon for a man on foot against a grizzly bear unless there are trees handy and the hunter is a good climber; for Mr. Grizzly, like the elephant and the brick, cannot climb a tree.

"I was up at what is now Glendive, Mont., in the spring of 1881, with a detachment of the fifth infantry, keeping the Cheyennes from swooping down on the men who were building the Yellowstone division of the Northern Pacific railroad—that is the division between Bismarck, on the Missouri river, to Glendive, on the Yellowstone. The road runs through the bad lands, an extremely rough, broken country, and at that time abounding in game of all sorts, as well as hostile Indians. Across the Yellowstone from where our camp was pitched there was scarcely a day when one could not see herds of buffaloes, strung out in long, black lines against the horizon, coming and going to water. There were not so many on the south side of the river, but occasionally a small band would wander almost into our camp.

"But to get back to the bear subject once more. One day the signal service man who had established a station on the military telegraph line on the north side of the Yellowstone came staggering into camp. He had rowed across the river at a heart-breaking stroke, and announced that there was a grizzly bear thumping around on the other side of the river. He had nothing but a Springfield carbine, he said, and his shack was not a very well-built affair, so he would be greatly obliged if a few well-armed, determined men who gloried in the chase would go back with him and finish up Mr. Bruin. There was no trouble to find volunteers. Indeed, the whole detachment would have been almost willing to swim the Yellowstone in order to get a chance at the expected sport. But Capt. Hargous, who was in command, knew a few things about grizzlies, and knew that the average soldier would simply be in the way in a bout with one of the big animals. So the captain selected three or four of his old men who were noted for their skill as hunters, and, with one or two of the officers, put out in boats for the other side.

"When they landed they found an old chap named Kenna sitting on the shore with his rifle across his knees and smoking his pipe very unconcernedly. Now this man Kenna was a most unique character. He was from somewhere in New England, and had drifted out west in the early frontier days, and had become a professional hunter. He always reminded me of some of J. Fennimore Cooper's characters. His vernacular was a combination of terse, odd, epigrammatic Yankee sayings mixed with the slang of the plains, with an occasional sentence of the Sioux thrown in, and all flavored with a liberal amount of profanity. He was a dead shot. He had a Sharp's rifle of .45 caliber that carried a cartridge with 105 grains of powder. He told me he had often lain down on the ground to leeway of a herd of buffaloes, so far away that they would not notice the report of his rifle, and knock down 20 or 30 animals before they would become alarmed and stampede. I know of his selling 1,700 buffalo pelts to a Missouri river steam-boat captain as a result of one fall's hunt.

"His outfit consisted of two Red River half-breed ponies, a burro, a rifle, a hatchet, a hunting knife, a frying pan and a coffee pot. The burro carried his grub stake and housekeeping outfit, together with his ammunition. He said a burro could always be trusted with one's most precious belongings. The burro never stampedes or strays off. For one thing he is too lazy and too much of a philosopher to engage in any such senseless performance, and besides he prefers the society of mankind to that of the lower animals. He will stand around a camp fire of an evening and gaze into its light with soulful eyes as if he were contemplating some abstruse question of ethics. And when the flapjacks are passed around he will gladly accept all that is offered him. Bits of bacon rind or anything else of the scant refuse from a plainsman's humble fare are accepted with a palpable if silent pleasure.

["]But once more, and finally, to get back to the bear. Kenna said he had struck the bear's trail about an hour before and had followed him up a coolie [sic] or sort of gorge, and found that the 'dratted cuss' had gone 'way up' under a pile of shelving rock, 'whar nobody could get him 'less as how sumbody went up thar to the fur eand and smoked the critter aout'. Kenna also explained that the bear had stuffed himself on the remains of a buffalo carcass which the old hunter had killed and would probably go to sleep for a day or two. After a short council of war it was decided to make an advance on Mr. Bruin, to boldly beard him in his den, as it were, to get him out by any means, fair or foul, and then finish his business outside. Kenna was authorized to direct the attack. A two miles' walk brought us to the bear's lair. Kenna directed two of the soldiers to go up and remove some of the rocks at the head of the canyon, and if possible start a fire and cover it so the smoke would be sucked back through the hole where the bear was hiding.

"The rest of us were to take station at the mouth of the opening and shoot the bear as he came out. The men got some grass and buffalo chips and soon had a volume of smoke pouring down the gorge that would rival one of Washington's soft-coal burning chimneys. The smokers then started to join us so as to get a chance for a shot. Before they got half way to us one of them spied Mr. Grizzly through a chink in the rocks making tracks for the opening. 'Look out! here he comes,' shouted the man. The rest of us, lined up on one side of the entrance with our rifles at a ready, and felt our hearts beat faster at the momentarily expected appearance of the bear.

"In less time than it takes to tell it, out came the bear at a lumbering gallop, puffing and snorting and occasionally passing his great paws over his head as if to claw out the smoke, which was stifling him. We opened fire on him as soon as he got clear of the opening, and I don't think anybody missed him. Except for turning his head and snapping angrily at the places where the bullets stung him he seemed to pay no attention to us at all. He had galloped off 50 yards perhaps before he seemed to realize what had happened. Meantime all hands had kept up a fusillade after him.

"Then bruin seemed to get the smoke out of his eyes and to 'tumble to the racket.' He made a short turn and started back for us. Now, it would be wholly idle to attempt to describe my own feelings under the circumstances. An over-powering wish that I was somewhere else, far away, took possession of me, and this was accentuated by the knowledge of the hopelessness of that wish. The others all acknowledged a similar feeling afterward. We all began to back away, but kept up a straggling fire at the bear.

"Old man Kenna was the nearest to the maddened animal, and it seemed only a few clumsy lunges before he was on the old hunter. Then Kenna did a thing which almost paralyzed the rest of us with astonishment. Instead of trying to run or get out of the bear's way, he threw down his rifle, pulled out the hatchet he always carried in his belt, and, raising it aloft, brought it down with all his might on the bear's head as the latter closed in on him with tremendous arms. Bear and hunter went down in a heap together. We all ran up, not knowing which was most hurt, but determined to save the old man if possible. But our efforts were unnecessary. Kenna squeezed out from under the huge beast, which was gasping his last, with a hatchet blade three inches long buried to the eye in his brain. Kenna was considerably shaken up, and the bear had managed to give him one swipe across the shoulder, which made a right ugly wound. But other-wise Kenna was smiling and intact.

"Well, to shorten a long story, the bear weighed 600 pounds, we found, by the commissary's steelyards. Capt. Hargous gave Kenna $25 for the pelt. I forgot how many wounds we counted on the bear, but none of them were fatal, and if old man Kenna had not been there with his hatchet I probably would not be here to-night."

# Bear Slaying Indian Style

*The following November 13, 1890* **Anaconda** *Standard news article reported an exciting encounter between an Alaskan Indian and a big black bear on Admiralty Island, in which a hunting knife was used to check the bear's charge. Besides relating this adventure, the article also described how some Alaskan Indians killed bears with spears.*

Both the courage and the brute strength of the Alaska Indian is phenomenal, as was recently displayed in one of many instances that have come under notice, in which a powerful native in Alaska came out victorious in a hand-to-hand struggle with a large and ferocious black bear, says a Juneau correspondent of the Denver *News*.

The Indian (Jim) with one companion, an Indian boy about sixteen years of age, were out bear hunting on Admirality Island, southeast of Juneau, when the dogs ran a large black bear out of the woods, when Jim, taking hasty aim, fired, slightly wounding the bear in the neck. The sting of the wound enraged the brute, and turning upon his assailants, he reached Jim with a few bounds, and together the Indian and the bear went rolling over the ground in a life and death struggle.

In the meantime the boy had taken to his heels out of harm's way, and, supposing that his luckless companion was clawed into strings, hastened to camp with the news. Immediately upon perceiving the bear coming, Jim whipped out his ponderous hunting knife, and the first affectionate hug of the bear was reciprocated on the part of Jim by thrusting this murderous weapon to the hilt in the brute's side. In the struggle Jim managed to keep a firm hold of the handle of the knife, never withdrawing it, but using all his strength to push the blade in deeper, until finally it reached a vital part, when the bear relaxed his grip and fell over in the throes of death. Jim, mangled and torn and bleeding from a dozen ugly wounds, lay exhausted upon the ground for some time, but finally, with a superhuman effort, he struggled to his feet, skinned his prize and throwing the skin over his shoulder, started for camp, meeting his companions on the way, who were coming to gather up his scattered remains for cremation.

Upon examination Jim found that he had come out of the fight with two broken ribs, a deep gash in the thigh and a horrible and dangerous wound from the brute's teeth, starting in on the left side of the nose, leaving the lower eyelid hung by a small particle of skin, running back under the left temple, where a deep hole was made, and ending down under the jaw, where the lower jawbone was broken. As fearful as this last wound is, the hero of this battle is now doing well and occasionally utters a sort of contempt at the cowardly action of his companion in running away and leaving him to the mercy of an enraged bear. Jim will keep the skin as a memento of the hardest fought battle of his life.

To the bear hunter the wilds of Alaska offer a paradise that can be found in no other country on the globe, as is attested by the yearly shipment of choice hides, which reach an enormous amount. The most choice of them are the black bear, which roam the woods by hundreds, and prime skins of which bring from $25 up to as high as $100 each in the market. During the excursion season, tourists from all parts of the globe make a thriving trade for Alaska merchants in the bear skin line. There are five distinct species of bear in Alaska—the black, brown or cinnamon and cross which inhabit all portions of southeastern Alaska and the upper portion of the Yukon country. Further north in the St. Elias alps, is the home of the St. Elias grizzly, which in size, ferocity and color much resembles the grizzlies of the Sierra Nevadas, and still further north along the lower reaches of the Yukon and the ice fields of the Arctic ocean is the white polar bear. As brave and sk[i]llful in hunting bear as the Alaska Indian is, he seldom hunts the St. Elias grizzly both for the reason that there is but little profit in the hides, and the great size and ferocity of the beast makes hunting them a most hazardous undertaking. Their mode, however, of killing them by shooting into them from a heavily-charged smooth-bore musket a heavy slug if either lead, copper or iron, then awaiting their charge, which never fails to follow the shot, with a long, heavy and strongly made spear, resting the butt of the weapon on the ground and planting one foot firmly against it. The point of the spear rests at angle to pierce the bear in the breast, and the bear's own weight, when it strikes the spear in its mad charge, is calculated to drive the weapon through him or pierce him deep enough to cause death. As will be readily seen, if at this critical moment the hunter's courage should fail him, or by a miscalculation the spear failed to impale the charging beast, the hunter would be knocked senseless and immediately torn into shreds. This mode of bear hunting may have its advantages, but there is none but the Alaska Indian who has the nerve and courage to try the experiment.

# An Arboreal Battle

*Eph.* Beaseley climbed a tree to escape a bear but soon found out that bruin could climb too. An aboreal battle between bruin and Beaseley pursued. This close encounter was related in the February 25, 1891 **Bozeman Chronicle**, titled "Beaseley and The Bear—How Eph. Beaseley Confronted a Big Grizzle Bear and Disposed of Him." Despite this heading, the bear was probably either a young grizzly or a black bear since it could climb.

All old-timers of Bozeman [Montana] remember Eph. Beaseley. He was a long, lank, hungry, naturally tired individual reared in the ague swamps of Arkan—saw. Beaseley was very fond of hunting and the number of bears he had slaughtered, to hear him tell it around some grocery store fire, was simply appal[l]ing. While Beaseley seemed indisposed to exert himself to any considerable extent on the family wood pile, the enthusiasm and hard work he would put in killing bear and other "varmints," led those who were not acquainted with his fondness for repose, to believe that he worked harder than a third-class postmaster under this administration.

Beaseley had one bear story which he frequently related, and which his friends say is truer than poetry. It seems that Beaseley did slaughter a bear once and in the following manner: Grub becoming scarce he and a friend went to the mountains early in the fall to kill grouse. One was armed with a muzzle-loading shot-gun and the other had an army rifle of the vintage of '62. While hunting, they flushed a bear which set Beaseley in motion in fine shape. Becoming winded Beaseley sought a tree which was leaning. This he mounted with wonderful rapidity, but the bear ascended it with the same agility and before Beaseley could get to the top the bear had him by the leg. With wonderful presence of mind Beaseley swung from a top most limb, at the same time swinging the bear from his perch. All efforts, however, to shake off the bear, who hung with a tenacious grip to Beaseley's breetches [sic] was unavoiding. Finally Beaseley yelled to his companion to shoot, but when he went to do so he found that the caps for the shot gun had been forgotten and the balls for the rifle was [sic] some four sizes too large. And so the bear and Beaseley hung, until finally Beasclcy with the free foot gave the bear a prodigious kick and broke his neck. Beaseley then dropped to the ground, skinned the bear and came home to forever relate instances of his prowness [sic] with bears big and small.

# | Baker's Bear Exterminator

*A former Butte, Montana, shoe salesman invented probably the most unusual method of killing bears in the West by devising deadly "honey rolls." These contraptions, called "Baker's bear exterminators," were certainly effective. Shortly after the introduction of these "infernal machines" the bear population in the Madison valley dropped dramatically. "Baker's Bear Exterminator," written by Dan R. Conway, appeared as an article in the June 30, 1927 Rocky Moun tain Husbandman, and despite the many typographical errors it is an interesting account.*

Many old-timers in Montana today can recall that unique character, J.H. Baker, who for more than 25 years operated a boot and shoe store in Butte, maintaining such a place on Park street.

J.H. Baker crossed the great divide in Idaho several years ago, and of him many an interesting story is told. After severing his connections with the retail business in Butte, he became associated with a number of friends in an organization known as the Granite Mountain company for the purpose of breeding "drivers" and thoroughbred cattle in the Madison river valley. This company had its home ranch near where Moose creek leaves the mountains. In that section is to be found some of the state's best land, and the Granite Mountain company acquired a vast area. Having obtained first water rights, they were assured of continuous good crops of forage and grain. It was a well-financed enterprise, and everything about the home ranch was the very best that money could buy. There was, however, one serious drawback to successful operation—an interference which sorely perplexed the operators. This drawback had its cause in the close proximity of the ranch to the mountains, which rendered the place altogether too convenietn [sic] for one of the big silvertips inhabiting that section of the main range of the Rockies. This denizen of the wilderness was wont to frequently lay tribute to a calf or a colt, either killing it and feasting upon the carcass where it had been found, or carrying it into the mountains with him.

To the rear of where the ranch was seated, are some of the wildest mountains in Montana. Many of the great cliffs arose almost perpendicular and abounded in caves and ledges. In these, numerous bears and mountain lions had their lairs.

On innumerable occasions, the herders who stood watch and [sic] tried to kill this old bruin, or his companions; but the beast proved altogether too wary.

Finally b[e]ar traps were resorted to; but this attempt as well, proved vain. Hundreds of hunters had tracked the animals but met with no better success than did the trapper; and the score or more of mon[s]trous predatory beasts haunting the caves and ledges up the canyons of Moose, Squaw and Wolf creeks seemed to live charmed lives.

The situation had reached a stage bordering on disastter [sic], when, one night, the bunkhouse conversation recalled a story of the fondness of bears for honey. Someone suggester [sic] that poisoned honey be scattered around and over the carcass of some recently killed horses as a means which might serve as an effectual means of exterminating the marauders. This suggestion gave Baker an idea; and with daylight of the following morning he was in a light wagon and on his way to the valley where, at an Ennis store, he telegraphed to Virginia City for 5,000 giant [p]owder caps and 200 gallons of honey. This came out on the stage the next morning, and he lost no time in returning to the ranch with his load of "bear exterminator" (as he was pleased to call his purchase.)

Bake rtraveled [sic] late that night as the road was long and the road rocky and rough. He was obliged at different points to proceed very slowly lest some sudden jar explode his cargo.

Arrived at the ranch, he hurriedly prepared for this experiment. Taking a number of burlap sacks, he spread them thick with honey, inserting at intervals, caps, and rolling up the entire mass into a large ball. He smeared honey on the outside of a dozen of these infernal machines; and the following morning, shortly after breakfast, with one of his men, took these out to a hill in the direction of Wolf creek, where they were planted around the carcass of a horse which had been dead for about a month, and hed [sic] previously been "worried" by a hungry bear.

Baker's scheme was a decided success. All of the men on the ranch spent two or three sleepless nights lying awake to hear the roar of the explosion which would declare in no uncertain tones that a member of the tribe of bruin had quit the world by the route of "the infernal machine." At first, no reports came.

For some reason or other the bears seemed to shun that horse meat as though it were a plague. However, while the boys were all in the bunkhouse discussing where would be the best point to plant the honey-combed bombs, there came a sudden dull roar from the vicinity of Wolf creek. It resembled the sudden detonation of a blast down deep under ground, and for a moment all thought it was the sound of thunder visiting the valley considerably out of season. But Baker knew what it was and entering the bunkhouse, he ordered one of the hands to saddle up his horse and accompany him as soon as possible, for he was sure that the bear trap had worked. Another man was directed to hitch up a team to one of the wagons and fol[l]ow, the plan being to bring bruin's carcass into camp.

Yes, the "honey rolls" had worked all right. When Baker and his man arrived upon the scene, they discovered one of the largest of grizzlies ever seen, as dead as the probverbial [sic] mackerel, and with his entire head blown off.

After taisting [sic] the horse meat, the bear discovered the "honey rolls." They looked good to old bruin, and they taisted [sic] much better. First he licked all the honeycoating from the burlap, and then discovered that there was more sweetness inside. He drove his sharp teeth through the burlap, and in the course of a few bites, his teeth closed down upon one of the giant caps. In an instant there was a flash, and in another instant the earth faded away before the bear.

Baker was elated that his scheme had worked so successfully, and the carcass was loaded and taken to the camp in great triumph. Thereafter the manufacture of "honey rolls" became a popular diversion among the ranch hands; and before another week had passed, the infernal machines could be found spotted around the carcasses of every dead animal within a mile or two in every direction. They proved more than a success, and before the season had passed a score of bears of all conditions, ages and sex had paid the full penatly [sic] for their crimes and depredations. There were no failures, except one. That was at a time when some inexperienced hand had made a "honey roll" to[o] small. It was "bolted bodily" by a young yearling cub, and he carried half a dozen giant caps off into the mountain[s] with him one day just as a bunch of cowpunchers were passing the spot where the bait had been planted. The boys were anxious for some sport and they decided to try and capture the cub alive. They were punchers from a neighboring ranch and were ignorant of the "honey roll bear exterminators". Consequently they were entirely unprepared for the surprise which followed their little diversion with the cub bear.

One of the boys who was a good roper, ran up to within easy throwing distance, and there his horse balked, as horses always do when they "smell bear." The puncher made a throw in the direection [sic] of the bear and succeeded in dropping the rope around its neck and over the forelegs. It was, however impossible for him to get his horse close enough to the quarry to permit him to take his "turn" on the saddle horn and he was obliged to turn the rope loose after the frantic, fleeing cub. Freed from restraint, the young bear ambled down the mountain side as fast as he could, resembling a big, furry ball rolling over and over. The further he went the more momentum he gained, until suddenly, just as he came close to a cliff, the loose end of the rope became entangled in some projecting rock. The bear was brought to a sudden standstill. Before the boys had time to realize what had happened, they saw the cub hurled over the side of the cliff which they knew was a sheer drop of about 150 feet. "Dear bear," said the foreman. "Now, Nosey, you'll get your rope back."

Scarcely ha dthese [sic] worws [sic] been spoken when there came a dull roar from the bottom of the cliff; and a few seconds later, the punchers, fully a quarteqr [sic] of a mile away, were deluged by a shower of fur and warm flesh. They realized that the bear had "been loaded," and the fall had exploded the giant caps which young bruin had been carrying internally.

Nesy [sic] got his rope all right—two or three strands of it— and then the punchers wended their way to Granite mountain camp. There they related their experience with the cub and asked for an explanation. This was explained by the proprietor, who stated that [the bear] the boys had chased was the only one that had got any distance from the carcass of the dead horse before the "honey rolls" did their stuff.

It is needless to state that thereafter the punchers who rode the Upper Madison range, gave every bear they met a wide berth. They could never be sure that any of the bears had not been feasting on "honey rolls"; and one experience with the effectiveness of "Baker's Bear Exterminator" was all they desired. No one would shoot at a bear unless the animal happened to be at least half a mile away.

Finally, however, the reign of terror among the bears of the upper Madison came to an end. It soon developed that there was scarcely a bear to be found in the entire country. All of those that had ever ventured down into the flats had been killed by the "honey rolls," and the few remaining told their furry friends of the awful contrivance that had sent their fellows to Bear Heaven in a blaze of glory, and without their heads. So, it soon developed that bears could not be induced by any means to come within 10 miles of the place; and the horses and cattle, ever afterward, grazed in perfect peace and comfort.

# Canned Black Bear

*A Butte, Montana, hunter killed a black bear under unusual circumstances. His friends claimed he took unfair advantage of the bruin, but the hunter asserted that he did the bear a favor—and perhaps he did. It is difficult to determine what one would do if faced with a similar situation. The incident was related in the December 2, 1937* **Rocky Mountain Husbandman.**

Friends of P.M. "Max" Sheriger, Butte [Montana] sportsman, claim he recently took unfair advantage of a 200-pound bruin by shooting the animal while it had its head stuck in a cream can. Sheriger, it is said, admitted the story was true, adding that he was taking no chances, cream can or no cream can. "I was doing the bear a favor," he stated.

The bear was killed while Sheriger and six Butte friends were enjoying an Armistice day holiday at the summer home of James T. Finlen Sr., located on Rock creek, 35 miles out of Missoula [Montana].

According to a description, or "construction of the crime," by members of the party, the bear had been foraging around a ranger's lookout station the night before. He broke into the place and made a complete shambles of it. On leaving he is believed to have found the five-gallon cream can which has been used all summer as a garbage receptacle. It evidently contained something that appealed to the nostrils of Mr. Bear and he went in after it. When he tried to back out the can came with him. He rambled about all that night, trying to get his head out of the can.

Leaving camp at noon Armistice day Sheriger thought he noticed a can moving about in the air. He was about 85 yards distant, but after some intense peering through the bushes he realized what it was. Not wanting to get too close, he let fly with his 30-40 rifle, but only nicked the bear. Stung by the steel-jacketed bullet, the bear let out a muffled roar and reared up on his hind legs and began thrashing about, the cream can waving crazily with every movement of his head. Again Sheriger let go, this time with excellent aim, sending a bullet through bruin's heart and dropping him.

Returning to camp, Sheriger told his pals. He left the bear in the woods, his head still tightly encased in a cream can. His story was regarded as some sort of a "Paul Bunyan" and Sheriger was invited to "take a drink" and he would "probably be all right in a minute."

Sheriger forced one of the gang to return with him the next day, taking along a pack horse to bring in the bear. But Sheriger was jobbed, being given a horse that was sure to go completely wild when led near a dead bear. Sheriger got around this by blindfolding the horse while the two men hoisted bruin into a tree fork. Then they backed the blindfolded horse under the carcass and lowered the beardown [sic] into the saddle.

"I tied the bear tightly to the saddle, " said Sheriger, "feeling that if the horse bolted when he realized what he had on his back he would have to lose the saddle before he could lose the bear."

The horse quieted down and was led, without incident, back to camp.

Another member of the party—Jim McGrath—shot a large buck deer. Returning to Butte, the big game hunters had evidence aplenty of their prowess, with the bear on one fender and the buck on the other.

In the party in addition to Sheriger and McGrath, were Dr. Pat Kane, Dr. John Kane, Tom Kelly, Dr. J.L. Donald and James Finlen Jr., who was host to the group.

# For Love of A Crumpled-Horn Cow

*One man's personal vendetta against grizzly bears helped exterminate the species from the Bitterroot Mountains, where they once freely roamed. George Solleder's feeling toward grizzlies exemplified the attitude of his day. However, he had more experience with grizzlies than the average man and killed well over one hundred of them. Besides taking pleasure in killing grizzlies, he teased, photographed and chloroformed them. His stunts were recorded in the* **Anaconda Standard,** *July 18, 1909.*

Some wise men hunt grizzly bears with rapid-fire repeating rifles, others pursue the sport in brigades after taking out life insurance policies; most men conclude that they have not lost any grizzlies, and there is one man in Darby, Ravalli county [Montana], whose favorite stunt is to chloroform grizzlies and then take their photographs at the only moment in their whole lives when they are looking comparatively pleasant. So far he has no competitors in this exhilarating diversion, which he insists is a positive cure for all neurasthenic disorders, provided the chloroform hunter proves a good sprinter when the bear wakes from the lethargy of the anesthetic.

George W. Solleder has killed more grizzlies than any other hunter in the United States. It is a record of which he is pardonably proud, but which he modestly excuses by saying that grizzly shooting is a habit which he contracted in his youth and for which he can find no cure. In addition to this there is a reason, as will be seen. Some men's sporting appetites are satiated with bags of quail and woodcock; others need moose or elk to stir the Nimrod pulse; but it takes half a ton of ferocious, maddened bear flesh in action to drive the Kansas ennui out of Solleder's blue eyes and to make his blood tingle with the lust of a battle really worth while. When necessary, of course, he will shoot dear [sic] and other game that drifts in his way; that is part of his business as a guide. But he does it in a perfunctory, apologetic sort of way as all in the day's work. His long suit is grizzlies, and in addition to a very unladylike disposition, the Bitter Root grizzly has an unstable temper barbed like a buzzsaw. [Theodore] Roosevelt says so in his essays on hunting big game, and Solleder admits that the colonel knows what he is talking about. Take it from Solleder—the Bitter Root grizzly is the only big game really worth the bother, and he has hunted them and shot them, and studied them, photographed them, teased them, chloroformed them and fought them hand to paw in a number of close calls that would have turned the hair of the ordinary hunter to snowy whiteness.

The origin of his long feud with the grizzlies is in substance like this: when, in the early '80s, Solleder located his homestead in the Bitter Root valley, Darby was practically a virgin wilderness. The creek abounded in trout unsophisticated and big, deer and elk pastured in the rich meadows and the grizzlies were undisputed monarchs of the great mountains. Over the long trail to the Bitter Root, Solleder and his young wife came on their honeymoon in a modernized prairie schooner. Their route lay through the Big Hole valley along the trail over which Chief Joseph and his Nez Perces had fled some three or four years before, and tied to the tail board of the great wagon, Angelique, the pet cow of Solleder and his wife, came also into the land of promise, which for Angelique was to be one of tragedy.

Angelique was a crumpled-horned mooley of more than ordinary intelligence, with great soulful eyes, in which slept the peaceful calm of Buddha. She possessed a gentle, well-bred, ladylike disposition, which endeared her to Solleder and his wife, but the soul of Angelique was soon to be called to even greener pastures than the rich meadows of the Bitter Root. One morning when Solleder arose with the sun for the morning milking he found that Angelique had broken loose in the night and wandered away. He followed the trail, and after a short search found her dead under a large tree, her back broken by the sledge-hammer blow of a grizzly's paw. Solleder, true to his type, is a man of few words and of suppressed emotions, but then and there he vowed that as votive offerings to the shade of Angelique, hectacombs of grizzlies should be sacrifi[c]ed. And he has kept his word. Both he and his neighbors have lost count of the number of his grizzly victims, but they are well up in the hundreds, and the ghost of Angelique chews the spiritual cud of satisfaction in Elysian pastures. She has had her revenge.

The memorial sacrifice began that very night. Solleder literally loaded for bear "Old-Meat-in-the-Pot" (he clings to the old style of a pet and expressive name for his rifle), and when the dusk of evening was settling went to the tree where the mangled body of the dead cow remained and climbed up into the lower branches and waited. He knew that the grizzly would return to the feast it had left, and he did not have long to wait. But let Solleder tell the story of his initial revenge in his own way as he told it to me:

"The sun was just dipping over the Bitter Roots when I settled myself on a big limb over the dead cow. It was a rather risky roost and it wasn't any too high for safety, but I wasn't going to take any chances of missing that there bear. No, sir. Well, there wasn't a breath of air stirring—not a whisper of a breeze— and it was so—quiet and lonesome you could hear yourself think. I figured it out that that bear wouldn't be around until it was plumb dark, and I was getting kinder sore on my job, and my legs were getting to cramp and my pants were developing bed sores, when I heard a stick snap back of me, and right then and there I knew it was time for Solleder to sit up and take notice. I heard the bear coming back of me, but I couldn't turn to see around the tree. A moment later he come out of the bushes and the sight of him in the half dark made me gasp. He was just simply a whale of a bear. I had been prepared to see a good-sized varmint, for I had studied the tracks around the dead cow but this cuss was the biggest bear I ever laid eyes on, and that is going some, I tell you.

"The bear went straight to the dead cow, and without a moment's hesitation jumped on it as if starving and began to tear and mangle it horribly. For a few moments, kinder fascinated, I watched the huge bulk of the beast beneath me as it ravenously gorged itself on cowflesh. Then I whistled. In an instant the bear was alert; its big head went up as it sniffed the air for danger. He was right under me, but still he wasn't in a position for a sure shot, and I jarred loose another whistle. That did the business for Mr. Grizzly and—near for me also, for that last whistle put the bear next in a hurry, and with a snort of rage at being disturbed at its meal, he rose up on his hind legs and I could see his eyes blazing with green fire. It was all quick as a flash of lightning and I had no time to think of home and mother, for when that bear got through raising himself his nose was on a level with the limb on which I was perched, and I caught a glimpse of an enormous great paw like a ham sweeping in my direction; then I fired.

"The next instant I was flying through the air as if shot out of a cannon—the bear had hit that branch a blow like a trip hammer, just missing me. My gun fell a short distance away from me, and you bet I scrambled for it, although every bone and muscle in my body seemed sore and bruised. I jammed another shell in and waited for some sign of what that bear was going to do next. It was all quiet—nothing doing in the sign line. It was getting pretty dark by this time and I could scarcely make out the body of the cow under the tree. After waiting a few minutes I crept cautiously towards the tree, and there stretched out over the carcass of the cow was the huge bulk of still quivering dead bear, with the top of its head literally blowed off. The muzzle of my rifle had been so close that the hair was scorched.

"That was the biggest bear I ever saw or ever killed. Next day when we dressed it for the hide one-quarter weighed 250 pounds. We couldn't eat it, for the flesh was so old and tough it smelled like carrion. But that was one bear that wouldn't ever again slaughter an innocent, harmless, pet cow. No, sir."

But while this little affair really started Solleder's long feud with the Bitter Root grizzlies, it was not his first bear killing. His initial performance in this line took place while he was yet a tenderfoot, and while on his way to establish his home in the Bitter Root. It was in the summer of 1881, and Solleder was on his honeymoon, which consisted in moving his Lares and Penates from Deer Lodge [Montana] over the old Indian trail through the Big Hole valley to the wild apex of the Bitter Root valley. Previous to this, Solleder had been guard at the territorial penitentiary at Deer Lodge, a position which he won by defeating Warden Hugh O'Neill, a crack shot, in a pistol tournament, so it may be seen that Solleder brought to his bear feud a trained and practiced eye. While serving as guard at the prison, Solleder saved enough money to send for his sweetheart back in Missouri. They were married soon after her arrival in the fall of 1880, and the next September, with a capital of about $300 in cash and about a million dollars' worth of hope, optimism and fearlessness, he and his bride started on the long trail across the mountains with two companions, who were likewise in search of the land of honey and promise.

About eight miles from the Big Hole battlefield, where Chief Joseph and General Gibbon had their bloody encounter, Solleder shot his first grizzly. The bear was seen crossing the "Long Prairie," a treeless stretch on Trail creek, soon after camp had been broken. Solleder's sporting blood began to burn for bear. He loaded his gun, an old .50-caliber needle, and, with a young setter dog, started in pursuit. His companions had lost no bears, and manifested little interest in the proceedings, save to inject into the conversation some derisive and scurrilous remarks about a she grizzly's ravenous appetite for tenderfeet and bird dogs. But it did not faze Solleder nor the dog.

A light snow had fallen during the night and the bear's trail was easily followed into the brush beyond the open prairie. The first glance at the huge tracks told Solleder that it was no baby he was after, but he was not wise then in bear lore, and probably it would have made no difference if he had been. The pursuit led over the hills on the south, across the ridge and down into a creek bottom. Here, squatted on her haunches in the willows that bordered the creek, the bear waited, and Solleder almost ran into her before he saw her. He took quick aim and let drive, and over went the bear in a heap. But before Solleder could reload, the bear was up again, and, with a roar of rage, charged him. Solleder was a tenderfoot then, and he frankly confesses that he was both surprised and pained at this radical change of front.

"The bear was within 30 feet of me," said Solleder, in recounting the adventure, "coming like a house afire, before I recovered myself. Then I sicked the pup on her, and that pup waded in like a veteran, except in discretion. For the fool pup was a tenderfoot like myself, and just didn't know how. He went for that bear as he would for a cat, and then that great paw made a half circle swing, and the next moment there was 15 pounds of surprised and yelping pup hurtling through the air like a skyrocket. When that pup landed, some 25 feet away, it let a mortified yip out of itself and then, with its tail plastered between its legs and with a pained and humiliated expression upon its face, which never wore off, it started for home, just hitting the high places up the ridge, mournfully looking back over its shoulder. That was sure a humiliated and depressed pup. But I reckon that that blamed pup just about saved my life. During the diversion the dog furnished Old Lady Grizz, I had reloaded, and I fired again as the bear came on towards me, the bloody foam dripping from her jaws. Down went the bear again with a savage grunt, but up again in a jiffy, and on she came, her little eyes snapping fire, and those great paws swinging likc pendulums.

"You bet I lived a long time in the few seconds that followed. But I didn't lose my head, no, sir; I didn't have time. I grabbed for another cartridge and in my hurry I tore the loops off my belt half way around. When I fired, square in the beast's face, the bear was only a few feet away and still coming. Quick as a flash, I reached for another cartridge and as I shoved it into the breech I began to run backwards, for that bear was too—close for either health or comfort. I had not taken a dozen steps before I tripped and fell over a small log. I fell headlong on my back and a second later the bear crashed down on top of me, a great, heaving, quivering, bloody mass. I threw the muzzle of the gun into her face, but there was no need of another shot—the bear was dead. My last shot had hit the bear in the mouth and shattered the brain. It was one of the closest calls in the bear line I ever had. Yes, sir.

"I dragged myself out from under the dead bear and scrambled to my feet. During the fight—it all happened so quick—I had kept my nerve. In fact, things were coming my way so fast I didn't have time to get scared, but as I looked over the big hulk of that dead bear I got scarder and scarder, and my nerves went to pieces like a house of cards in a Kansas cyclone. I had to sit down on a log to shake myself together."

For 27 years Solleder has kept up his feud against the grizzly, and some years he would get 10 or more, and in the bad seasons he would be able to reduce the bear population by only five or six in revenge for the slaughter of Angelique. When the camera became a popular fad, Solleder added it to his arsenal, and has taken the keenest interest and pleasure in humiliating various grizzlies by making them pose for their pictures. It is a field of sport which Solleder has almost to himself with very little danger of ruinous competition—the life insurance rates are too high. An experience during February last, however, came near writing finis to Mr. Solleder's camera studies in grizzly home life. The phenomenon of hibernation has always had for Solleder a keen interest, and he has neglected no opportunity to investigate it on the spot. He has his own theories about hibernation, and he believed that the evidence of the camera would prove his contention.

"Now, it's the theory," said Solleder, in relating to me his attempt to snapshot a hibernating bear, "that bears den up and suck their paws all winter. Now, that doesn't apply to all bears. Where the den faces the sun I've seen them out in the middle of winter, but their forefeet are so soft and tender they leave bloody prints on the crusted snow. The 1st of February last I got track of a bear which had wandered out from its hibernating den. It struck me that it would be a fine think [sic] for me to chloroform the beast and take his picture—just one of those fool ideas a man will have at times.

"Well, I got two men to help me, and on snowshoes, with guns, rope, camera and two bottles of chloroform, we hiked to my hunting cabin on Hunter creek and camped for the night. The next day, by an early start, we crossed the middle range and struck the bear's bloody trail going up the side of a mountain toward a ledge of rock. We climbed up, and just at the top of the slide rock we came upon the den. Softly we crawled up to the mouth of the den and peeked in cautiously. Our eyes were used to the glare of the snow and the den was as dark as a pocket. It was an uneasy moment, for we didn't know whether the bear had returned to its hibernating sleep, or was wide awake and ready for a scrap. However, as our eyes got used to the darkness, we could see the bear, way back in the den, crouched up asle[e]p.

"I then made a cone of a piece of paper, tied it on the end of my snowshoe stick, saturated it with the dope and crawled into the den, after posting my companions where they could shoot in a hurry if necessary. When I got near enough to reach, I poked the chloroform cone under the bear's nose. As this was my first attempt at chloroforming grizzlies, I was just a shade nervous to see what would happen. After the first good whiff of the stuff, the bear lazily lifted a paw and poked the cone away, much as a man would hit at a fly, but you bet your life I was ready for one of those flying exits. I breathed easier, however, when the bear dropped back to sleep like a man with a snoring jag. I gave him the cone again, and d—m me if he didn't take to it this time like a baby to a bottle of milk. You would have thought he had been raised on it. Pretty soon, after I'd given him almost all of the two bottles, he fell over, dead to the world.

"Taking the thongs off our snowshoes, I re-entered the den and tied the bear's forefeet together and then tied the rope to the thongs in between his feet. Then we dragged him out and took a snub around a tree with the rope. I got busy right quick with the camera, for the medical dope sheets failed to state how long a grizzly would stay chloroformed. The dramatic climax came about five minutes after the bear struck the fresh outside air. I had the camera about 15 feet away from him and my head was under the black cloth as I was trying to get a focus. The blamed thing wouldn't work, somehow, and as I was fussing around trying to find out what the matter was, one of the boys let out a yell like a Sioux buck on the warpath.

"I grabbed the cloth off the camera just in time to see the bear lift its head and look around. The next instant the thongs were snapped like sewing thread and in another instant that bear was coming hell-bent for the camera. I could tell by the look on his face and by the way he growled that he didn't like cameras and resented the indignity of chloroform. Well, I didn't wait to argue the question with him. I just hit the high spots and shouted to the boys to shoot. It was a mighty fine skin and I sent it to Dr. Williams of Minneapolis. But I found out one thing—when you chloroform grizzlies you want a barrel of the stuff and you'd better apply it with a hose. Yes, sir."

But Solleder has had better luck in photographing other game which abounds in the Bitter Root, as the accompanying illustrations show, and he numbers among his camera trophies a number of bear pictures. It has been his experience during his 27 years of hunting and guiding in the Rockies, that a bear, if unmolested, generally will not attack a man, although the Bitter Root silvertips frequently spring the unexpected. But when wounded a bear will fight while there is breath in his body, displaying a wonderful tenacity for life. A wounded bear, Solleder says, if the bullet is not immediately fatal, will plug the wound with pitch which it scrapes off the trees, stopping the hemorrhage and incidentally showing a high order of intelligence.

Mr. Solleder has just announced that his plans to corral a big grizzly which during the past year has killed 23 head of cattle in the valley and which so far, through its evil cunning, has foiled all attempts of hunters to capture it. Solleder writes that this is a "bouncer" of a bear.

# Loaded for Bear

*Forester George L. Dally wrote about a bear story told to him one evening by his supervisor. It seems that there was a big bear roaming the mountains in Arizona, and an old sourdough determined to have its hide. After setting up an elaborate trap for bruin one evening the old-timer got quite a surprise. Dally's story appeared on pp. 69-76 of* Rangers of the Shield, *a collection of stories told by foresters, edited by Ovid Butler and published by the American Forestry Association; copyright 1934.*[25]

Another dry camp, with only a quart of water in the canteen.

It was almost dark, and as the supervisor and I reined up for the night I knew I was tired—it had been a day of steep climbs and deep ravines. No wonder neither of us spoke till our animals were turned loose and we had some supper under our belts. Even then we preferred to push the dirty dishes aside.

As the supervisor lit his pipe I could see by the light of his match the trace of a smile spread over his face. I knew I was elected to hear another yarn. I thought a lot of the boss. He was an interesting chap, but he was sometimes powerfully long-winded.

I did not have long to wait. As our tiny campfire blazed up for a moment, he peered out into the shadows.

"Somehow, George," he said, "this country and just the way the sky and the trees look tonight remind me of when I was a youngster. Open range then— cattle everywhere—game was a downright nuisance. Guess I've told you my dad was foreman of a big cattle outfit. Well, about a week after we'd finished the new ranch camp near the Breaks—old loghouse is standing yet near where Riley salts over in Humbug Valley—the queerest hombre I ever met comes into our place. And following close to his heels comes a big burro—snow white."

"Did the burro remind you any of Deputy," I ventured. "Deputy" was one of the mules in our government pack-train, and the last time we'd used him he'd bucked off our pack and kicked a hole in our can of syrup, to say nothing of losing all the salt.

The boss swore softly to himself and then continued. "Not by a dang sight! This burrow [sic] was intelligent. He had a kinder look than that cockeyed Deputy mule, and how he loved that master of his."

"You ain't formally introduced his master yet," I prompted, hoping to pep up the story a bit.

"By gravy! That's right. He sure was a queer hombre." The boss chuckled. "He was a big-framed chap—must a been fifty past— long, white hair and whiskers, and he had a walk about half old man's shamble and half easy swing of a tramper. Curious talking chap, too. Dad and I were sitting on the step. The old boy stopped at the gate and looked us over.

"Apparently satisfied, he walked up and stuck out a big hand to Dad and said 'Howdy, stranger, glad to see ye here. Don't know ye, but me, Pat Garr's me name, and this is me burro, Jock,' and danged if that burro didn't bob his head. 'I live down in the box canyon,' he went on. 'Me and Jock here has to come out once or twice a year for grub—little flour, tea, and a pinch o' salt. Me and Jock gets on fine with that. Glad to see ye here, stranger.'

"We got pretty well acquainted with old Pat. He stuck around camp for a week or two. He had prospected all over the West. Dad and I figured the length of time he told us he'd spent in each state and we calculated he'd have to be 462 years old. He'd shot one pure black panther, came within a hair of being scalped by the Sioux, and got lost twice in Death Valley. But him and that burro Jock! By gravy! the two loved each other like father and son. They'd been alone a lot together, and you know how that is, George."

Did I know? Hadn't I sat down like a big overgrown kid and bawled my eyes out when Trump, my collie, got salmoned over in the Tahoe country, and wasn't I with grizzled old Dan Hufford when he rolled Prince and found him at the bottom of the canyon with a broken neck? The boss had paused. I couldn't say a word, and as we sat there under the stars the silence of the night was broken only by the periodic jingle of the bells on our horses nearby. Yes, we knew— knew what companionship with a faithful animal meant.

"From time to time Pat visited our camp," drawled the supervisor again finally, "and we came to look for him ever so often for a stay of a week or two. Always he wanted us to come down and see him, but somehow we never went. Then came a long stretch when Pat and Jock never showed up. Dad and I got downright worried, so I saddled up one morning and started out to see what had happened to the pair. You know how you'll get a little nervous when you're worried, and after I got started from camp I hit it through the sagebrush hell bent. But that trail into the canyon!"

"Like the one we put down off of Barley Flats?" I asked.

"Steeper and narrower, a whole lot," declared the boss, "and winding down for a good thousand feet of narrow canyon wall. Every time I jarred a rock loose it bounced and echoed from wall to wall 'till it sounded like a boiler factory at full speed. By gravy! it was beautiful country though, and when I got down a ways I could see below me a small mesa with some grass and one big yellow pine—and that dang white burro grazing. It proved to be Pat's camp, and as I neared the bottom here came the old boy running toward me. His long white hair and his whiskers were streaming in the breeze. He was yelling at the top of his voice. 'Oh, I'm glad ye chose today to come! Ye're welcome any time, but this is the best day.'

" 'What the—' but he gave me no chance to finish.

" 'The bear—biggest one in Arizona—get him tonight sure. Come along, boy, show ye his track. Glad ye came!'

"He sort of pranced along ahead of me to a little stream I'd crossed on the way down and there, sure's you're born, was a bear track twice as big as I ever saw, and you know, George, I been roaming these mountains for thirty years."

"Pat was all excitement and he had me over to the pine tree on the little mesa. 'This is me trap,' he cried. We'll git the brute—biggest bear in the country!' And such a trap!

"He had a hind quarter of a mountain sheep suspended from one of the lower limbs and trained upon it from every conceivable angle was some dang firearm. The collecting of firearms, new and antique, had been Pat's only vice. He was a born collector, and now he had them all collected in that tree and pointed just below that quarter of sheep. Six-guns, single-shots, muzzle-loaders, needle-guns, little guns and big guns, all manner and kinds of guns, and they were loaded with all kinds of loads—rocks, pieces of lead, cartridges, slugs, bolts—every sort of thing. And the whole outfit was connected with pieces of string that led from the bait to the triggers like a regular Boob McNutt picture. He was tickled with his fixings and he was probably saying to himself, 'Gawd help that bear when he tries to take the bait.' On our way back Pat stopped for a minute and stroked the burro's head and neck.

"Pat's home was nothing to brag about; sort of a place where the rock had split and left a big gap fifteen feet across. Over this Pat had thrown some poles and rocks and dirt. On the front he'd just stood some poles upright and hung a deer skin for a door. Where he ever got the poles is hard to say, but he must have brought them in on Jock.

"We had deer meat and tea for supper and then the old man was for going back to his bear trap, but I made him wait. He lay on his bed of grass and skins while I lay just outside in my saddle blankets. Lord, that was a long night! Longer by the fact that Pat was nervous and talked all the time about killing the biggest bear in Arizona.

"About midnight, though, we did get a few winks, only to be jarred awake by a terrific roar. The world, it seemed, had exploded, and kept all the sound within that canyon. The walls magnified the noise, tossed it from side to side— played with it. It must have been nearly five minutes before that jumbling, rumbling, terrifying roar died away. Pat was out in the open dancing like a wild maniac and yelling, 'I've killed the bear, I've killed him!' He was for going at once, but I fought him back. It was pitch dark. The bear might only be wounded, and to meet up with him would have been a bad proposition in the daytime, let alone in the middle of the night. We didn't get any more sleep, though, and when things began to get just a shade lighter I couldn't hold the old man, so we hurried over the rocky trail to his trap.

"I can see him now as he sort of crouched and worked his way up that steep slope. Every muscle was tense, every motion showed excitement. When we got near the top we could see some object lying at the base of the tree. Pat hesitated for a second or so, then throwing his arms up wildly he screamed as a women would in mortal agony, dashed ahead of me and threw himself on the object under the tree. I couldn't understand, so I ran to him. There he sprawled, grasping that dead, lifeless thing, tears in his eyes, and wailing 'It's Jock! It's Jock! I've killed him!' "

The Supervisor shifted his position a little and kicked the outer embers into the fire. He sighed and there was a catch in his voice as he continued. "Old Pat was pretty badly shocked. I managed to get him to come up to the ranch. Dad kept him busy about the place. Once or twice each year he would ramble off for a week or so—where he went we never knew, but I doubt if he ever went again into that canyon."

"And the bear?" I asked after a bit.

"Never saw or heard of him again."

Our fire had burned out. The night had become cold. We could hear our horses cropping not far from our camp. We got up and threw the canvas manties over our supplies and turned in. Tomorrow would be another hard day.

# The Bear
# Hunt At San Pascual

*Lots of cowboys talked about and tried to lasso bears on the frontier range, but none perfected the art as well as the Spanish cowboys around California. Hancock M. Johnston described in detail how the vaqueros skillfully roped grizzlies and brought them back to town for bull fights in a two-part article published in the August and September 1917 issues of* **Forest and Stream**. *Part I appeared on pp. 341-343; 368 in August; Part II appeared on pp. 428-431 in September.*

['] Juego la copa de oro y gano" (I play the cup of gold and win), said José Guero, as we were all seated in the big sala [parlor] of the old adobe house on the San Pascual ranch playing burro tisnado.

"That's all right," said the big Missourian, yawning noisily; "why don't you fellows show us some of your celebrated bear hunting you talk so much about? I've been on this ranch a year and haven't seen a bear lassoed yet, though there's tracks around pretty near every day; blamed if I don't begin to think it's a California yarn about lassoing bears, anyhow."

"Well," said Chato, "if anybody wants to lasso a bear, one nailed the old mare's colt last night down by the oak corral, and from the number of tracks there must have been at least six of them; anyhow, there was an old one with some half-grown cubs. They made a close call on the old mare; but only tore a strip of meat off her side."

Don Jose Sotelo, a gray-haired man of sixty years, who had been major domo [horse-breaker] of the Chino ranch in its palmiest days, looked up from the corner where he was preparing hair from a horse's mane to be made into a hair rope, and began to manifest an interest in matters going on around him.

"Carrai! you can revenge the old mare if you want to. There's nothing I'd like better."

Jose Navarro, the head vaquero [cowboy], replied: "We'll trade her for a bear— perhaps two; if we don't, some of the Doctor's fine colts will get a call one of these nights; besides the mare is old, and if we are lucky we can have a good time and a big bear fight on the Diez y Seis de Septembre" [September 16].

Don Jose's eyes shot a glance of contempt at the "if" in his son-in-law's remarks. The old man was said to have lassoed and tied a dozen bears at Chino without assistance.

"Well," said one of the boys, "let's do it now, while Don Jose is here and we have a full moon to work by." This was greeted by a yell of approval.

After being urged by all present, particularly the Yankees, Don Jose consented to lead the bear hunt. After a general discussion of the subject it was decided, this being Sunday, that all could be gotten in readiness for the necktie party by Tuesday night.

El Burrero viego (the old donkey herd[er]) and El Cir, a young nephew of the owner, were delegated to invite Jose lenero [sic] (the wood cutter) a noted bear sharp, and also to have the bait prepared and make all arrangements. Don Jose and Navarro were detailed to select each man's best broken and bitted horse and put it in condition for the work ahead. These horses are so skillfully trained that with only a twine string for reins, they can be stopped at full speed, whirled around or even thrown on their side.

Poking a good deal of fun at each other, the Californians and the skeptical Americans went to bed in first-class humor, looking forward to any amount of fun and enjoyment in the next few days; the Americans feeling that when the hunt was over, if there was no bear tied, they would have the laugh on the natives for all time.

Next morning long before daylight all had breakfasted and scattered to carry out their respective duties connected with the big hunt. By daybreak the horse band was corralled, and as we rode away we saw Don Jose and Navarro selecting our horses. We three went to find the old mare, the others to search for the bear's regular trail from the mountain. We roped the mare without difficulty and led her along the edge of the bajeo [lowland], meeting El Cir and his party as agreed near the oak corral. They had found the trail along a wood road which filed down a very narrow cañon into the Arroyo Seco [Dry Creek], a general place of refuge for thieves and murderers in those early days. The trail was immediately above the corral de robles [of oaks], so-called because it was built of oaken logs placed on end; it was used for conveniences when branding horses and cattle.

After carefully examining the location, we brought the old mare up to the edge of the bajeo, which is a low, flat piece of land; this one was as smooth as a floor, a mile and more wide and about three miles long, running southeasterly across the San Pascual ranch, the site of the present City of Pasadena. Here we killed the mare, and dragging the paunch, made a circuit of about ten miles by way of the Cañada de las flores [of the flowers] and Precipice Cañon, thence across the Plain of Flowers above Loma Colorado (now Monk's Hill), down through the Rincon to the Arroyo Seco bank, from whence we followed the bank back to the mare's body. This was done to enable the bear to follow the scent of the carcass.

By the time we had finished it was late in the afternoon; we had long been thinking of bean stew and coffee, so we left for the ranch, where we found that Don Jose and Navarro had been as busy as we. We reported to the Don, attended to the tired animals and seated ourselves to a savory supper, to which we did ample justice.

When the candle light came each man busied himself putting on new latigos, replacing all weak strings in every part of the saddle, bridle and spurs; going over every strand of his riata, until nearly midnight, when we all turned in. Next morning by sunrise a messenger was despatched to visit the carcass. By early breakfast time he reported that there was about one-third gone; that where the paunch had been dragged over sandy places in the roads, the bear tracks were so thick it looked as though they had been patted smooth by human hands; in fact, he could not tell how many bears had followed that trail by the tracks; for his part he thought about a thousand.

"Ah! calabacero" [ignorant one], said Don Jose, "don't you know that one bear will sometimes walk up and down the paunch track just for fun? They are devils. To-night, it is a sure shot on their coming again, as they evidently did not find the old mare until too near daylight to finish her, so to-night as the moon rises, we must be within earshot of the carcass, and we won't give up the bear until the moon sets. She's most likely to come in the half lights."

After breakfast we saddled up to our favorites, and went out over the bear trail to make a guess of how many bears, and of what size they were, also to select our road for the raid upon them, and take in the accidents of the ground in daylight. The bear sharps decided that there was an enormous she bear, with three half-grown cubs, which would make it amply exciting for the eleven hunters.

Those horses were fed all the grain that was good for them that day, and were as well cared for as any Kentucky thoroughbred ever was the day before the race, for we knew there would be plenty of hard work for them sometime between dark and daylight.

By early dusk Tuesday night, every man's horse was carefully saddled and bridled, riatas coiled and hung on the pommels and the latigos left so that one pull would tighten them sufficiently for the journey. Anxiously we waited, loafing around the corridors with occasional glances at our horses, discussing the prospects of the hunt from every standpoint and relating incidents and accidents of previous hunts engaged in by different individuals.

About ten o'clock Don Jose put new life into the circle by shouting out of the door of the house, "A las armas, muchachos, adelante!" (To arms, boys, forward!) In less time than it takes to tell every man was in his saddle and we were strung out on the trail by twos and threes. A finer looking cavalcade could not have been picked out for perfect pose in the saddle, mounts and equipment for the prospective work.

Don Jose, sitting [on] his beautiful and graceful tordillo (gray) chineno straight as an arrow in spite of his sixty odd years; Navarro on his high-strung, merry sabino; Chato on El Mohino; El Cir, my brother, on his Arab-shaped Garfia cream; I, on a Sanchez with four white feet, and the others equally well mounted, set off merrily at a fox trot up the wood road and along the easterly bank of the arroyo [stream] through the Potrero [Ranch] Chiquito and Potrero de las Aguages, through the magnificent live oaks, which then abounded there, and came out on the mesa, just above the old Tejon trail leading by the Piedra Gordo, or Eagle Rock. There we stopped, and throwing our feet up over the horses' withers, tied our spur chains to prevent their clinking against the stirrups.

Don Jose rode slowly ahead, listened intently for a moment, then said in an undertone, "The old woman has arrived, sons." El Burrero wanted to know how he knew. The old man replied, "The dog that eats does not bark. Don't you hear the coyotes yelling? In other words, the bear is eating horse, the coyotes want to eat horse, but are afraid of her, so stand off and yell at her; if the bear was not there, the coyotes would be eating and could not yell."

"Well," said the burrero, "that is easy to guess after you know how."

"Now," said Done [sic] Jose, "as you see, the moon is just coming over the sierras [mountains], and in about two minutes she will have her horn hooked over the top of one of these pines, and give us light to do our work, so cinch your saddles and be ready for the word; remember, the unskillful and Americans must stay back and keep between the bears and the edge of the arroyo, so as to make them take to the plain for it, if they run, which I doubt very much their doing, as a grizzly bear with cubs at her side will generally stand her ground and fight to the death. The cubs of course are most likely to cut across and break for the arroyo, so you who can't do any work keep between them and the arroyo, and if they make toward you, charge them and hammer them over the head with your rope-ends. Navarro, El Lenero and I will attend to Mrs. Oso [Bear]. El Cir, El Guerro [sic], Jose Ybarra, Chato and Ambagsio ought to be able to take care of the three cubs and tie them up."

When all were ready we rode along the mesa just behind the brow of the hill very quietly until we arrived at a point between the bear and the arroyo bank; wheeling about, we divided ourselves in accordance with the work allotted to us, when our attention was called to the fact that it was light enough to see the bear. Every man shook his feet in the stirrups to see if everything was tight, and Don Jose, pressing his gray with the calves of his legs, and slightly leaning forward, went off with a bound like a shot, yelling "Santiago! At the bear, boys, don't be cowards or gourd sellers."

Every man followed at like speed, over the mesa, down the steep slope to the bajeo, hooting and yelling like demons. In the dim light we could see a massive form which looked to me, as I got nearer, more like my small boyhood's idea of an ogre than anything I had ever seen. It was terrifying, but upon near approach my ogre resolved itself into an enormous grizzly standing with her fore paws hanging purposelessly before her. Two cubs were sitting on their haunches at her side looking at us in wonder and curiosity; the other was hidden behind her and the carcass.

We all expected her to stand her ground and fight for her cubs, as bears generally do, but she evidently thought them big enough and old enough to take care of themselves, so when we got within about sixty feet of her, she lit out with a snort (about the same sound that a large hog would make if she did her very best) for Precipice Cañon.

According to instructions, Don Jose, El Lenero and Navarro only put out after the bear. El Georchy, El Burrero and I deployed as scouts between the cubs and the arroyo; El Cir, El Guero, Ambagsio, Ybarra and Chato charging the cubs, which stood their ground and made a game fight from start to finish. Don Jose led the trio after the old bear, a little to the right and about sixty feet in her rear.

Navarro was immediately behind him, El Lenero about a hundred feet behind and somewhat to her left. They all gained on her in the run across the bajeo, and Don Jose planted his lasso around her neck, but it was promptly jerked off and thrown to one side in a very contemptuous manner. Don Jose slowed down to prepare his rope again, giving Navarro a chance which he improved as well as he could, but unfortunately, just as he was about to throw, the bear gave a snort that sent Navarro and his sabino a hundred yards off their course; by this time, "the necktie party" had struck the hog wallow on the other side of the bajeo and the bear had the advantage, so she increased the gap between herself and El Lenero considerably, for by this time he was leading the trio of lassadores; but as soon as the hog wallow was cleared and the smooth slope dotted with elder bushes on the other side gained, El Lenero ran on to her rapidly and planted his riata over her neck and behind one shoulder—"aluso ladron" (thief fashion), as we used to call it.

It was too much for the bear's ingenuity. She could not get it off, so she charged with one foreleg lashed to her neck. Don Jose was right there, and as she came the old chap met her with a beautiful overhang [sic] throw, caught both hind feet, and whirling the chineno 'round on his feet, and her stretched out full length on her side quicker than I can tell it.

The other two horses having given courage by their actions to the cowardly Sabino, Navarro came up, and taking down his horsehair rope to hold his horse with, wrapped the reins very tight around the pommel, got down and went to Don Jose's assistance; Don Jose now took a reef in his riata, riding up within ten feet of the bear, leaving about twenty feet of the loose end beyond his horn. Navarro took this, slipped it through the neck rope and passed it back to Don Jose; catching that between Don Jose and the bear in his hands, he pulled hard on it to keep it tight; Don Jose, taking up the slack of the end, tightened the riata at about the same point as before, drawing the hind feet chock-a-block to the neck riata and rolling the bear into a big ball. Of course this is one way of roping a bear, but there are many other ways.

Navarro now took down some bale rope and half-hitching it several times 'round the bear's nose, fixed at least one female so that she would have to keep her mouth shut. He then added his riata to the other two and the trio dragged the bear up to a tree about a foot in diameter, pulled her hind feet around it on opposite sides with riatas, then with many knots and half-hitches known only to sailors and vaqueros, tied them together, hugging the tree, at the same time leaving plenty of space between the tree and her body, so that she could describe as many circles around the tree by springing and walking around it with her forelegs as she chose, but could not reach the riata on her feet.

Navarro now took all the other riatas off, and cutting the bale rope on the bear's nose, left her as free as air, except as to her two hind feet. She availed herself of the opportunity to make up for long silence and enforced inaction. She screamed, kicked, bit, scolded and threatened, and we poked fun at her in several different languages until she lapsed into sullen silence, when we left her to solitary meditation and went back to the bait.

Guero succeeded in catching a cub the first throw, and Chato and Ybarro [sic] helped tie it; the chambones [bunglers] and greenhorns were all busy with the other two; one of the cubs ran for the arroyo. I threw my riata, but having buck fever somewhat, the cub ran through the loop and kept his course. I whirled my horse and whacked him on the nose a couple of times with the hondo (rawhide lasso loop) which turned him back. By this time the big Missourian had gained courage and wanted to be in, so about the time the cub was turned El Georchy was pretty close to him and coming head on at full speed. The cub probably thinking that as Georchy had no riata here was his meat, immediately changed his tactics and charging the Bayo Coyote, caught about four pounds horse steak off the stifle, hanging on like a mortgage.

You should have seen the bay buck and squeal! Instead of standing the usual three bucks, as most gringos [foreigners] do (one up, one down, and the other to the ground), that gringo simply was great; you could not have slipped a piece of tissue paper under him at any stage of it. Chato, who had been trying to learn English all winter before, became so excited and enthusiastic that he vented all his vocabulary in one long sentence, and though not to the point, was more appropriate than he knew. "Bully, Coche, I'll keel you now; I'll wheep you! I'll let you know to-morrow! Oh, by—-!" he screamed.

El Cir said, "I thought you couldn't ride broncos, George?"

"Well, I'd like to see the color of the horse that could dump me down among them bears, ride or no ride; I'd fly if I had to."

This put every one into a hilariously good humor. El Cir caught the cub with his riata as he was flung off by the crazed bucking Bayo Coyote, and Ybarra and Navarro, who had gotten back by this time, tied the others. The fight had lasted about an hour and a half, and we had bagged four grizzly bears. "But," asked the burrero, "what kind of an outfit is going to load and haul this menagarie to the house and town, I want to know?"

"Well," said Don Jose, "it's pretty near daylight. Let's go back and gct some good hot breakfast and fresh horses, and we will show you how easy the thing is when you have the sabe" [know how].

## Bringing Home a Grizzly

*Part II*

So we went home, and after a delightfully hot breakfast, selected fresh horses, this time with reference to strength and education among mad bulls and steers. We took with us also a large beef's hide.

When we got back we found one cub dead; Don Jose said from anger. I thought from being tied too tightly; otherwise everything was as we left it, so we went to visit the old bear, to see if her temper had been improved; but we found her still in hysterics; she had dug holes all around the tree until it was almost uprooted, and all we could see was a part of her hind legs tied around the tree.

"Now," said El Burrero, "what figure does that beef's hide cut? Are you going to feed it to her?"

"You'll see," replied Don Jose. Measuring more or less the length between Mrs. Oso's front and hind legs when stretched at full length and width between, he made like measurements on the beef's hide and cut holes about an inch and a half in diameter at each point; the forelegs of the bear were then pulled taut with riatas wrapped with sheep skin, wool side in and the strongest and thickest riatas in the outfit wrapped and half-hitched around each leg, the hind legs being treated the same.

The bear was pulled out from the tree by the fore feet; the hide was stretched in front of her and the rumps of the hide slipped under the forefeet; the ends of the riatas were passed through the holes made about the forearms of the steer's hide and she was dragged up on the hide until the riata drawing through the holes pinned her feet close to the hide. The riatas on her hind feet were passed through the holes made in the gaskins of the hide and tightened, fastening the hind feet to the hide. She now presented the appearance of being pinned to a card like a bug for a specimen.

The gringos looked on open mouthed and gussing from time to time. "Well, I thought I knew it all before, but I didn't."

"Sure," was the burrero's comment.

By this time a fifth riata was attached to the head of the beef's hide. Three vanqueros [sic] now took the forward riatas, and two, the one's attached to the hind feet, taking a turn on their pommels and pulling all together, Mrs. Oso slid over the grass on her rawhide sled as slick as a toboggan; the rear vaqueros keeping just enough tension to hold the bear flat on her stomach. The gringos took off their hats and yelled with delight. We left the five men hauling Mrs. Oso back to the ranch house, and turned our attention to the two remaining cubs.

First, their mouths were tied with bale rope and the whole body enveloped in a horse blanket (to prevent fright of horses), leaving a breathing hole at the head. Four men put each on a horse, one man lead the horse, and one walked on one side holding on to the blanket to steady the cub. In this way they were taken to the house very comfortably.

At night, seated in the corridor in the cool breezes coming up from the arroyo from the ocean, El Burrero said, "Don Jose, they told me you caught and tied seven bears alone at Chino, and that such a thing was not uncommon among the Californians, even Romulo, an eighteen-year-old son of Don Andres Pico, doing the trick alone; but I put them down as Californy lies, and didn't take the trouble to ask you how it was done; but since I have seen four bears tied up like shoats by you fellows, I am going to ask you to tell me how one man surrounds a bear all alone. If you tell it straight, I will believe it; but I think it will stump you before you get him backed up to a tree."

"Diablo, viejo! [old devil] a vaquerito del-pais [any young cowboy] can do the work for me, because I frequently send one to kill and butcher a steer alone, and Carrai! if he can't do one, he can't do the other, because it is almost equally dangerous and takes about the same nerve. Anyhow, a man who is a coward has no business being a vaquero, which requires plenty of courage whether you are breaking a colt or throwing a cape at a bull or gathering up a riata at full speed.

"Well, I will tell you of my last bear which I was not hunting, as I had lost none that day and was only looking over the different bunches of cattle, to jud[g]e their condition. In going through some thick willows that grow in the big swamp at Chino, I felt my horse stagger and heard such a slap that I knew instantly that a bear had intended to slap my face as a surprise, but had missed me and struck my horse on the rump, so instantly I put spurs and went flying out of the willows to the open grass beyond, meantime trailing my riata which had hung loosely coiled on the horn—our custom when on the range—and prepared my lasso.

"The bear was full charge behind me, and with his mouth wide open. I took in the situation and slowed down, letting him come within about ten feet, circling until I was pretty close to a lone curly willow, slid the horse on his haunches a little to one side, and as the bear came up, caught him by one hind leg; quick as thought I tightened the riata, running around the tree and drawing Mr. Oso close up to it. He had fallen and rolling over, was biting at the rope on his leg. I rode around the tree four or five times encircling it tight with the riata and tied the end to an outside limb.

["]Mr. Oso never thought to follow me at each turn, so I tied the hind foot to the tree. I then drew near to him, he trying to get at me all the time, and taking my macate threw it around his neck; taking a few turns on my pommel brought the end of the rope along the opposite side of the horse's neck from that which was fast to the bear and tied it to the rope between the bear and the horse, to prevent my horse from turning tail to the bear and getting into all kinds of difficulty. Then I reached down and pulled my cinch straps as tight as possible, so he could not budge the saddle. Getting off, I took my silk sash, went on the opposite side of the tree and tied his two hind legs tight together, my horse pulling away from him in the opposite direction, keeping him from whirling on me. Now my bear was backed up to the tree and tied. You saw the rest last night."

We selected a large post that stood under the shade of three large live oaks that grew at the corners of the triangle, about 250 feet north of the house on the wood road, and tied the bear as before, giving her water and meat. Leaving her alone we planned to kill the day, rest, loaf and feast; the third succeeding day would be the grand function at El Pueblo [the town], and meantime we must move Mrs. Oso six miles, provide a toro bravo [ferocious bull] for her to fight, also a suitable place for spectators. We decided, as the most fitting way of celebrating our prowess, upon a barbecue!

El Cir gave the order for a fat calf of ten months to be killed. The lenero went down to a spot designated and dug a circular hole two feet deep and wide. Selecting water-worn cobbles, with which the arroyo abounded, he lined the hole with them; taking several armsful of dry oak branches and breaking them to fit the cobble-lined hole, he quickly struck a match and had the pile in full blaze. Soon it was only a mass of beautiful coals. I wish I could give you the picture of this spot as it looked on that summer day. A great live oak casting its shade a hundred feet around its gnarled trunk, overhanging a spring, cool and clear; its rim was surrounded by ferns, coarse but graceful, a belated mariposa lily stalk was there, and a lupin[e] bloomed scantily. We scarcely noticed it all so much then, but I recall it now, forty years later, perfectly.

The boys arrived with the calf, butchering it in Spanish style as it lay dead on the rails that had been put under it. Cutting off the head and taking the liver and the feet from the knees down, they turned them over [to] the lenero, who soaked clean barley sacks in water and enveloped the meat in them, putting in a few cloves of garlic for seasoning. He scooped the coals and ashes out of the hole and put the wet sacks in on the red hot rocks, placing a layer of green sycamore leaves about two inches thick over all, then covering them with the freshly dug earth to the depth of a foot, packing it hard with the spade.

While the lenero was thus engaged, the other boys had been as busy as a lot of gophers. Some had made a rousing bed of beautiful clear red coals, the best broiling fuel in the world, others had gone to the house bringing back bread, salza, green pepper, salt and claret.

Every man was his own cook, and every dish was a broil. Some used a long, slim oak or sycamore stick, others laid the juicy morsel directly on the coals, each one selected his favorite bit, and what a menu to choose from! Each had its own particular flavor; salted, eaten piping hot from the stick with a spoonful of salza or bit of green pepper and washed down with a swallow of claret or spring water.

Sitting on the roots of the tree, as large as a man's leg, some forming the seat, some the back, of as restful an arm chair as one could wish, one had the whole range of the Lincoln Park Hills, and looking through a gop [sic] in the arroyo, the cupola of the town courthouse, the misty outlines of the homes on the south, and through a gap the profile of the recumbent Indian or Washington, as the face seemed to resemble, in the Los Felis Hills. To the north the beautiful sage-covered hills, fringed with the dark green live oaks and beyond in the distance the blue Sierra Madres; to the east the hills covered with oak surrounding the rodeo.

Then the siesta; stretched under the closely woven boughs of the live oak, with the cool breeze playing around our heads, the music of the water as it fell among and ran over the boulders down the bank of the arrayo [sic] to a garden below, and the enjoyment of the dreamy cigarritos, until soft sleep fell among us. Those days, those times! They will never more return.

By daylight we had loaded the bear on and added an extra new skin to the hide gondola, to better protect her from the rocks, and under the escort of eight men—five only being necessary—started on our journey down the sandy road of Arroyo Seco to the pueblo [town], the other three going on ahead to secure suitable corrals, etc. The bear procession met a train of several two-yoke oxen drawing carretas [wagons], which the bueys [oxen] with a snort scattered all over the arroyo, not paying any attention to the "Ho! parate [stop], Chanate! vete Barcino, carajo!" A burro train also scattered off with its pack-saddles, rushing through the willows; in fact, Mrs. Oso seemed to inspire every animate thing with new life on sight, and no wonder, for she was about as ugly as a "kick on the shins," with the question of whether it hurts or not added on to it.

The crowd having all the seats and standing room, Mrs. Oso and Mr. Toro were brought in and introduced to one another, by making fast a log chain twenty feet long to the bull's foot, and the other end to Mrs. Oso's neck, this to prevent a scattering in case they did not face the music.

When all was ready, the vaqueros retired, letting both animals loose at the same time. For a moment they stood looking at each other. The bull concluded first that he had her sized up, lowered his head and charged her. The bear half rose on her hind legs and swatted him on the shoulder, taking about four pounds of beefsteak off, but the bull in the supplemental rush knocked her over, and backed off, pawing the dirt as he went. The grizzly got up, shook herself and rushed like lightning at the bull, grabbing him at the withers, but hardly had she taken hold when the bull, throwing up his head with enormous force, ended her hind-quarters up almost over her head, and as her body came down, with a quick side thrust he rammed his horn in behind her short ribs clear to the heart.

The bear let go her hold and fell over on her side, dying in less than a minute. The bull was all right, with the exception of the lost beefsteak and the bite on his neck, and just as mad as ever, he pawed the dirt and bellowed for more bear.

"Another surprise," El Burrero said; "who would ever think a bull could kill a bear in three minutes?"

The bear, though very thin from raising a large family, weighed 1,100 pounds; fat, would have easily weighed 1,500 pounds or more. I can't remember what became of the cubs, but they were sold to a man called Round House George, who kept a few animals and sort of pleasure garden, on a small scale in Los Angeles.

# Endnotes

1. From *Friends of My Life As An Indian*, by James Willard Schultz. Copyright 1923, James Willard Schultz. Reprinted by permission from the Museum of the Rockies.
2. Grizzly bear.
3. Pahk'sikwoyi (sticky-mouth), another name for grizzly bear.
4. "A Bear Hunt in Montana," by Authur Alvord Stiles; *National Geographic*, February 1908, pp. 149-154. Reprinted with permission.
5. Later that fall, while elk hunting young Randall surprised a grizzly 100 feet in front of him. He had a 30-30 cal. Winchester carbine and planned to shoot the bear but lost his nerve. Randall quickly recalled his father saying a 30-30 was no gun for a grizzly and also remembered the horrible fate of Johnny Graham. He decided to get out of the bear's way. On the following day, young Randall and his father rode to the spot where he had encountered the grizzly and discovered that the tracks were those of Old Two Toes.
6. Reprinted with permission.
7. Article's headline said 3,000-foot.
8. "Smokechaser's Bear," by E.A. Woods, (pp. 153-160), in *Rangers of the Shield*, ed. by Ovid Butler and published by the American Forestry Association in Washington, D.C.; copyright 1934 by the American Forestry Association. Reprinted with permission.
9. From *Tough Trip Through Paradise*, (by Andrew Garcia, edited by Bennett H. Stein, The Rock Foundation, 1967) is reprinted with permission of Houghton Mifflin.
10. Copyright 1926, by J.W. Schultz. Reprinted with permission from the Museum of the Rockies.
11. Copyright 1919, by J.W. Schultz. Reprinted with permission from the Museum of the Rockies.
12. Copyright 1984, by Museum of the Rockies. Reprinted with permission from *With the Indians in the Rockies*, Confluence Press, Lewis-Clark State College, Lewiston, Idaho.
13. Reprinted with permission.
14. "Cowboy Lore in Colorado," by Honora DeBusk Smith (pp. 37-43), *in Southwestern Lore*, edited by J. Frank Dobie, published by the Southwest Press in Dallas, Texas; copyright 1931 by the Texas Folklore Society. Reprinted with permission of the Texas Folklore Society.
15. So called because he was said to be the originator of the "sourdough" raised biscuits so popular on the range. He was for years a cook for the Mackenzie Cattle Company. He was not so widely known as "Puggy-Hoo," witty old Irish cook at Crossell Ranch in the early eighties.
16. Reprinted with permission.
17. Reprinted with permission.
18. Reprinted with permission from Irvington Publishers, Inc., 740 Broadway, New York, N.Y. 10003.
19. Reprinted with permission from Irvington Publishers, Inc. 740 Broadway, New York, N.Y. 10003.
20. From typescript copy in the Montana Historical Society Archives, SC 1436. Published by permission of the Montana Historical Society.
21. Grinnell puts Pickett's location at Black Butte or Cone Butte in his notes on "Memories of a Bear Hunter" in *Hunting at High Altitudes*.
22. Pickett encountered a grizzly at an elk bait which required six bullets from a high-powered rifle loaded with 106 grains of C.H. No. 6 powder, with 340 grains Express bullet—according to an account in *Hunting at High Altitudes*.
23. Reprinted from *The Grizzly Bear: The Narrative of a Hunter-Naturalist*, by William H. Wright. University of Nebraska Press. 1977. Reprinted with permission.

24. Probably Frank Welch of Corwin Springs. See story introduction in Close Encounters, "Two Toes Kills Again."

25. "Loaded For Bear" by George L. Dally, *Rangers of the Shield*, edited by Ovid Butler and published by the American Forestry Association in Washington, D.C.; Copyright 1934 by the American Forestry Association. Reprinted with permission.

# Index

# About the Author

Jeanette Prodgers was born in 1958 in Helena, Montana, where she was raised. She graduated from the University of Montana in 1980 with a B.A. in journalism and liberal arts, and has published articles in *Montana Historian, Montana Outdoors, Montana: The Magazine of Western History,* and *Old West.* In 1985, Prodgers traveled to Alaska's Admiralty Island to study grizzly bears, living in a Forest Service cabin. She now lives with her husband, Rich, in Butte, Montana.

Jeanette Prodgers began work on *The Only Good Bear is a Dead Bear* in 1984, while researching other facets of western history and noticing the abundance of bear stories in turn-of-the-century newspapers. She eventually collected more than 200 bear stories, from which she selected the best for this book.

Any reader interested in lavish descriptions of bear encounters will praise this book forever.